BEER

A TASTING COURSE

DK

BEER
A TASTING COURSE

MARK DREDGE

CONTENTS

NAVIGATING BEER BY STYLE

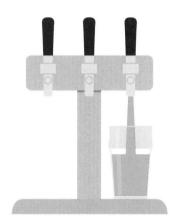

INTRODUCTION

This book is all about the flavor of beer.

Discover how beer's many wonderful, enticing, delicious flavors are created with the base ingredients, and how different brewery processes impact those flavors. Learn about the defining flavor profiles of classic beer styles and how beers within the same style category are similar or why they're sometimes different. Gain confidence in understanding and identifying the flavors in whatever beer you're drinking.

I love the flavor of beer, and it was flavor that first excited me and made me curious enough to try every beer I could find. I love how each beer presented me with new flavor experiences, whether it's the pungent citrus of an American IPA, the comforting malt familiarity of a pint of Dark Mild, or the layered complexity of an aged Barley Wine. Beer became more than just a drink: it became an adventure in flavor.

When I first started discovering the wider world of beer, with every new style, I found new things that excited and fascinated me. As I swirled my glass around trying to understand the beers, there were new aromas, new flavors, and new characteristics, and the more I drank, the more curious I became.

As I read tasting notes, I could practically taste them in my imagination, but I wanted to drink them for myself. I wanted to taste more, taste them better, and get better at drinking beer. I knew that meant one thing: I had to drink more.

As I learned and understood more about beer, I was able to connect flavor to ingredients and brewing processes, and then I could also link flavor to a broader appreciation of regionality, history, and beer-drinking cultures.

As I continued to study flavor, judged beer competitions, and taught classes about beer, it became clear how challenging it can be to understand and identify flavor and how others were also challenged. I realized that it came down to language and confidence. We need to know the words to use, to know how to use them in the context of beer, and have the confidence to use them. In *Beer: A Tasting Course*, I hope to give you the words and confidence to appreciate the flavors of beer, as well as exploring in more detail many of the world's most delicious beers.

WHEN I WAS TEACHING,
"IT JUST TASTES LIKE BEER!"
WAS SOMETHING I HEARD
OFTEN IN MY CLASSES.

Beer: A Tasting Course is a flavor-focused approach to beer. We look at the specifics of flavors, why beers taste the way they do, and how to identify and communicate about those flavors. The ultimate goal is that this book helps people to be better able to choose the beers they most want to drink.

It's possible for everyone to become a better beer taster, and the best way to do it is simply to drink more broadly, eat more varied foods, and think more when you drink. I love how the flavor of beer can be evocative or elusive, familiar or challenging, comforting or thrilling, complex or simple, and sometimes simply unforgettably wonderful. Many years after I discovered the joy of drinking different beers, I'm still just as excited about opening every beer I drink because every beer can offer me a new flavor experience.

ABOUT THE BEERS IN THIS BOOK

The beers I've selected in this book are representative of their style and are widely available regionally, nationally, or internationally. There's a bias in favor of the traditional brewing nations and modern centers of craft beer because that's where the majority of these styles originated. This is not a book about the world's rarest or highest-rated beers, and it includes huge international brands alongside beers from small independent breweries. Rather, it seeks to set foundations of flavor with beers that are regarded as being true to their style, regardless of brewery size or ownership. Most beers are well known and are common in many beer books, but they are classics for a reason. By knowing them well, we can taste everything else within their context, allowing us to make better critical and analytical assessments of beer.

WHAT
----- IS -----
BEER?

IN THIS SECTION WE look at the fundamentals of beer, brewing, and drinking. The flavor of beer is created by the ingredients and processes, and it's important for us as drinkers to understand those flavors. The senses combine to create the experience of flavor, which is uniquely personal. We'll look at how to identify flavors, how to evaluate beer, and how to improve as tasters. Then we'll discover the main ingredients in beer, how they contribute different drinking qualities, and the way processes in the brewery influence flavors, some of which might not always be good. Finally, we look at fresh and aged beer, and different approaches to enjoying beer with food.

THE STORY OF BEER

Beer is the most popular alcoholic drink in the world. There are dozens of different beer styles, and great variety within each of those styles.

WHAT A LOT OF BEER!

After water and tea, beer is the most-consumed drink in the world. Some 49 billion gallons (185 billion liters) of beer are brewed and drunk annually. Around 90% of all beer that people drink is pale and refreshing lager.

WHAT IS BEER?

Beer is a fermented drink, primarily made with water, grain, hops, and yeast. There are tens of thousands of breweries making beer in the world, ranging from global megabrands to people brewing in their garage, and whether large or small scale, beer is basically brewed the same way. Most beers take two to four weeks from the day they're brewed until we can drink them.

HOW BEER IS BREWED (THE QUICK VERSION)

Brewers mix warm water and grain together and heat the mixture, extracting fermentable sugars and color from the grain. They draw off the sweet liquid from the grain, bring it to a boil, and add hops to give bitterness, flavor, and aroma. Then brewers strain the bittersweet liquid, cool it, and move it into a new tank where they add yeast.

The yeast ferments the grain sugar into alcohol. After a week or so, the beer is cooled further and left to mature until it's ready to be drunk, which is typically another one to four weeks.

ALES, LAGERS, AND WILD/SOUR BEERS

There are three main categories of beer: ales, lagers, and wild/sour beers. These groups use distinctly different yeasts (and bacteria in sours) to produce the beers (see pp.64–65). Within the overarching family of beer, there are many different types, or styles, of beer, each with its own expected characteristics. Some of those styles are traditional and have been brewed for decades or centuries, while others are contemporary and have been shaped by ever-changing modern trends.

ALE
Fermented warm with ale yeast

- Pale Ales & IPA
- Stout & Porter
- British ales
- Hefeweizen
- Witbier
- Saison
- Belgian Dubbel, Tripel, & Quadrupel
- Kölsch
- Altbier

LAGER
Fermented cold with lager yeast

- Pilsner
- Helles
- Festbier
- Dunkel
- Schwarzbier
- Bock
- Doppelbock
- Hoppy Lager
- IPL

WILD/SOUR
Uses wild yeast and bacteria

- Lambic
- Gueuze
- Kriek
- Belgian Red-Brown
- Wild Ale
- Berliner Weisse
- Gose

WHO BREWS (AND DRINKS) THE MOST?

China brews more beer than any other country, and the United States, Brazil, Mexico, and Germany make up the top five. By consumption, almost one-third of all beer is drunk in Asia, one-third in the Americas, and one-quarter in Europe. The world's biggest per capita drinkers are the Czechs, followed by Austrians, Poles, Romanians, and Germans. The Czechs average 40 gallons (180 liters) per person per year, almost double that of second-place Austria.

DRINKING BEER

Most beer contains alcohol (ethanol). Ethanol is water soluble, and when we drink it, it passes into our digestive system. Some enters the body through the bloodstream in the stomach, and the rest enters via the small intestines—if we've eaten, it can slow down the absorption.

The alcohol travels around the body, and as it does so, we begin to feel its effects. While those first few sips can make us feel good, the body treats alcohol as something to break down and process quickly, and prioritizes the metabolization of it—in other words, it wants to get rid of it.

Mostly via the liver, the body can process about one standard drink an hour—say, a pint of 4% ABV beer. If we drink more quickly than the body can process the alcohol, it builds up in our system and begins to make us feel drunk. The more we drink, and the quicker we drink, the more we will be negatively affected by alcohol. Enjoy beer, but drink responsibly.

THE FLAVORS OF BEER

This book is focused on the flavor of beer. Those flavors can come from all the individual ingredients and different processes in the brewery, plus interactions between the ingredients. Here are the most common flavor terms used to describe beer and their derivation.

HOPS	FLORAL (GRASSY & FRUITY)	Grassy (fresh or dried), hop leaves/pellets/cones, fresh flowers/blossom, honey/marmalade / Lemongrass/lime leaf
	CITRUS	Lemon/lime, orange/mandarin, grapefruit
	TROPICAL FRUIT & SWEET AROMATIC	Passion fruit, pineapple, mango, guava/papaya, coconut
	STONE FRUIT, BERRY, & ORCHARD FRUIT	Peach/apricot, cherry/plum, grape/lychee, gooseberry, black currant, blueberry
	SPICE	Aniseed/mixed spice, black pepper, cumin/curry spices
	PUNGENT & VEGETAL	Tangy berry, onion/garlic
	HERBAL & WOODY	Marijuana/dank / Resinous/pine, cedar/woody, herbs (rosemary, dill), mint/menthol, earth/soil
MALT, GRAIN, & ADJUNCTS	GRAINY & MALTY	Straw/grassy, malt/rich malt, creamy/oaty
	BREADY & BAKED	Fresh dough / Bread, graham cracker, cereal, savory cracker, toast, nutty/toasted nuts / Sourdough bread
	FRUITY & CARAMELIZED	Light citrus, tea, dried fruit/tea cake, licorice, marmalade/honey, fudge / Molasses/maple syrup
	ROASTED	Chocolate/cocoa, coffee (fresh/grounds), roasted barley, smoke (wood/meat/peat)
WATER	SOFT	Fuller/sweeter
	HARD	Drier/crisper
YEAST & FERMENTATION	ESTERS	Sweet apple/plum, rose/honey, banana, peach/tropical, vanilla/creamy, aniseed/dried fruit
	PHENOLS	Black/white pepper
	BRETTANOMYCES	Clove/smoky/medicinal / Barn/farmyard, pineapple/tart fruit
	BACTERIA	Acetic (vinegar), acidic (lemon), lactic (tart dairy)
	ALCOHOL	Light fruitiness, vinous/warming
AGED BEER	GENERAL AGED CHARACTER	Dried fruit/sherry, nutty/almond / Soy sauce/umami
	BARREL-AGED CHARACTER	Oaky/wood, ex-alcohol (wine/whiskey), coconut/vanilla

THE HISTORY OF BEER

For thousands of years, beer has been evolving with new scientific discoveries, technological developments, cultural advances, and societal changes.

THE ORIGINS

Beer has been a constant in the history of humankind, and it's widely believed that dedicated brewing dates to the Agricultural, or Neolithic, Revolution of around 10,000 years ago. Beer became an everyday drink, consumed by everybody. It was a source of hydration and nutrition, and it was a social drink shared with others.

While the earliest millennia of beer drinking reveal fascinating insights into life, for drinkers today, the story becomes more relatable from the 1500s onward.

PRE-16TH CENTURY

Beer was a staple across northern Europe, and hops became the primary bittering ingredient in beer; before hops, a mix of herbs was commonly used. Beer was mostly brewed by women for domestic consumption, but larger households and monasteries were creating breweries on a bigger scale. Mash tuns, fermenters, and serving vessels were all made of wood.

Brewing was still an empirical process, but these breweries created the foundation for contemporary brewing. Almost all beer was ale, with much local and regional variety. It's likely there were two main qualities of beer: pale wheat-based beers, which likely developed a tart flavor, and dark, sweet, and probably smoky-tasting beers.

16TH TO 18TH CENTURIES

Brewing and malting was now a skilled trade, and beer was a commercial product. Britain was the foremost brewing nation, and British colonization took beer around the world. By the late 1700s, the Industrial Revolution saw large-scale breweries growing in Britain, utilizing steam power and other advancing technologies. Porter became the world's first great beer style.

In central Europe, Bavaria had brewing laws in place to help control quality, and that, combined with its unique process of storing beer in cool underground cellars, created lager beers. Most brewing was seasonal and undertaken only in the winter months. Beer was stored to drink through the summer and was mostly drunk locally.

WHITBREAD BREWERY
In the 18th century, breweries in Britain relied mostly on horsepower. Here, George Garrard's painting of 1792 shows the Whitbread Brewery, one of the most successful of the big London brewers.

YUENGLING
Founded in 1829 and located in Pottsville, Pennsylvania, Yuengling Brewing Co. is the oldest continuously operating brewery in the United States.

20TH CENTURY

A shift took place from varied and sweeter dark ales to more consistent and refreshing pale ales and lagers, a move that took beer from a form of nutritious "liquid bread" to a primarily social drink. Beer, and specifically lager, was now brewed globally.

Major events such as Prohibition in the United States (1920–1933) and the World Wars (1914–1918 and 1939–1945) had a huge impact on beer, leading to a new development of styles from the 1950s. Paler and less challenging beers became the most common, though many classic and traditional styles remained. Marketing began to have an important role in the industry.

By the 1960s and 1970s, pale lager was the ubiquitous drink, and the beer industry consolidated to be dominated by a handful of huge global companies. The microbrewery and craft-brewery revolution began in earnest from the 1980s.

21ST CENTURY

The small-brewery revolution has taken over the world with its aim of brewing great-tasting and diverse selections of beers for local customers. There's never been a greater variety of beers available, with classic styles sitting alongside modern innovations. The most common beers are dominated by hop aromas and flavors. With ever-more interest in craft beers, global brewing companies have begun to take over small breweries. Regardless, wherever you go, small breweries have become a cornerstone of local communities.

19TH CENTURY

This was the great century for beer development and saw a technological and scientific shift from the old empirical ways of brewing. At the beginning of the century, British ale brewing was the global powerhouse, but by the end, lager was dominant.

New instruments to measure and control beer, such as the thermometer and hydrometer, which measures sweetness, helped to improve beer quality, and then industrialization increased scale.

New techniques, such as malting to produce paler malts, changed the fundamental flavors of beer, and specific new styles emerged such as the Munich Lager, Vienna Lager, and Pilsner. Fermentation became better understood and then more controllable. Artificial refrigeration made temperature control and year-round brewing possible, which also meant beer could be brewed in more countries.

Wood was replaced by other materials in the brewery, with stainless steel eventually becoming the most-used material by the 21st century.

Large-scale bottling was possible, and transportation became quicker, meaning beer could fundamentally change from a local (draft-only) product to a national bottled one.

Many central Europeans emigrated, and they took their lager-brewing traditions with them. This importation was most significant in North America, which became a new brewing powerhouse.

HOW FLAVOR WORKS

Before we even open a beer and think about flavor, it's good to have an understanding of how our senses and our brain work together to create our experience of flavor.

SMELL & TASTE
Smell and taste combine as aroma compounds reach the olfactory nerves and are registered in the brain.

EXPERIENCE
Our knowledge and our flavor experiences stored in our memory help shape the specific characteristics we identify in the beer.

SIGHT
We see the beer and our brain begins to create an expectation of what we're going to drink, using clues like color, clarity, and even the name of the beer.

AIR FLOW
As we exhale, internal smells of food and drink register as flavor.

SMELL
We smell the beer as we raise it to our lips, and volatile aromatic chemical compounds register in the olfactory nerves.

SOUND
We take clues from things we hear, like someone telling us to expect a certain flavor or quality in the beer.

TOUCH
We can feel the beer's temperature, carbonation, viscosity, and more in the mouth.

TASTE
We sense the tastes (sweetness, bitterness, sourness) on the tongue as the beer moves through the mouth.

FLAVOR IS CREATED IN THE BRAIN

Our experience of flavor is uniquely personal, and it's fully formed within our brain as a construction of all our senses—smell, taste, touch, sight, and sound—plus the context, our mood, expectation, and previous experiences. Whatever we taste, it's true to our own experience of it. Just because someone else tastes something quite different, it doesn't mean we're wrong. We might be able to express ourselves better or identify flavors more specifically, but whatever you think about a beer is true for you.

IDENTIFYING FLAVOR

Our senses, preferences, and experience help shape the specific flavor characteristics we identify in beer.

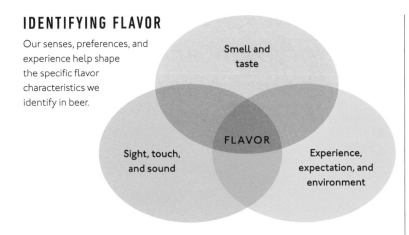

Smell and taste

Sight, touch, and sound

FLAVOR

Experience, expectation, and environment

HOW SMELL WORKS

Smell helps us safely navigate through life as it adds refinement to the other senses and aids in decision-making. All our senses combine to understand flavor, but smell is the most evocative and gives us the most enjoyment. It also helps us assess if food and drink are safe to consume.

Smell works in two distinct ways: orthonasal and retronasal. Orthonasal is what we smell in the world around us when we inhale—we can call this aroma. Retronasal is the sense of smell linked to what we're in the process of consuming. We experience it when we exhale, creating our impression of flavor.

THE SMELL OF BEER

Beer contains hundreds of aromatic compounds. When we inhale those aromas, they are drawn in through the nose and up to olfactory receptors, which send signals to the olfactory bulb. When we drink a beer and then exhale, more and different aroma compounds, which can react with saliva, are also sent up to the olfactory receptors. The olfactory bulb tries to identify the smell before sending information on to other parts of the brain, specifically the areas that deal with memories and emotions. To help the brain make a decision on what we've just inhaled and tasted, it uses cues from all the other senses to quickly present back to us a basic impression of that beer.

When we try to consciously analyze a beer, we're going against the brain's natural simplifying instinct and challenging it to work in new ways, while also applying pleasure to the process.

THE SENSE OF TASTE

We can identify five basic tastes: sweet, bitter, sour, salty, and umami. Taste helps us consume good food and avoid harmful ones, and the tastes connect with the aromas to create the impression of flavor.

Sweetness is always good as it means a source of calories in the form of carbohydrates. Bitterness, however, could mean a food is poisonous, so we're alerted when we taste something bitter. The taste combines with smell and other information to help us make a decision.

We need salt to survive, but too much can be dangerous, so there's a level at which it's unpleasant and hard to swallow.

Likewise, sourness is good in a small amount as it evokes ripe fruit or fermented foods, but too much can mean food has spoiled.

Umami often reminds us of cooked proteins, the flavor of fermentation, or just foods that are delicious. Ongoing research is exploring whether fat, the other macronutrient alongside carbs and protein, is also a distinct taste.

A LIBRARY OF SCENTS

In order to help the decision-making process, we subconsciously remember almost everything we've ever smelled before, and there's a part of the brain that is like a big library of scents, which we can draw from at any time. Because of how smell is processed via memory and emotion, the smells that are stored alongside an emotion (a food from childhood, a loved one's perfume) are often recalled more viscerally. We can consciously add smells to this banked library, which is part of flavor training with beer. When we consciously think when drinking a beer, our brain is scanning through countless smell memories and not just those related to beer. That is why we sometimes recall unexpected flavors, such as breakfast cereal or candy. Our memories are unique to us, which is why smell and flavor are evocative personal experiences.

A SENSE FOR BEER

All of our senses combine with our previous life experience to create the perception of flavor in every beer we drink. Here's how it works.

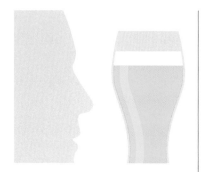

SIGHT

Sight is more accurate and nuanced than smell for most people, and the way a beer looks can greatly influence our expectations. We expect color to be an indication of flavor. If we're given a cherry-flavored soda that's an orange color, we may fail to realize it's cherry. We anticipate a bright yellow beer to taste different from a dark brown one. If a beer looks great, and is served in an attractive glass with the right amount of foam, we have higher expectations than if it's poorly served.

The branding or the name can influence flavor experience, too. Many people choose beers based on the label. We anticipate a beer called Mango Dream to be very different from one called Coffee Monster. Using visual cues like flavor wheels or a list of terms can help us identify flavors.

SMELL

Smell is infinite, nuanced, and elegant. We can smell complete "smell-scapes" of thousands of different aromas as well as singular chemical compounds. Nuance allows us to smell the difference between lemon and grapefruit, Saaz hops and Citra hops, and it also lets us smell a beer and pick out a dozen different descriptors.

We're able to take in the whole aroma, but can also direct our attention to specific parts of the beer, smelling past hop aroma to work out the malt, or bypassing yeast esters to try to identify the hop character.

From the hundreds of chemical compounds, our brain seeks patterns of aromas that it recognizes and can recall smells very accurately. The more smells we know, the more we're potentially able to recognize in beer.

TASTE

Almost every beer has at least two of the five basic tastes—sweet, bitter, sour, salty, and umami—while some may have all five. Taste combines with aroma to create a nuanced flavor experience: the flavor of lemon is perceived differently if the base beer tastes bitter (lemon peel), sweet (lemon curd), or sour (fresh lemon).

We're able to distinguish between low, medium, and high volumes of the tastes, though they can balance each other out or emphasize each other: we perceive high bitterness as lower if the beer is very sweet. Sweetness is in all beers to varying amounts, and most beers have a bitter taste, except sour beers.

Sourness could be acidic/lactic or acetic. A small amount of sourness is pleasant, but can be unpalatable if too high.

EVERY MEMORY OF A GREAT BEER IS ATTACHED TO AN EXPERIENCE RATHER THAN SIMPLY THE FLAVOR OF THE BEER.

CULTURAL REFERENCES

Flavor exists in cultural spaces with different reference points, so the flavors we grow up with are the ones we're more likely to identify in beer. Every country has different specific flavors that resonate, which is particularly relevant with hop-forward beers with exotic and fruity aromas, and with stronger beers, where a lot of those reference points come from a place of nostalgia, like candy. Drinkers from Seoul, Mumbai, Wellington, Milan, and Denver will all know a different mix of flavors.

TOUCH

We can identify characteristics of a beer by the way it feels in the mouth. We notice temperature differences down to the degree, and carbonation can be still, fizzy, or creamy. Some bubbles are small and tight (like Champagne), while others are big (like soda).

Viscosity could be light like an American Lager or thick like Imperial Stout, as in the difference between skim milk and cream.

Astringency (tannins) has a drying feeling, like grape skins, and it could come in very dry, very bitter, or oak-aged beers.

Alcohol can sometimes be felt as a warming sensation in strong beers. Other characteristics we can detect in the mouth include spiciness from chile, pungency from ingredients such as ginger, and the cooling quality of mint or menthol.

SOUND

Sound might not seem like it can influence flavor, but it can have an effect in some important ways. The sound of a beer being opened is a cue to make you thirsty, as is the sound of a beer fizzing in the glass.

More relevant is the impact of human interaction: if someone hands you a beer and says "This smells like chocolate truffles," then you're likely to smell chocolate truffles. If they hand you a beer and say "This was voted the best beer in the world," then you have a higher expectation than if someone says "Does this smell weird to you?"

EXPERIENCE, EXPECTATION, & ENVIRONMENT

Our knowledge and experience help shape the flavors we find. If we have a broad understanding of different foods and flavors, we have a larger library of scents to recall and identify in beer.

Understanding different beer styles can mean we're able to assess a beer more quickly. If we're experienced tasters, we should be able to identify a wider range of drinking characteristics.

Drinking a beer we know is rare or highly rated can increase our expectation of it and perhaps mean we're biased toward a more positive evaluation.

Environment is also important: drinking a fresh pint of beer in the brewery where it's made will often be an elevated experience compared to drinking that beer at home.

SENSORY EVALUATION OF BEER

Here we look at tasting techniques and evaluative characteristics that you should consider when drinking and evaluating a beer.

HOW TO TASTE BEER

We all find our own ways of tasting that work best for us, but there are certain techniques that can help.

I. Look at the beer. What's the color and clarity like? Is there good foam? Does it look attractive to drink?

2. Swirl the beer to release some of the volatile aroma compounds. Can you smell anything at arm's length? As you get closer, can you smell anything different? Is it fruity, malty, spicy, or something else?

3. Smell again and this time inhale deeply. Then take shorter, sharper breaths (we can detect more aromas with rapid inhalations). Can you pick out any specific aromas? Are the aromas delicate or intense?

4. Take a sip or a mouthful. Move the beer around your mouth and, if you can, breathe in through the mouth at the same time—it'll help move all the aroma compounds around, while also coating your tongue.

5. Swallow and exhale, trying to push the air back through your mouth and up and out of your nose. Think about the flavors, the tastes, the mouthfeel, the finish, and the overall quality of the beer.

KEY CHARACTERISTICS

As we get more confident at tasting, we can begin to apply more evaluative critiques, like comparing beers and understanding if something is what we expect or not, adding scale (low sweetness, high bitterness), identifying different ingredients and flavors, and considering it all in context. Evaluate in order from the beer's appearance to its lasting qualities. Here are some things to consider.

APPEARANCE AND FOAM

- Straw to black.
- Bright, hazy, cloudy, opaque (is there any unwanted sediment?).
- No foam to lasting foam and look at the foam color (white to dark brown).
- Does it look good?
- Is it appropriate to the style?

AROMA

- Light, medium, or intense.
- The character and origin of the aroma (hops, malt, fruity, spicy, wild yeast, aged, and so on).
- Is it what we expect in the beer?
- Is there anything negative in the aroma?

TASTE

- How sweet is it (dry to syrupy)?
- Is the bitterness low, medium, or high? Does it arrive immediately or does it grow as you drink?
- If relevant to the beer, can you distinguish between hop and malt bitterness (think grapefruit peel versus espresso)?
- Is there any acidity and is that appropriate to the beer?
- How is the balance of flavors? Is it appropriate to the beer style?

MOUTHFEEL AND DRINKING CHARACTERISTICS

- Light, medium, or full-bodied.
- Crisp and dry to heavy/sweet.
- Carbonation: low or flat like water to high like Champagne.
- Intensity: subtle/delicate to very strong.
- Depth of flavor: often one of the main qualities of a world-class beer is a greater depth of overall flavor complexity.
- Finish: does the flavor linger or disappear quickly (and either way, is that good)? What are the lasting characteristics?

OVERALL IMPRESSION

- Is it a good beer, an excellent one, or is it poor or faulty?

IS IT APPROPRIATE?

Comparing a beer to what we expect from the style is a good way to assess its character. A Helles might have a great tropical fruit aroma, for example, but it's not right for the style.

TASTING SHEET

Use this tasting sheet as a guide to the characteristics to consider when tasting and evaluating a beer. Start with flavors and aromas, and then list more specific tasting terms in the comments section. For example, if you smell something bready, try to identify what it is.

APPEARANCE			COLOR		
CLEAR	HAZY	OPAQUE	STRAW	YELLOW	GOLD

MALT & ADJUNCT	HOPS	ESTERS
GRAINY	FLORAL/GRASSY	PEAR/APPLE
CREAMY	FLORAL/FRUITY	BANANA
BREADY	CITRUS	ANISEED
BAKED	TROPICAL	FLORAL
TOASTY	MELON	DARK FRUIT
FRUITY	STONE FRUIT	VINOUS
SPICY	BERRY	WARMING
CARAMELIZED/SWEET	SWEET AROMATIC	VANILLA
ROASTED	SPICE	TROPICAL
SMOKED	PUNGENT	STONE FRUIT
	HERBAL/WOODY	OTHERS

MOUTHFEEL AND DRINKING EXPERIENCE		
CARBONATION	BODY	BITTERNESS
None → High	Thin → Full	Low → High

BALANCE			
APPROPRIATE	INAPPROPRIATE	FAULTY	POOR

				FOAM		GENERAL COMMENTS

ORANGE	AMBER	BROWN	BLACK	NONE	LASTING

WILD/SOUR/ PHENOLS	OTHERS	FERMENTATION
LACTIC/ACIDIC	WOOD/OAK	CLEAN/NEUTRAL
ACETIC	SHERRY/AGED	FRUITY
FRUITY BRETT	NUTTY/AGED	SPICY
FUNKY BRETT	ADDED FLAVOR	WILD/BRETT
PHENOLIC	ALCOHOL	SOUR

NEGATIVES/INAPPROPRIATE TO STYLE

DIACETYL/BUTTER	OXIDIZED
ACETALDEHYDE/APPLE	PHENOLIC
DMS/CORN	SOUR
SULFUR	OTHER

SWEETNESS	INTENSITY	FINISH
Low → High	Subtle → Intense	Short → Lasting

OVERALL IMPRESSION

ADEQUATE	GOOD	VERY GOOD	EXCELLENT

UNDERSTANDING BEER STYLES

Styles categorize beers and help us understand them. They have an expected flavor profile, guiding drinkers to the beer they want to buy and helping brewers create their recipes.

WHAT IS A BEER STYLE?

Some styles are traditional, often closely associated with a particular country, region, city, or even a singular brewery. Historically, those styles developed because of the local ingredients and brewing processes, and they became the regular kind of beer in that place.

As interest grew in world brewing, beer styles were formulated into guidelines, categorizing and differentiating the flavors, ingredients, and qualities—such as amount of bitterness, alcohol content, sweetness—we expect. Those style guides created a foundation for all beer types and helped to further the wider world's understanding of beer.

WHY BEER STYLES?

Defined beer styles were developed more theoretically in beer writing in the 1970s and 1980s. As beer competitions became more popular, these styles formed the common reference points by which to compare and judge beers, and committees of experts put parameters around the expected characteristics of classic versions of a style. As craft beer became more popular, beer styles were one of the most important ways of differentiating the flavor profiles of beer. Styles help us determine whether we want to order the Dubbel or the Double IPA, the Pilsner or the Porter.

UNDERSTANDING THE PREFIX OR SUFFIX

Nowadays, many classic beer styles come with a prefix or suffix that helps us understand what to expect.

Beer style guides create lines between styles based on typical examples, but those lines are not strict and no style guide is completely rigid in its definition— there's overlap in flavor between

SESSION OR TABLE

Lower alcohol version of the style (Session IPA, Table Saison).

IMPERIAL OR DOUBLE

Higher alcohol version of the style (Imperial Brown Ale, Double IPA).

styles. The nature of beer means that brewers are always looking to create their own versions of typical beer styles, brewed in their own way. They can use the classic recipe as a foundation to produce something new, while still giving the drinker an expectation of a beer's underlying characteristics, such as a Citra-hopped Belgian Blonde, for example.

RECIPE AND FLAVOR

Much like cooking, each beer is a product of its recipe, including ingredients, processes, temperature, equipment, and a sense of place— a specific location and inspiration. Classic recipes enable brewers to brew authentic versions of beer styles or see how they can tweak a recipe in a nontraditional way.

CONTEMPORARY & INNOVATIVE BEERS

New styles are emerging all the time, often as an evolution or revolution of an existing style, while other styles change and form into new sub-styles. Some of the new styles stay with us and become increasingly popular, like Hazy IPA, while others are a brief trend. But every beer comes with a context to it, whether it's a sub-style (Sour IPA) or the use of a prefix (Imperial Pilsner). Styles become a reference point, and while it's still possible to create an entirely new type of beer, it will always rely upon an older style for inspiration.

IPA OR INDIA

Used anywhere to mean aromatic hops (Red IPA, India Porter).

JUICY/ HAZY/NEW ENGLAND

A cloudy, hop-aromatic beer (Juicy Pale, Hazy IPA).

AMERICAN

A hop-aromatic beer using American hops and often stronger than a typical version (American Stout).

BEER STYLE FLAVOR MAP

A knowledge of beer styles helps us understand what we're drinking. Styles exist in a continuum of flavor, where each beer style is a combination of hop, grain, fermentation, and maturation flavors. This map of flavor and beer styles shows how styles are placed within the overall world of beer. The scale is biased toward the flavor impact of an ingredient, rather than the intensity of the flavor, so Mild and Imperial Stout can sit close to each other thanks to their malt-forward flavor, even at completely different intensities.

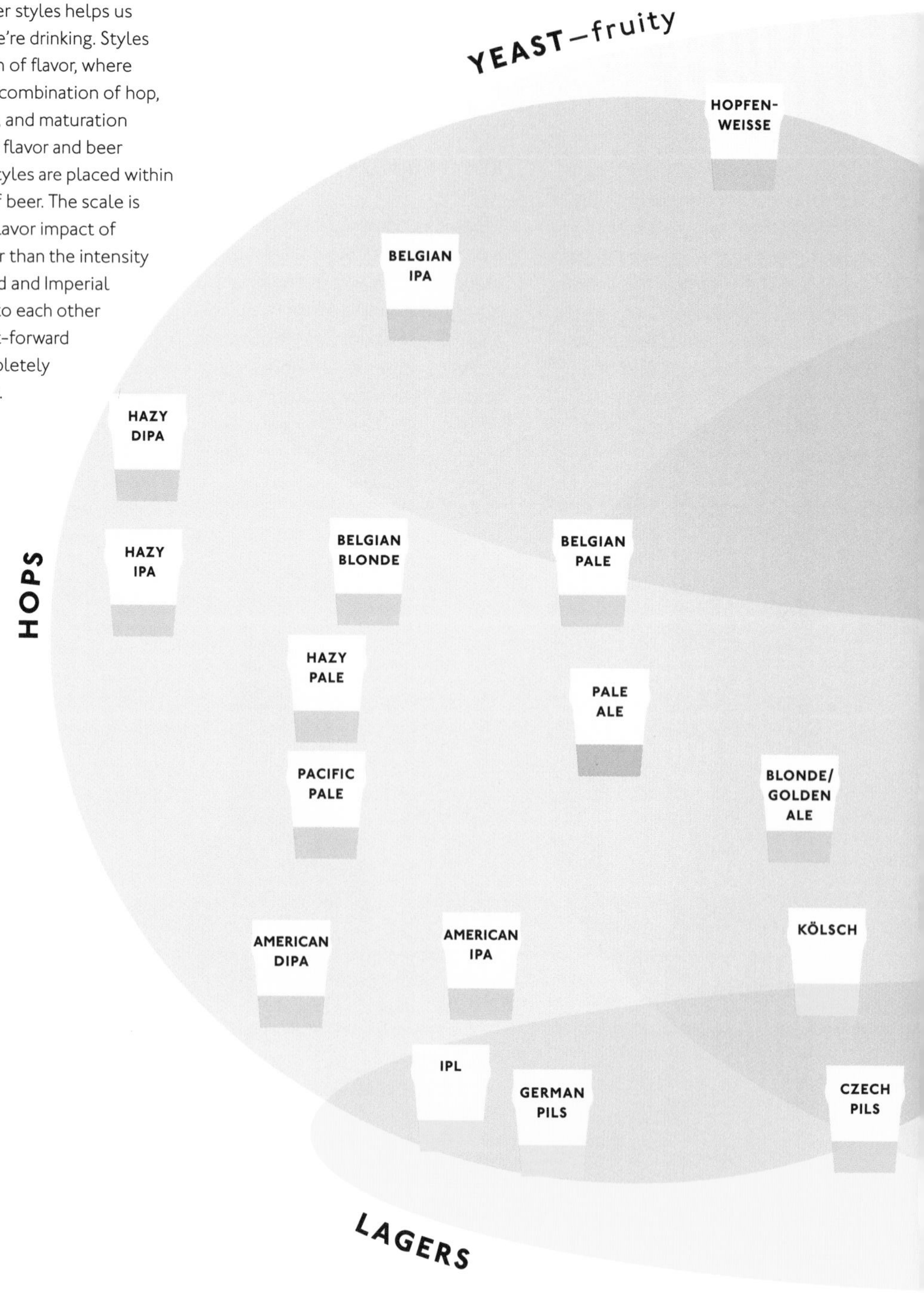

YEAST—fruity

HOPFEN-WEISSE

BELGIAN IPA

HAZY DIPA

HOPS

HAZY IPA

BELGIAN BLONDE

BELGIAN PALE

HAZY PALE

PALE ALE

PACIFIC PALE

BLONDE/ GOLDEN ALE

AMERICAN DIPA

AMERICAN IPA

KÖLSCH

IPL

GERMAN PILS

CZECH PILS

LAGERS

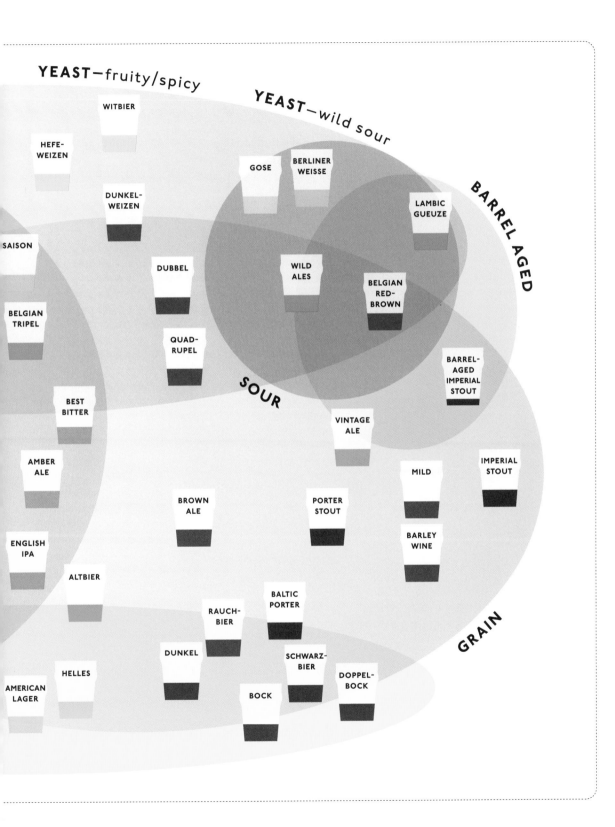

YEAST—fruity/spicy

YEAST—wild sour

BARREL AGED

SOUR

GRAIN

WITBIER

HEFE-WEIZEN

DUNKEL-WEIZEN

GOSE

BERLINER WEISSE

LAMBIC GUEUZE

SAISON

DUBBEL

WILD ALES

BELGIAN RED-BROWN

BELGIAN TRIPEL

QUAD-RUPEL

BARREL-AGED IMPERIAL STOUT

BEST BITTER

VINTAGE ALE

AMBER ALE

MILD

IMPERIAL STOUT

BROWN ALE

PORTER STOUT

BARLEY WINE

ENGLISH IPA

ALTBIER

BALTIC PORTER

RAUCH-BIER

DUNKEL

SCHWARZ-BIER

DOPPEL-BOCK

AMERICAN LAGER

HELLES

BOCK

BEER FOAM

When you pour a beer into a glass, bubbles of gas head to the top of the glass, forming foam. Foam is one of the most distinctive features of a beer, and while lots of other drinks have bubbles—such as soda, Champagne, and hard cider—no other drinks naturally form a lasting foam when they're poured.

PRESSURE CHANGE

The beer inside a can or bottle is saturated with gas, usually carbon dioxide (CO_2). When you open the beer, you change the pressure inside the container and the gas starts to escape (that's the pssst you hear when you open it). If you leave a can or bottle of beer open, then the carbon dioxide gradually escapes and the beer goes flat. When you open a beer to pour it out, it's the action of pouring that encourages foam to form.

The carbon dioxide is knocked out of the beer as it hits the glass, but it doesn't simply pop or float away like balloons released from a net. Inside the glass are tiny nucleation points—slight imperfections on the smooth surface, or an etched pattern in the base of the glass (see opposite). The gas collects in those points and grows into bubbles, which are released into the beer. Bubbles continue to form in those nucleation sites while you drink, and the more saturated carbon dioxide in the beer, the more bubbles you'll get.

The bubbles head up through the beer until they reach the surface. What makes beer special is that the bubbles don't immediately pop at the top; instead, they form into foam and grip the glass. They will eventually burst, but a constant supply of new bubbles rising through the beer maintains the foam.

LOOK AT THE LACING

When you walk into a bar or pub, don't look at the full glasses, look at the empty ones. If you can see foam clinging to the inside of the glass like a lace pattern, then you know you're in a well-maintained place. The foam will cling to the glass only if the beer has been well brewed and is served well in a clean glass. You can also tell how quickly a person has drunk the beer based on how many rings there are—the fewer the rings, the bigger the gulps they've taken.

BEER BUBBLES DON'T POP

The hydrophobic protein in barley—which is not found in Champagne, hard cider, or soda—means bubbles form into foam and grip the glass.

BUBBLES HEAD UP THROUGH THE BEER

The bubbles move up through the beer to the surface. A supply of new bubbles forming at the bottom of the glass maintains the foam.

DIRTY GLASS | **CLEAN GLASS**

NO FOAM
Beer in a dirty glass will have poor or no foam.

IMPERFECTIONS INSIDE THE GLASS
If the glass has tiny spots of grease, dirt, or detergent, bubbles will cling to the sides of the glass, spoiling the appearance of the beer.

LACING
Foam will only form lacing on a clean glass.

GOOD FOAM RETENTION
Beer that retains a good layer of foam is an indication that the glass is clean.

NUCLEATED GLASSES

Look at the bottom of your empty beer glass. Do you see an etched design there, such as the brewery's logo, a pattern, or a series of lines? These are nucleation marks, which help create more bubbles and maintain good foam.

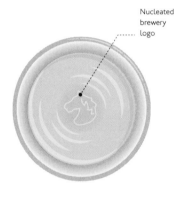

Nucleated brewery logo

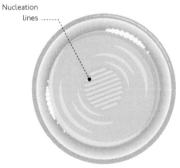

Nucleation lines

BEER-CLEAN GLASS

Ever seen bubbles on the inside of your glass? They're not a good sign. Those bubbles are stuck to tiny spots of dirt, detergent, or grease, which will affect the appearance (they look terrible) and the beer won't have good foam. Even a glass straight from the dishwasher might not be perfectly clean. At home, before pouring any beer, it's a good idea to wash your glass well with warm, soapy water, rinse it in cold water, and then pour the beer into the wet glass.

WHY FOAM MATTERS

Beer foam is a mixture of beer and carbon dioxide. If you pour a beer with a lot of foam, the liquid part always settles back to beer. The foam is important because it's able to hold on to aroma compounds, especially from hops and yeast, while it can also give a nice textural drinking experience, especially with a nitro-poured beer (see p.30) or a proper Czech lager pour.

POURING THE PERFECT BEER

Serve yourself the perfect glass of beer every time. For the majority of beers, you simply need to start pouring with the glass tilted at 45 degrees, but bottle-conditioned and naturally cloudy beers require a slightly different approach.

BOTTLE-CONDITIONED BEERS

Many British and Belgian ales are bottle conditioned (see p.69), meaning a small sediment of yeast remains in the bottom of the bottle. To avoid serving the yeast, store the bottle upright in the fridge for at least 24 hours before opening. Pour in one motion so you don't disturb the sediment, leaving a small amount of beer in the bottom of the bottle.

NITRO STOUT

Picture a pint of Guinness. It's a beer infused with nitrogen gas as well as carbon dioxide, and it's the nitrogen, and the way that the beer is poured, that give Guinness its distinctive foam.

Nitrogen is quite insoluble in liquid, but it's held inside a beer by the pressure of the can, bottle, or keg. When the beer is served, the nitrogen comes out of solution, creating the cascading appearance. To help it out, the gas needs to be knocked out with some force. Canned nitro beers, such as Guinness, usually contain a "widget," a small plastic ball infused with nitrogen, and this breaks the bubbles out of solution while also disturbing the bubbles as the beer's being poured. In draft nitro beer, there's a restrictor plate in the tap, which is rather like a shower head punctuated with lots of holes, and the plate disturbs the gas out of solution.

At home, you can pour nitro beers like a bartender would serve a Guinness—stop pouring near the top, let the foam settle, and then top up the glass—but it's not essential.

THE PERFECT POUR

For most beers, including lagers, pale ales, and dark ales, open your beer and hold a clean, wet glass at around 45 degrees. Pour the beer with some vigor down the inside of the glass, allowing foam to form as you continue to pour down the inside of the glass. As the beer fills up the glass and the foam rises, straighten the glass and pour until it is full.

1

45°

TILT THE GLASS
Start with a clean, wet glass tilted at an angle of about 45 degrees.

2

POUR VIGOROUSLY
Foam should form as you pour the beer vigorously down the inside of the glass.

3

STRAIGHTEN UP
As the beer fills the glass and the foam rises, straighten the glass and pour until it is full.

HEFEWEIZEN AND WITBIER

These are naturally cloudy beers, and the cloudiness, which is composed of grain proteins and yeast, should remain in the glass.

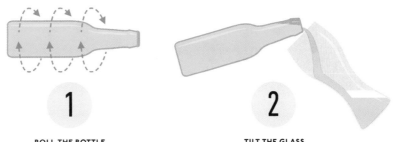

1

ROLL THE BOTTLE
Gently roll the bottle before opening it to rouse the yeast.

2

TILT THE GLASS
Hold the glass at an angle of about 45 degrees and pour the beer down the inside of the glass.

3

STRAIGHTEN UP
Straighten the glass when it is about three-quarters full.

Rotate the bottle to mix up the yeast

4

SWIRL THE BOTTLE
When the glass is almost full, swirl the bottle around to mix up the yeast.

5

TOP UP
Then top up the glass so it has a full foam and a lightly hazy appearance.

BEST SERVING TEMPERATURE

What temperature do you serve beer at? Some experts prefer to serve every beer cold from the fridge (39°–45°F/4°–7°C). Others may give suggested temperatures for certain styles (see right). Pale, light beers are often served colder than strong, dark beers because the colder a beer is served, the more dulled the flavors might be, so if it's a richer and more complex beer, you might not want it icy-cold. However, it's best to serve beer at the temperature you most enjoy it. And remember that if it's too cold, it'll warm up in your glass, but it's not so easy to cool it once it's too warm.

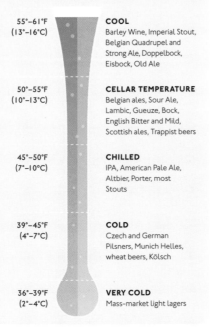

55°–61°F (13°–16°C)

COOL
Barley Wine, Imperial Stout, Belgian Quadrupel and Strong Ale, Doppelbock, Eisbock, Old Ale

50°–55°F (10°–13°C)

CELLAR TEMPERATURE
Belgian ales, Sour Ale, Lambic, Gueuze, Bock, English Bitter and Mild, Scottish ales, Trappist beers

45°–50°F (7°–10°C)

CHILLED
IPA, American Pale Ale, Altbier, Porter, most Stouts

39°–45°F (4°–7°C)

COLD
Czech and German Pilsners, Munich Helles, wheat beers, Kölsch

36°–39°F (2°–4°C)

VERY COLD
Mass-market light lagers

DOES THE GLASS MATTER?

Glasses from around the world have different characteristics, but do differences in shape affect the flavor or does it all come down to personal preference?

DIFFERENT GLASSES

The easy answer to this question is yes, the shape of the glass can make a difference to the appearance, aroma, flavor, and drinking experience of a beer:

- A tulip rim on a bowl glass will intensify the aroma, so these suit complex and stronger beers that you want to swirl and contemplate.
- A wide-mouthed glass such as a *Krug*, shaker, or pint is designed for easy drinking, so it is best for pub beers such as lagers, standard ales, and IPAs.

- A small taper to the top of a glass is good for IPAs, focusing on the hop aroma without making it too intense.

PERSONAL TASTE

At the same time, though, it's important that you drink from a glass you like. If you prefer to drink beer from a stemless wine glass because you like the shape, feel, and consistency it gives to the tasting experience, that's perfectly fine. If, on the other hand, you just want to open a beer, pour it out, and drink without thinking, then

IN A GLASS OF ITS OWN

Belgium is famous for every beer having its own specifically designed glass. Each vessel celebrates the best aspects of that particular beer, so matching the beer to the glass creates an elevated drinking experience.

the traditional Willibecher glass is a good option.

More than any other advice about beer glasses, though, the most important is to make sure the glass is really clean and at the right temperature for the beer you are drinking (see p.31).

STEINS AND MUGS

A thick wall ensures your beer remains cool, while the dimples make the wider glass easier to hold. This glass type is particularly popular for traditional British ales and for German and Czech lagers.

DIMPLED MUG/MAß
Helles, Dunkel, Festbier

STEINKRUG
German lagers

MUG
Czech Pilsner, British ales

WEIZENS AND LAGERS

The gently curved shape, with a slightly narrower top than the more traditional mugs, allows the beer to remain carbonated. It's perfect, then, for a lager, Pale Ale, Blonde, or wheat beer. The tall shape makes the rising bubbles visible, and there's enough room at the opening for a foam head.

WEIZEN
Weissbier

TALL FLUTED
Pilsners

WILLIBECHER
*German lagers,
British ales, Pale Ales*

EVERYDAY GLASSES

These glasses are designed for everyday beers. They are simple, easy to drink from, and work with a wide variety of styles, though they aren't necessarily the first-choice glasses if you want to properly evaluate a beer's flavor.

BELGIAN TUMBLER
Saison, Sour Beers, Witbier

IMPERIAL PINT
*British ales, Stouts,
Pale Ales, IPAs*

SHAKER
*American Lagers,
Pale Ales, IPAs*

GOBLETS AND CHALICES

The curved bottom of these small glasses enhances the flavor and aroma of the beer. As with wine glasses, the stem gives drinkers the ability to swirl their drink, enhancing the aromatics and the overall drinking experience. This glass shape is perfect for stronger and more complex beers.

STEMLESS WINE GLASS/TUMBLER
Any beer style

STEMMED GLASS
Any beer style

SNIFTER
*Strong Ales, Barley
Wine, Imperial Stouts*

GOBLET
Belgian ales

HOW BEER IS MADE

There are several distinct stages in the process of making beer (brewing) to take the raw ingredients to the finished drink. The following is a basic overview for brewing a typical ale or lager.

HOT SIDE

Before brewing begins, the brewing liquor (water) is warmed to around 158°F (70°C) in the hot liquor tank. The grain is weighed out and milled (crushed), like grinding whole coffee beans.

- **The mash** Warm water combines with milled grain in the mash tun. The water draws color, flavor, fermentable sugars, and other compounds from the grain. Temperatures and specific processes have an important impact on flavor (see pp.42–43). The sweet liquid produced is called wort.
- **Lauter** Wort is separated from the grain, either in a lauter tun, with wort and grain transferred across and then separated, or the wort is drawn from the mash tun into the next vessel, the kettle, leaving the grain behind. The grain husks create a natural filter bed as the wort flows through it, and more warm water is sparged (sprinkled) over to extract as much fermentable sugar as possible. Spent grain is removed.
- **The kettle** The wort transfers to the kettle, where it's brought to a rolling boil for 60–90 minutes. Hops are added into the kettle, with additions at the beginning of the boil giving bitterness, and later additions giving flavor and aroma (see pp.56–57).
- **Whirlpool** The hopped wort flows through a whirlpool or hop back to remove hop plant matter and other unwanted particles, together known as trub. Brewers can also include additional hops here.

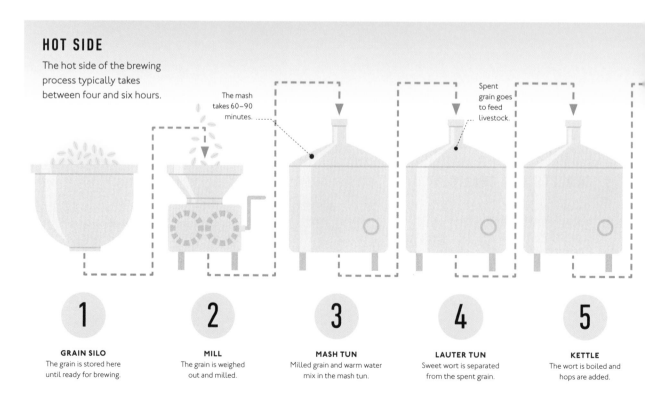

HOT SIDE

The hot side of the brewing process typically takes between four and six hours.

The mash takes 60–90 minutes.

Spent grain goes to feed livestock.

1
GRAIN SILO
The grain is stored here until ready for brewing.

2
MILL
The grain is weighed out and milled.

3
MASH TUN
Milled grain and warm water mix in the mash tun.

4
LAUTER TUN
Sweet wort is separated from the spent grain.

5
KETTLE
The wort is boiled and hops are added.

COLD SIDE

- **Cooling** The hot hopped wort flows through a heat exchange alongside cold water as it cools to fermentation temperature (50°–68°F/10°–20°C) on its way into a fermenter.
- **Fermentation** Yeast is added to the fermenter. The yeast converts the grain's sugars into alcohol, carbon dioxide, and numerous flavor compounds. The fermentation temperature and the amount of time taken will vary based on the yeast (see p.65), but most primary fermentations take two to nine days. It finishes when the desired amount of sugar has been converted into the target alcohol content.
- **Maturation & conditioning** The beer is chilled further, usually down to around 32°–36°F (0°–2°C) over the process of a few days. During this time, the beer could be dry hopped (see p.56) and left to mature and condition, developing its final flavor profile. This process could take anything from a couple of days to a couple of months (see pp.68–69).
- **Filtration or centrifuge** Some beers will have the yeast removed or reduced by a filter or centrifuge on their way to a packaging tank or bright beer tank—"bright" is an old reference to the beer "dropping bright" (being clear and without yeast).
- **Packaging** Finished beer is filled into either cans, bottles, kegs, or casks. It might be pasteurized during the packaging process, which heats the beer—often inside the cans or bottles—to kill

CARBONATION

Beer can be naturally carbonated in the conditioning tank; it can be force-carbonated, meaning carbon dioxide is pushed into the beer inside a pressurized tank; or it can be carbonated and conditioned inside the bottle or cask (see pp.68–69).

any potential microbiological spoilage and to keep the beer shelf-stable for longer (see p.69). The beer might be left to condition a little longer, as with bottle-conditioned beers, before it heads out to bars and stores.

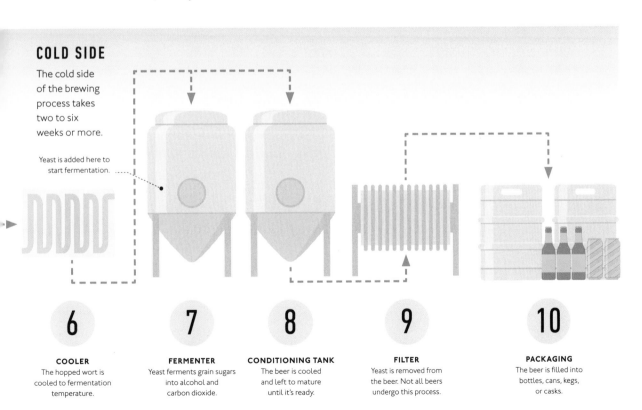

COLD SIDE

The cold side of the brewing process takes two to six weeks or more.

Yeast is added here to start fermentation.

6

COOLER
The hopped wort is cooled to fermentation temperature.

7

FERMENTER
Yeast ferments grain sugars into alcohol and carbon dioxide.

8

CONDITIONING TANK
The beer is cooled and left to mature until it's ready.

9

FILTER
Yeast is removed from the beer. Not all beers undergo this process.

10

PACKAGING
The beer is filled into bottles, cans, kegs, or casks.

WATER IN BEER

Your glass of beer is around 90 percent water,
and when it comes to beer, water isn't just water—
it can have a big impact on drinking characteristics.

WATER IN THE BREWERY

Beer is basically flavored and fermented water. The water that enters a brewer's mash tun and lauter tun will emerge as delicious beer a few weeks later. In the intervening time, it's been mixed with grain, heated, strained, boiled with hops, strained again, and cooled, then fermented and left to condition. The one constant thing is the water, which is now carrying all the flavor and the alcohol.

Every source of water is slightly different in its mineral content, and those minerals affect qualities in beer, with different styles requiring subtly different water compositions. Brewers are able to adjust their water to suit whatever beer they're brewing.

BREWING-WATER SCIENCE

Some minerals affect the mash pH, which in turn influences the quality of the beer, while other minerals can have a more significant impact on drinking characteristics. The optimum mash pH for brewing a non-sour beer is 5.1–5.5pH. Pale beers need to become more acidic (lower pH), and dark beers more alkaline (higher pH)—water and steps in the mashing process influence this. Getting the pH correct is important to ensure the malt enzymes are active in the mash (see pp.42–43). If a pH is too high, then flavors can be dulled, while if it's too low, it can encourage bacteria to develop.

Calcium is arguably the most important mineral in beer because it lowers the pH, helps with clarity and stability of the beer, and is a nutrient for yeast. Magnesium helps lower mash pH and is also a yeast nutrient. Carbonate and bicarbonate raise the pH, so they work well in darker ales, while also enhancing malt flavors. Sodium can contribute to a fuller mouthfeel and richer sweetness, but won't affect pH. Sulfate and chloride are important as a duo: sulfate can accentuate hop bitterness and give a drier and crisper quality, while chloride can make a beer feel fuller bodied or sweeter; brewers seek to find a ratio balance between these two minerals in all beers.

COMPOSITION OF BEER

In a standard 5% ABV beer, water makes up more than 90 percent of the total composition. The rest is composed of alcohol, carbon dioxide (CO_2), and minerals and extract, which include all the flavor compounds.

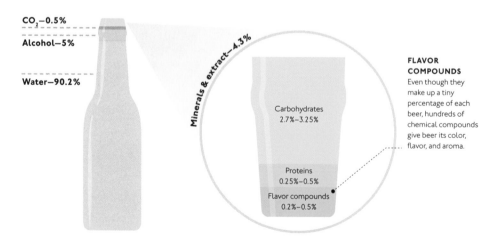

CO_2—0.5%

Alcohol—5%

Water—90.2%

Minerals & extract—4.3%

Carbohydrates
2.7%–3.25%

Proteins
0.25%–0.5%

Flavor compounds
0.2%–0.5%

FLAVOR COMPOUNDS
Even though they make up a tiny percentage of each beer, hundreds of chemical compounds give beer its color, flavor, and aroma.

HISTORIC LEVELS OF MINERALS IN BREWING WATER

The world's classic beer styles all come from a particular place, often a specific city: Pilsen's Pilsners, Munich's Dunkel Lagers, London's Porters and Bitters, Burton's India Pale Ales (IPAs), and Dublin's Stouts. The reason is not simply that drinkers there had a preference for those kinds of beers, it's that the natural water source available to brewers only allowed them to brew certain kinds of beers successfully. The data in this table are from the mid-19th century. The higher the numbers, the harder the water.

The very soft water of Pilsen gives a softer hop bitterness and allows the malt flavor to dominate.

Munich's water is relatively balanced, but it's on the hard side with higher alkalinity from carbonates, which balance darker malts, while low sulfates increase the malt flavor.

The dark malts in London Porters and Bitters are balanced by the water's high carbonates, while the chloride and sodium give those darker beers a richer malt flavor.

Water in the IPA of Burton has high sulfates (specifically gypsum or calcium sulfate) to enhance the hop bitterness and give the beer a dry finish.

In Dublin, the water is high in bicarbonates, giving a hard alkaline water that is essential to lower the pH from the roasted dark malts in the mash.

MINERAL	CITY AND BEER STYLE				
	Pilsen Pilsner	Munich Dunkel	London Porter/ Bitter	Burton India Pale Ale	Dublin Dry Stout
CALCIUM Lowers mash pH, helps beer stability, important yeast nutrient.	10	109	52	352	118
MAGNESIUM Lowers mash pH, helps beer stability, important yeast nutrient (less so than calcium).	3	21	32	24	4
CARBONATE/BICARBONATE Raise pH and can enhance malt flavors and residual sweetness.	3	171	104	320	319
SODIUM No effect on pH but gives a fuller/smoother mouthfeel and malt flavors.	3	2	86	44	12
SULFATE Accentuates hop bitterness, gives a crisper, drier quality.	4	79	32	820	54
CHLORIDE Makes beer feel more full bodied and taste sweeter.	4	36	34	16	19

WATER TREATMENT

When brewers understood water science and how to manipulate it, they were able to brew beer styles anywhere in the world, which changed the future of brewing. Most brewers source water from the city system, though some have a natural water source. Either way, the water almost always undergoes some treatment in the brewery to purify it, removing trace minerals, ions, and particles. Brewers can add extra minerals back to adjust the water profile to their exact specification, depending on the beer.

GRAINS & MALTING

Grain gives beer color and flavor plus the sugars
that ferment into alcohol. Its journey from
field to brewery has several stages.

THE BREWING GRASSES

Barley is the principal brewing
grain. Alongside that, brewers
often use wheat, oats, corn,
and rice, and, less frequently, rye,
spelt, and non-gluten grains such
as buckwheat and sorghum. Each
grain gives different qualities to
beer. Barley is the main grain
because it naturally contains
enzymes that can convert its
unfermentable starches into
fermentable sugars during the
brewing process. In order to
activate those enzymes, the grain
first has to be turned into malt
through the malting process.

SMOKED MALTS

Smoked malts follow the
same steeping and germination
process as other malts, but they
are dried in direct-fired kilns over
wood fires, where they absorb
the smoke aromas.

THE MALTING PROCESS

Malt is a grain that has been harvested then allowed to
germinate before being dried (kilned) and sometimes
roasted. All the principal brewing grains can be malted,
but different processes are required for corn and rice.
This illustration shows the process for barley.

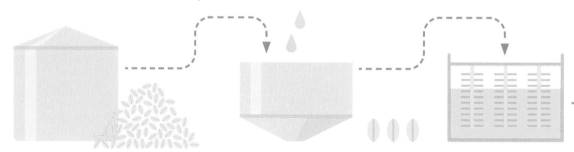

1
HARVEST
Barley is harvested, checked,
cleaned, and then stored in silos
until it's ready to begin the
malting process. It's essentially
a dormant seed at this stage.

2
STEEPING
The barley is soaked in water
(54°–59°F/12°–15°C) for around
two days, where it hydrates to
around 45 percent from 12
percent moisture. Enzymes in
the grain come back to life.

3
GERMINATION
The barley is transferred to a
humid germination compartment
at 55°–64°F (13°–18°C). Over the
next four to six days, the grain's
cell wall begins to break down,
starch-degrading enzymes are
released, and the barley begins
to sprout. The grain is regularly
turned (raked) during this stage.

BEYOND BARLEY

Brewers can add supplementary, or adjunct, ingredients to the mash, with some adding body and sweetness, others creating a dry beer, and some adding flavor.

Candi sugar (light or dark) is common in strong Belgian ales.

Dark sugars leave behind a dried fruit and brown sugar flavor. Honey, molasses, and maple syrup add fermentable sugars as well as flavor. Dextrose (glucose) is highly fermentable and can give a lighter body and drier finish. Some brewers use glucose to replace some of the malt in their budget

lager brands. Lactose (milk sugar) is unfermentable, so remains as a smooth and creamy sweetness. Rice and corn give a clean, light, crisp beer.

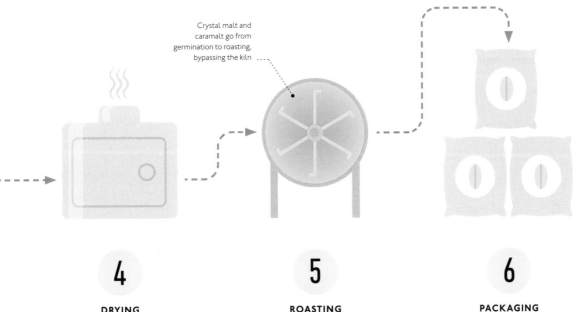

Crystal malt and caramalt go from germination to roasting, bypassing the kiln

4
DRYING
Germination is stopped by moving the barley to a kiln and passing warm air through it. It dries to 3 to 6 percent moisture, which could take about 24 hours. The temperature and time depend on the malt being produced. This creates the base malts such as Pilsner malt, pale ale malt, and Munich malt.

5
ROASTING
Darker malts like amber and chocolate are roasted after being kilned, adding new flavors and a different color. Time and temperature range from around 212°F (100°C) for 20 minutes for lightly roasted amber malts, to over 392°F (200°C) for two hours for chocolate malt. Roasted barley is unmalted barley that's been roasted.

6
PACKAGING
The malt is bagged or stored in silos before being sent to breweries.

TYPES OF MALT

The wide variety of malts brewers can use give
a range of different flavors and colors to beer.

MALT	TYPE	ADDS	FLAVORS
PILSNER	Base malt	Pale color, fermentable sugars	Straw/hay, grassy, bread
PALE ALE	Base malt	Pale color, fermentable sugars	Light malt flavor, bread, graham cracker
MARIS OTTER	Character/base malt	Pale color, fermentable sugars, rich malt flavor	Graham cracker, rich malt flavor, light toast
VIENNA	Darker base malt	Amber color, fermentable sugars, rich malt flavor	Toasted malt, toasted nuts, light caramel
MUNICH	Darker base malt	Amber color, fermentable sugars, rich and aromatic	Toasted malt, light to dark toast, bread crusts
AMBER/BISCUIT	Kilned/color malt	Rich grain flavors, more texture, darker color	Toasted nuts, toast, graham cracker
CRYSTAL/CARAMALT	Crystal/caramalt	Texture, caramelized flavors	Malted cereal, dried fruit, caramel
CHOCOLATE	Roasted malt	Dark color, roasted flavor	Dark chocolate, cacao, coffee
ROASTED BARLEY	Roasted malt	Dark color, roasted flavor	Bitter, espresso, burned toast
DEHUSKED	Roasted malt	Dark color, low roast flavor	Mild roast, mostly used for color
SMOKED	Smoked	Smoky aroma and flavor	Meat smoke, wood smoke, peat smoke
DEXTRIN MALT	Crystal/caramalt	Texture, foam	Low flavor, just light nutty sweetness
RICE/CORN	Adjunct	Lightens body, adds crispness	Rice, corn, creamy
WHEAT	Base malt	Higher protein for texture, haze, foam	Creamy, dough, cereal, bread
OATS	Base malt	Higher protein for texture, haze, foam	Creamy oats, cereal, bread
RYE/SPELT	Character/base malt	Different kilned malt flavors	Nutty, toasted, light spiciness

TYPES OF MALT

- **Base malts** are pale and lightly kilned malts like Pilsner and pale ale. They make up the majority of the grain bill and give most of the fermentable sugars.
- **Character malts** are like base malts but often a specific variety like Maris Otter and Chevallier, which impart a more distinctive flavor. They could also be flavor malts like rye or spelt.
- **Kilned malts** are darker in color, such as Dark Munich. These are a small percentage of the grain bill, adding color and rich malt flavor.
- **Crystal/caramalt** are crystallized malts that add a caramel, dried fruit, and malt-loaf quality, plus a fuller texture.
- **Roasted malts** include black and roasted barley. They're used in small volumes. They give color and flavor but no brewing enzymes and low to no sugars.

BEER COLOR

Color is measured in three ways: the European Brewing Convention (EBC) and Standard Reference Method (SRM) are numeric representations, with the higher the number, the darker the beer. The other is simply the color name. For almost everyone, the name is sufficient. Fruit can add color, from pink to dark purple.

NAME THE COLOR

It's most common to use established colors, such as straw, gold, amber, brown, and black, with modifiers like pale and dark.

STRAW
SRM 2
EBC 4

YELLOW
SRM 4
EBC 8

GOLD
SRM 6
EBC 12

ORANGE
SRM 9
EBC 18

PALE AMBER
SRM 14
EBC 28

DARK AMBER
SRM 17
EBC 33

RED BROWN
SRM 20
EBC 39

BROWN
SRM 32
EBC 63

BLACK
SRM 40
EBC 80

GRAIN IN THE BREWERY

Through a series of different techniques and processes, brewers turn water and grain into the various types of beer.

THE SCIENCE OF THE MASH

Barley is a complex kernel, with many different enzymes working in different ways and at different specific temperatures—if they go beneath their specific temperature range, they won't work, and above it, they'll be denatured ("killed").

During the mash, when the milled grain and hot water combine in the mash tun, insoluble compounds like unfermentable starches and amino acid chains (proteins) are broken down by different enzymes to become soluble. A successful mash uses temperatures to release enzymes, which convert those starches into fermentable sugars, like maltose (about 50 percent of the sugar content of wort), glucose, fructose, sucrose, and maltotriose.

All enzymatic activity is dependent on the specific conditions of the mash, including pH and density/gravity, but temperature is the most important.

ENZYMES IN BEER

If the wort is held at a certain temperature, enzymes are broken down and become soluble. If brewers hit all the right temperatures, they'll maximize the enzymes produced and create good wort.

Phytase is useful in pale lagers to help lower the mash pH (known as an acid rest). Beta-glucanase helps to dissolve starches, making the next step more efficient, though it's not so important with modern malts. The protein rest breaks down proteins, but many brewers might skip this as they want to keep protein in their beer for foam and haze.

The most important enzymes are beta- and alpha-amylase as these are responsible for the majority of the conversion of malt starches into sugars. Brewers perform a saccharification rest (or rests) to optimize this. The temperature range of 144°–162°F (62°–72°C) gives them some control over the fermentability of their beer and its final character: holding lower temperatures results in a more fermentable and crisper, drier beer, while higher temperatures give a fuller-bodied beer with more residual sweetness. It's common to hit 151°–153°F (66°–67°C) as a midpoint between beta and alpha. Some brewers may perform a mashout temperature rest, stopping any extra enzymatic activity.

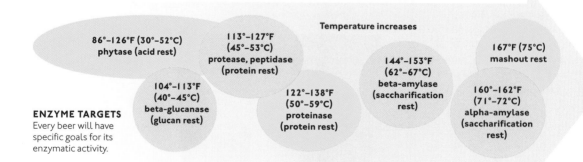

Temperature increases

86°–126°F (30°–52°C)
phytase (acid rest)

113°–127°F (45°–53°C)
protease, peptidase (protein rest)

144°–153°F (62°–67°C)
beta-amylase (saccharification rest)

167°F (75°C)
mashout rest

104°–113°F (40°–45°C)
beta-glucanase (glucan rest)

122°–138°F (50°–59°C)
proteinase (protein rest)

160°–162°F (71°–72°C)
alpha-amylase (saccharification rest)

ENZYME TARGETS
Every beer will have specific goals for its enzymatic activity.

DIFFERENT MASH TECHNIQUES

There are three main mashing techniques: infusion, step, and decoction. Infusion and step are used for ales and lagers. Decoction is typically only used for lagers and some Weissbiers.

An infusion mash is the simplest mashing technique. It requires "mashing in" the water just above the desired temperature, then holding it there for the entire mash, which is usually 60 minutes. The ideal temperature is 151°–153°F (66°–67°C), which allows beta- and alpha-amylase to convert the malt's starches into sugars.

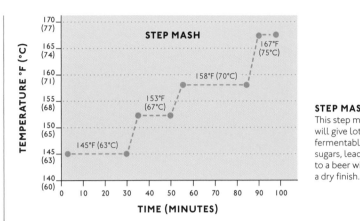

STEP MASH
This step mash will give lots of fermentable sugars, leading to a beer with a dry finish.

STEP MASH

A step mash requires ascending temperature steps and rests in order to maximize different enzymatic activities in the mash.

There will typically be two to four different steps (see above), correlating with the enzyme activity discussed opposite. This mash might take 60–90 minutes.

THE DECOCTION MASH

A decoction mash is a traditional German process. It works similarly to the step mash but involves removing a portion of the mash (grain and wort) and boiling it, then returning it to the overall mash, resulting in a jump in temperature plus the creation of new flavor compounds. These are due to the boiling and Maillard reaction (the latter gives more toasted and caramelized qualities). Brewers can do a single, double, or triple decoction (see right). This mash is more time consuming than the other methods and may take several hours.

Some breweries might add melanoidin malt instead because it adds strong malt flavor and Maillard qualities reminiscent of those given by a decoction mash.

TRIPLE DECOCTION
A triple decoction can take more than five hours to complete. Here, a mashout temperature rest is performed at 167°F (75°C).

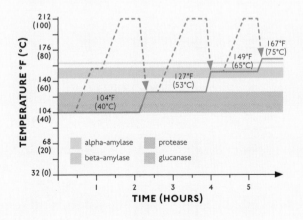

THE FLAVORS OF MALT

Malt, grain, and other starches or sugars give beer a range of flavors, which are reminiscent of grain-based products, baked goods, and caramelized and roasted qualities.

MALT FLAVORS

In malt-forward beers, malt flavors are more prominent than hop and yeast flavors. Some flavors overlap between the different groups shown here.

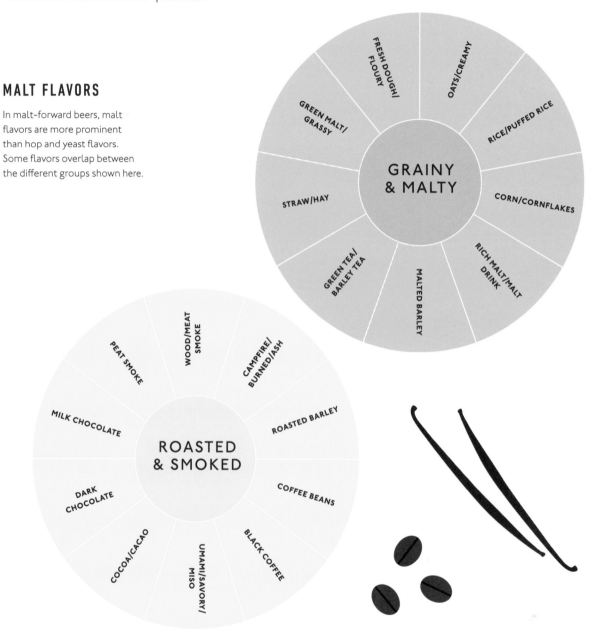

GRAINY & MALTY

- FRESH DOUGH/FLOURY
- OATS/CREAMY
- RICE/PUFFED RICE
- CORN/CORNFLAKES
- RICH MALT/MALT DRINK
- MALTED BARLEY
- GREEN TEA/BARLEY TEA
- STRAW/HAY
- GREEN MALT/GRASSY

ROASTED & SMOKED

- WOOD/MEAT SMOKE
- PEAT SMOKE
- CAMPFIRE/BURNED/ASH
- MILK CHOCOLATE
- ROASTED BARLEY
- COFFEE BEANS
- DARK CHOCOLATE
- BLACK COFFEE
- COCOA/CACAO
- UMAMI/SAVORY/MISO

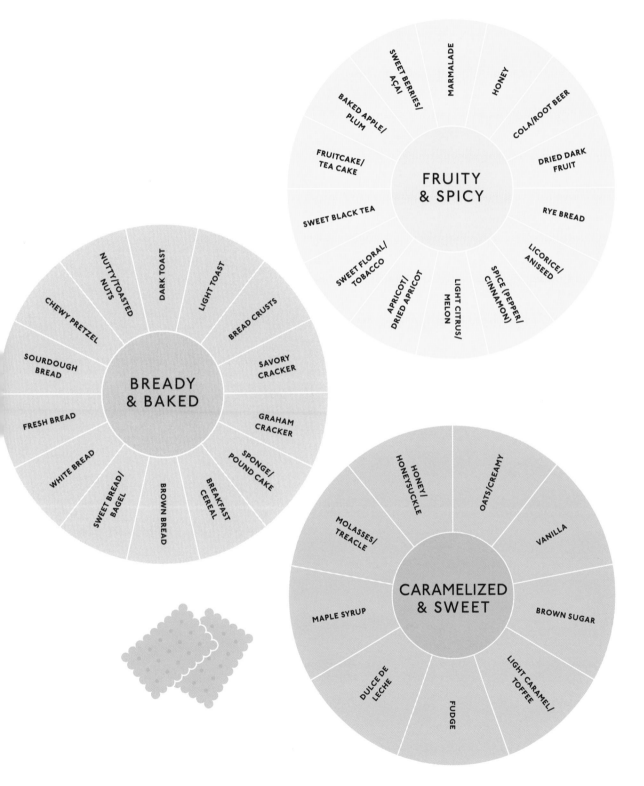

FRUITY & SPICY

SWEET BERRIES/ AÇAI

MARMALADE

HONEY

BAKED APPLE/ PLUM

COLA/ROOT BEER

DRIED DARK FRUIT

FRUITCAKE/ TEA CAKE

RYE BREAD

SWEET BLACK TEA

LICORICE/ ANISEED

SWEET FLORAL/ TOBACCO

SPICE (PEPPER/ CINNAMON)

APRICOT/ DRIED APRICOT

LIGHT CITRUS/ MELON

BREADY & BAKED

NUTTY/TOASTED NUTS

DARK TOAST

LIGHT TOAST

CHEWY PRETZEL

BREAD CRUSTS

SOURDOUGH BREAD

SAVORY CRACKER

FRESH BREAD

GRAHAM CRACKER

WHITE BREAD

SPONGE/ POUND CAKE

SWEET BREAD/ BAGEL

BROWN BREAD

BREAKFAST CEREAL

CARAMELIZED & SWEET

HONEY/ HONEYSUCKLE

OATS/CREAMY

MOLASSES/ TREACLE

VANILLA

MAPLE SYRUP

BROWN SUGAR

DULCE DE LECHE

LIGHT CARAMEL/ TOFFEE

FUDGE

BEER RECIPES

Every beer is made to a recipe, with different ingredients, processes, temperatures, and times combining to produce the final drink. Here are some typical recipes for popular beer styles.

STYLE	AMERICAN LAGER	CZECH PILSNER	DUNKEL
AVERAGE ABV/IBU	5% ABV, 15 IBU	4.5% ABV, 35 IBU	5% ABV, 25 IBU
GRAIN	80% Pilsner malt, 20% rice/corn	100% Pilsner malt	80% Munich malt, 20% Pilsner malt
BITTER HOP	Low bitter, German hops	High bitter, Saaz hops	Medium bitter, Bavarian hops
AROMA HOP	None	Saaz, late boil	None/low
BALANCE	Low malt, low hop	Bittersweet	Malt forward
YEAST & FERMENTATION	Lager yeast, cool fermentation 46°–54°F (8°–12°C), low–medium esters	Lager yeast, cool fermentation 46°–54°F (8°–12°C), low esters	Lager yeast, cool fermentation 46°–54°F (8°–12°C), low esters
TIME	2–4 weeks	4–6 weeks	4–6 weeks
OTHER INFORMATION	Rice/corn adds characteristic dryness	Decoction mash, cool and long maturation, very soft water used	Decoction mash, cool and long maturation

DOPPELBOCK	BEST BITTER	PORTER	IMPERIAL STOUT
7% ABV, 25 IBU	4.5% ABV, 35 IBU	5% ABV, 25 IBU	10% ABV, 75 IBU
70% Munich malt, 30% Pilsner malt	90% pale ale malt, 6% crystal malt, 4% oats/corn/amber/Vienna	85% pale ale malt, 5% caramalt, 5% brown malt, 5% chocolate malt	85% pale ale malt, 8% crystal malt, 5% chocolate malt, 2% roasted barley
Medium bitter, Bavarian hops	Medium bitter, English hops	Medium bitter, English hops	High bitter, any hops
None/low	Late hop & light dry hop	May have some late hops	None/low
Malt forward	More bitter but with balanced malt	Malt forward	Strong malt with deep bitterness
Lager yeast, cool fermentation 46°–54°F (8°–12°C), medium esters	Ale yeast, warm fermentation 61°–64°F (16°–18°C), medium esters	Ale yeast, warm fermentation 61°–64°F (16°–18°C), medium esters	Ale yeast, warm fermentation 61°–64°F (16°–18°C), medium esters, higher alcohol
6–12 weeks	2 weeks	2–3 weeks	4–10 weeks
Longer maturation than most lagers to smooth out flavor profile	Classically has lower CO_2 than other styles	Shouldn't be as roasted as a Stout	Can have longer in tank to mellow stronger flavors, additional ingredients often added

STYLE	AMERICAN PALE ALE	AMERICAN IPA	HAZY DIPA
AVERAGE ABV/IBU	5% ABV, 40 IBU	6.5% ABV, 60 IBU	8% ABV, 40 IBU
GRAIN	92% pale ale malt, 8% crystal malt	93% pale ale malt, 4% light crystal malt, 3% Carapils malt	75% pale ale malt, 10% oats, 10% wheat, 5% dextrin
BITTER HOP	Medium bitter, US hops	High bitter, US hops or hop extract	Medium bitter, US hops or hop extract
AROMA HOP	Late boil & dry hop with US varieties	Late boil & heavy dry hop with US varieties	Late boil, whirlpool, & heavy dry hop
BALANCE	High aroma with balance of malt	High aroma with light but balanced malt, strong bitter	High aroma, full texture, low bitter
YEAST & FERMENTATION	Ale yeast, warm fermentation 61°–68°F (16°–20°C), low esters	Ale yeast, warm fermentation 61°–68°F (16°–20°C), low esters	Ale yeast, warm fermentation 61°–68°F (16°–20°C), medium–high fruity esters
TIME	2–3 weeks	2–3 weeks	2–3 weeks
OTHER INFORMATION	Cascade, Centennial, Simcoe, & Amarillo hops often used	Should be dry & bitter with high aroma from citrusy US hop varieties	Oats & wheat give fullness to texture, should have tropical & fruity aromas

WITBIER	HEFEWEIZEN	QUADRUPEL	WILD ALE
5% ABV, 10 IBU	5% ABV, 15 IBU	10% ABV, 25 IBU	5% ABV, 5 IBU
45% wheat, 45% Pilsner malt, 10% oats	50% wheat, 50% Pilsner malt	80% Pilsner malt, 10% crystal malt, 10% dark candi sugar	60% Pilsner malt, 40% wheat
Low bitter, German hops	Low bitter, German hops	Medium bitter, German/English hops	Low bitter with aged hops
None/low	None	None/low	None
Low bitter with full texture & aromatic yeast	Rich wheat & malt flavor, aromatic yeast, dry finish	Rich malt flavor with dry finish	Dry & tart, but not too sour
Witbier yeast, warm fermentation 68°–72°F (20°–22°C), medium–high esters & phenols	Hefeweizen yeast, warm fermentation 68°–72°F (20°–22°C), medium–high esters & phenols	Ale yeast, warm fermentation 68°–72°F (20°–22°C), medium–high esters	Mixed fermentation of wild yeast & bacteria, high aroma
2–3 weeks	2–3 weeks	4–6 weeks	12+ weeks
Coriander & dried orange peel added in whirlpool, should have yeast aroma & flavor	Distinctive banana-like yeast aroma & a full-bodied texture	Sugar helps keep the strong beer dry	Typically matured in barrels for months to develop acidity & flavor

THE ROLE OF HOPS

The hop is a versatile ingredient that plays an essential role in the brewing process of most beer varieties today, giving beer its characteristic bitterness and aromas.

ANATOMY OF A HOP

The leafy green exterior of a hop flower (the petals, or bract) protects a sticky yellow substance containing the lupulin glands (the pollen, held within the bracteoles). Inside these glands is a complex mix of compounds that give beer much of its bitterness and aroma. The most important compounds are alpha acids and essential oils.

HOP ALPHA ACIDS

Alpha acids give beer its bitterness. The alpha acid content of a hop will vary from very low (2 percent) to very high (over 20 percent). Based on the percentage, brewers work out how many hops they need to add to achieve the desired level of bitterness. The main alpha acids are humulone, cohumulone, and adhumulone, with each hop variety having different quantities of each acid. Some hops are specifically prized for their bittering qualities.

NOBLE HOPS

Czech Saaz and German Hallertau, Tettnang, and Spalt are regarded as being the noble hops. They are highly esteemed for their elegant and distinctive aromas. Several other traditional landrace hops—those that grew naturally in their area and predate breeding—could also be considered "noble": Golding and Fuggle from England, Strisselspalt from France, and Cluster from North America.

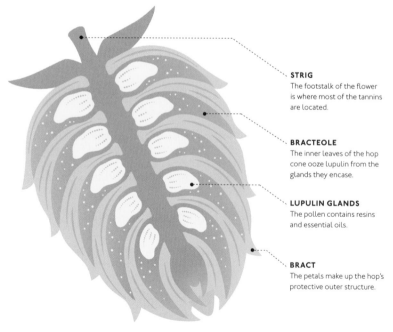

STRIG
The footstalk of the flower is where most of the tannins are located.

BRACTEOLE
The inner leaves of the hop cone ooze lupulin from the glands they encase.

LUPULIN GLANDS
The pollen contains resins and essential oils.

BRACT
The petals make up the hop's protective outer structure.

INSIDE A HOP
This cross section shows a hop's component parts. Hops act as bittering, flavoring, and stability agents in beer.

HIGH ALPHA ACID

20

POLARIS (18%–21%)
PAHTO (18%–20%)
APOLLO (17%–21%)

15

BRAVO (15%–18%)
HERKULES (14%–17%)

HOPS BITTERNESS SCALE
The highest alpha hops include those bred specifically for high bitterness, so brewers can add fewer hops to achieve the same overall bitterness level. Historically, the lowest alpha hops have been known as aroma hops but are still used for bittering beers.

10

5

GOLDING (3%–6%)
FUGGLE (3%–6%)
SPALT (2%–6%), TETTNANG (2%–5%), & SAAZ (2%–5%)

LOW ALPHA ACID

HOP OILS AND AROMAS

Each hop variety has its own unique mix of aromatic and flavorful essential oils, which are also found in numerous other ingredients. Here are the most common hop oils.

HOP OIL	CHARACTER	IN NATURE	IN HOPS
Myrcene	Resinous, spicy, "hoppy"	Pine trees, cannabis, bay leaves, lemongrass, mandarin, mango	Citra, Centennial, Mosaic, Cascade
Humulene	Pine, woody, herbal, light citrus	Celery seed, sage, cannabis, black pepper, clove, ginseng, tobacco	Admiral, Golding, Hallertau
Pinene	Pine, spicy, citrus	Juniper, black pepper, rosemary, orange peel, cannabis	Centennial, Columbus, Simcoe, Mosaic
Caryophyllene	Woody, spicy, floral, pepper	Black pepper, cinnamon, clove, basil, oregano, lavender	Saaz, Tettnang, Admiral, Golding
Farnesene	Floral	Lemon thyme, apple, chamomile, perilla	Tettnang, Northern, Brewer, Saaz
Linalool	Floral, orange	Coriander and cilantro, papaya, orange juice, lychee, black tea, ginger	Amarillo, Centennial, Citra, Crystal, Loral
Geraniol	Floral, lemon	Lemon peel, lemongrass, bergamot, peach, geranium, rose	Cascade, Centennial, Chinook, Ekuanot
Limonene	Citrus, orange, lemon	Lemon, orange peel, lime, grapefruit, dill, sumac, pine	Citra, Simcoe

HOP THIOLS AND ESTERS

Thiols are sulfur-containing compounds that have a low flavor threshold—we can taste them when only a small amount is present. Pronounced tropical and tangy aromas, such as grapefruit, passion fruit, black currant, and gooseberry, are characteristic of thiols.

Other sulfur hop compounds, which might give onion, leek, or garlic aromas, can suppress or cover up some of the brighter citrusy aromas. These allium aromas are often euphemistically described as "savory."

Hops also contain a number of fruity-smelling esters that are transformed and revealed through fermentation. They are distinct from aromas produced from either yeast or hops. Hops with the highest ester content include Ekuanot, Citra, Loral, Simcoe, and Centennial. Hops added into actively fermenting beer will produce a range of aromas not found if the hops are added when fermentation is complete. This interaction between yeast and hop gives a broader selection of fruity esters and aromas and is known as hop biotransformation.

GROWING HOPS

Hops are perennial plants that need specific seasonal weather conditions, preferring cold winters, frost-free springs, and sunny summers.

HOP BREEDING

Hop plants are either male or female, and each plant reproduces its own sex. Growers have bred hops for more than 100 years, and they cross-breed male and female varieties. Through cross-breeding, they aim to raise new seedlings that have the desired qualities of each parent. It's a long process— up to 10 years—to go from the initial cross to the hop being commercially available. Typically, male hops grow well and have good resistance to disease, while female hops impart flavor. Only female hops are cultivated for brewing.

THE HOP-GROWING YEAR

Hops grow on tall (up to 23 ft/7 m) framework structures, winding around string as they grow tall during spring. They then grow outward and come into flower over summer. In the northern hemisphere, the hop-growing year starts in March, with harvesting in late August and September. In the southern hemisphere, hop growing starts in September, with harvesting taking place in March and April.

MARCH
The first job of the growing year is stringing the hop poles with biodegradable twine.

OCTOBER–FEBRUARY
Hops have been cut back to their rootstock and now will lie dormant for a few months. The hop gardens undergo any repairs or reconstructions.

AFTER HARVESTING, GROWERS CUT THE PLANTS BACK TO THEIR ROOTSTOCK READY FOR NEXT YEAR'S GROWTH.

APRIL–JUNE

In spring, the hop plant begins to grow back from its rootstock, and the first hop shoots appear. When the shoots are large enough, growers train (tie) two or three shoots clockwise around each string. The hops continue to grow upward until around the longest day of the year.

JULY–AUGUST

The hop plants grow to their full height by July, and then they begin to grow outwards. First they come into "burr," with bud-like growths, which then turn into hop flowers (cones).

LATE AUGUST–SEPTEMBER

The hop flowers reach maturity and are ready for harvest. Growers cut down the whole bine and string of tall plants, and a picking machine separates the hop cones. The cones are then dried from 80 percent to 10 percent moisture, before being baled in large sacks. After harvesting, the growers cut the plants back to their rootstock ready for them to start growing again in a few months' time.

TYPES OF HOPS

After hop flowers have been harvested, the flowers can be used fresh, or dried, pelletized, or processed further. There are several ways in which these fresh or processed hops can be used in the brewery.

HOP PELLETS

Hop pellets are the most common format of hops used today. Compared to flowers, pellets give a more intense flavor, have a higher efficiency of flavor, tend to stay fresher longer, and are more efficient for brewing and storage.

Pellets are made by chopping up the whole flowers and pressing them tightly into pellets. Much of a hop flower is just plant matter that doesn't contribute acids or oils (bitterness or flavor). There are two main types: T90 and T45. In a T90 pellet, the plant matter remains. In a T45 pellet, the whole hops are frozen to −4°F (−20°C) and chopped up, allowing the lupulin to be separated from the plant material, with about 45 percent of the plant matter added back to the lupulin. Overall, T45 is more concentrated.

WHOLE-FLOWER HOPS

Harvested and then quickly dried and pressed tightly into bales, this is the traditional way of using hops. Whole-flower hops can give more elegant and floral aromas compared to other types of hops as they hold onto more of their volatile oils, but adding lots of flowers can also leave vegetal and harsh flavors, especially if used in high amounts for bitterness. Flowers are typically more expensive than pellets.

POWDER IS MORE
EXPENSIVE THAN
OTHER TYPES OF HOPS,
BUT IT'S POTENT AND
LESS WASTEFUL.

HOP EXTRACT

Acids and oils extracted from hops can be made into liquid. Extracted alpha acids give a clean bitterness without the need to add lots of plant matter. Brewers can use aromatic oils to add or correct hop aroma.

FRESH/GREEN/WET HOPS

Taken straight to the brewery without being dried, fresh hops create some of the only truly seasonal beers. The flavors tend to be lighter, fresher, and more delicate, like the flavor of a fresh tomato compared to a roasted one.

HOP POWDER

By subjecting hops to very low temperatures using liquid nitrogen, the lupulin can be separated from the plant material, leaving a concentrated powder of pure hop aroma and flavor. Known as lupulin powder or Cryo hops, it's about twice as strong as the equivalent in pellets and without the vegetal matter. Powder is more expensive but it's potent and means less waste.

HOPS IN THE BREWERY

To get the desired bitterness, flavor, and aroma, brewers have different timings and methods for adding hops in the brewery.

DOUBLE DRY HOPPED

Double dry hopped (DDH) can mean either adding double the typical amount of dry hops or including two or more dry-hop additions. This process produces particularly aromatic beers such as Hazy IPAs.

HOPS FOR BITTERNESS

Hops are typically added into the brewing kettle when the wort is boiling. Hops contain alpha acids, which give beer its bitterness, and essential oils, which impart aroma and flavor. The alpha acids are mostly insoluble compounds, but by heating them, they isomerize and become water soluble (iso-alpha acids). The longer they boil, the better they're utilized and the more bitterness they'll give. The hops need to boil for 60 minutes or more for optimum bitterness.

High alpha hops are typically favored for bitterness as fewer hops are needed to achieve the same bitterness level—a brewer would need to add more of a 4 percent alpha hop than one that is 12 percent, for instance, to get the same amount of bitterness.

DRY HOPPING HAZY IPA

Every brewery dry hops its beer differently. This is an example of the fermentation and maturation of a Hazy IPA, including when it would be dry hopped.

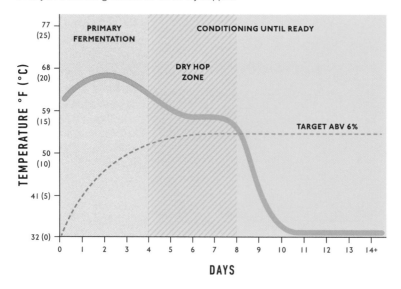

DRY HOPPING

Brewers use dry hopping to increase hop aroma and flavor. It involves adding hops on the cold side of brewing, typically when the beer is near the end of active fermentation and temperatures are still warm (55°–64°F/13°–18°C)—the warmer temperatures encourage more hop aromas and some hop biotransformation. The hops are mixed into the beer and left for one to four days. When the beer is cooled, the hops drop out of solution and can be removed via an opening in the bottom of the tank, or the beer can be transferred into another tank for conditioning until it's ready to be packaged.

HOP USE: BITTERNESS VS DRY HOP

As tastes change in beer, so has the way in which brewers add their hops. The earliest India Pale Ales from Burton on Trent in England were high in bitterness with a relatively small dry hop. As IPAs grew in popularity in the 2000s, they got very bitter with a moderate dry hop, while Hazy IPAs have decreased in bitterness but increased significantly in aroma. On the graph below, the vertical lines at each point plotted show the range in International Bitterness Units (IBUs; green) and dry-hop volume (orange), respectively.

HOPPING HAZY IPAS

The modern trend for Hazy and Hoppy IPAs has revolutionized the traditional practice of adding hops throughout the boil. To maximize the hop aroma and flavor, some brewers add only a small amount of hops into the kettle. This is to achieve low-level bitterness and to help with foam retention. They add most of the rest of the hops in the whirlpool and then again as dry hops.

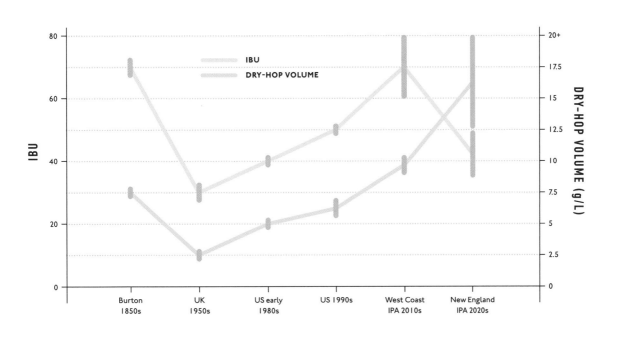

MEASURING BITTERNESS

Beer's bitterness is measured in International Bitterness Units (IBUs). It's a measure of the parts per million of iso-alpha acids in the beer, and it's calculated by factoring in the hop alpha acid, the amount of hops added and their utilization—determined by when they're added, with early additions utilized more—and the gravity (sweetness) of the wort.

There is no upper limit to what a beer's IBU can be, but it's effectively a scale of 0–100 as almost no beers go beyond that range.

While IBU gives a quantifiable value, that number alone doesn't tell us about the perception of bitterness and the overall balance of the beer. It's important to consider sweetness alongside bitterness: a 4% ABV Golden Ale with 40 IBUs, for example, will taste more bitter than a 7% ABV

IPA with 40 IBUs, with the residual sweetness balancing the bitterness.

HOW BITTER?

The science tells us that to get bitterness in a beer, the hops have to be boiled for an extended time. Yet even hops added to the whirlpool will contribute some bitterness to the beer.

HOP REGIONS & KEY VARIETIES

The local weather, soil, and other growing conditions combine with different hop varieties to produce the wide range of characteristics in hops. These are the main hop-growing regions and some important varieties.

TOP OF THE HOPS

The three most-grown hops in the world are German Herkules, American Citra, and Czech Saaz. The American top five are Citra, Mosaic, CTZ, Cascade, and Simcoe.

ENGLAND

Bramling Cross	black currant, spicy, vanilla
Bullion	black currant, lemon, spice
Challenger	cedar, green tea, spice
Golding/EKG	honey, lemon, curry
Fuggle	mint, woody, grassy
Jester®/Olicana®	passion fruit, grapefruit, herbal
Target	dried herb, marmalade, tangerine

REST OF EUROPE

Saaz (Czech Republic)	hay, tobacco, herbal
Styrian Golding (Slovenia)	green tea, herbal, lemon
Strisselspalt (France)	herbal, grapefruit, grass

GERMANY

Hallertau Blanc	grape, lemongrass, tropical
Herkules	pepper, spicy, bitter
Hersbruck	grass, tobacco, bergamot
Hüll Melon	melon, strawberry, vanilla
Magnum	cedar, pepper, resinous
Mandarina Bavaria	tangerine, lemon, grapefruit
Mittelfrüh	grass, floral, lemon
Perle	floral, tea, pepper
Saphir	lemongrass, floral, juniper
Spalt	woody, tea, spice
Spalter Select	lemon, floral, woody
Tettnang	pepper, black tea, floral
Tradition	grass, floral, lemon

ENGLAND

First planted by Flemish farmers, hops have been grown for brewing in England since the 1500s. They were first grown in the southeast and spread to the Midlands, which remain the main growing areas today.

Most varieties have an underlying earthiness, like fall leaves or hedgerows. Flavors and aromas are of fresh flowers, spice (cumin, pepper), mint, black currant, honey, orchard fruit, light citrus, and dried stone fruit. Modern varieties have a light tropical quality. They are typically used in classic British styles like Best Bitter, Pale Ale, Golden Ale, Mild, Stout, and Porter, and some Belgian Ales.

EUROPE

Hops have grown in many European areas for millennia. They are found in Belgium, France, Germany, the Czech Republic, Poland, and Slovenia, plus a few other pockets such as Spain, where they grow several American varieties. Germany is the world's second-largest hop-growing country, with the main growing regions being Hallertau and Tettnang.

Classic qualities include grassy, spicy, herbal, botanic, floral, and light or dried citrus flavors, often used in lagers to add a crisp bitterness. Modern varieties might be more common in hop-forward beers and have more tropical, citrus, and melon qualities.

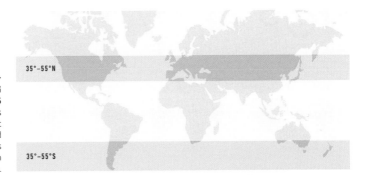

HOP-GROWING REGIONS

Globally, hops grow best between 35 and 55 degrees latitude north and south.

35°–55°N

35°–55°S

UNITED STATES

Amarillo®	grapefruit, peach, resinous
Azacca®	mango, papaya, orange
Cascade	grapefruit, floral, pine
Centennial	blossom, orange, resin
Chinook	grapefruit, pine, spice
Citra®	citrus, mango, melon
CTZ	dank, pepper, bitter
Ekuanot®	mandarin, melon, mango
El Dorado®	apricot, tropical, citrus
Idaho 7®	pineapple, pine, berry
Mosaic®	mango, berry, stone fruit
Sabro®	citrus, coconut, tropical
Simcoe®	pine, grapefruit, berry

NEW ZEALAND

Kohatu®	tropical, pine, floral
Motueka™	tropical, lime, lemon
Nelson Sauvin™	gooseberry, grape, passion fruit
Pacific Gem	berry, oak, pepper
Rakau®	apricot, resin, dried fruit
Riwaka®	grapefruit, passion fruit, lime
Wai-iti™	peach, lime, apricot
Waimea™	pomelo, pine, herbal

AUSTRALIA

Aus Cascade	grapefruit, berry, floral
Eclipse®	mandarin, citrus peel, pine
Ella™	floral, anise, peach
Enigma®	grape, berry, melon
Galaxy®	passion fruit, peach, citrus
Topaz™	lychee, tropical, resinous
Vic Secret™	passion fruit, resinous, pineapple

NORTH AMERICA

Responsible for some 40 percent of the world's hops, the United States is the world's leading hop grower. The majority grow in Washington State, with most of the rest in Idaho and Oregon. Hops had grown on the East Coast since the 17th century and reached the West Coast in the 1850s. Over time, all growing went west.

There are higher intensities of aroma, flavor, and bitterness compared to European hops. Flavors are citrus, tropical and stone fruit, melon, pine, onion/garlic, dank/marijuana, coconut, and fruit candy. They are best expressed in Pale Ales, IPAs, Double IPAs, and any hop-forward style.

SOUTHERN HEMISPHERE

Hops have grown in Australia and New Zealand since the early and mid-1800s. Breeding programs helped develop new varieties, often crossed with American or British plants. Most Australian hops grow in Tasmania and Victoria. New Zealand hops grow in the Nelson area of the South Island. Hops are also grown in South Africa and in parts of northern Patagonia.

These hops tend to have vibrant tropical fruit qualities, with passion fruit, mango, pineapple, grape, gooseberry, grapefruit, lime, orange, and stone fruit. They are commonly used in hop-forward styles and are a key flavor in Pacific Pale Ales and IPAs.

HOP FLAVORS

Hops give us some of the most vibrant aromas and flavors in the beers we drink, but being able to describe those flavors is often a challenge. Let's look at some ways to help refine our flavor language.

DESCRIBING FLAVORS

When trying to describe the flavor in a hoppy beer, we're often nosing through a variety of different aromas, like citrus fruits, tropical fruits, and herbal and spicy notes. The challenge is to refine that down to different individual aromas, getting as specific as we can while also ensuring the flavors we pick out actually mean something to us. If we've never tasted a guava, then we can't truthfully say we experience it in a beer, even if others find that flavor.

Taking fruit flavors as an example, here's a systematic approach to follow. We all have different flavor memories and experiences and there are no incorrect flavors—if you smell or taste something, it's in the beer, no matter how obscure it might seem.

WHAT'S THE FAMILY OF FRUIT?
Is it citrus, tropical, stone fruit, orchard fruit, melon, or berry? Can you narrow it down to a specific fruit, such as grapefruit or peach?

WHAT'S THE VARIETY OF FRUIT?
If possible, can you go further and name a specific variety of that fruit—ruby grapefruit, white peach, Alphonso mango, or sour cherry?

WHICH PART OF THE FRUIT?
Then get even more specific: is it a particular part of the fruit, such as skin, pith, flesh, or juice?

WHAT'S THE CONDITION OF THE FRUIT?
Is the fruit underripe, ripe, overripe, dried, or fermented?

HAS THE FRUIT BEEN COOKED OR PROCESSED?
Is it a combination of other ingredients or processes, such as grilled pineapple, marmalade on toast, mango lassi, orange soda, or lemon cake?

HOP & MALT TOGETHER

Malt flavor can change the flavor of hops. Imagine four 5% ABV beers, each identically hopped with Citra and Cascade to be aromatic like a Pale Ale. In each, the malt flavor will change how those hops present.

PALE LAGER

LIGHT/FRUITY

Malt flavors are clean, light toast, and dry. Hop flavors are pineapple, grapefruit, light herbal, and orange.

HAZY PALE ALE

SWEETER/TROPICAL

Malt is sweeter and full bodied. Hop flavors are juicy tropical fruits, sweet tangerine, grapefruit, and pine.

RED ALE

DARK/COOKED

Malt flavors are caramelized, dark toast, and berries. Hops are grilled grapefruit and herbal liqueur (Campari).

BLACK IPA

BITTER/ROASTED

Malt flavors are roasted and bitter dark chocolate. Hops are grapefruit pith, marmalade on toast, and roasted pineapple.

SINGLE OR COMBINED FLAVORS?

Let's say you smell something in your beer that reminds you of marmalade on toast. What you've got is flavors of bittersweet stewed oranges, orange peel, sugar, and toasted bread. Here we should consider whether it's better to describe the individual flavors or the combined ones. Usually, it's down to the audience: marmalade on toast is a nice evocative description for tasting notes, while the individual approach will be more useful for brewery tasting panels.

TROPICAL & STONE FRUIT HOP AROMAS

Among the most common hop aromas are tropical fruits and stone fruits. Fruity flavors can be described as singular or combined (see p.61). Singular flavors are the fresh ingredients, including the specific part of the fruit and degree of ripeness (green mango vs ripe mango). Combined flavors are a mix of different ingredients, or ingredients that have been processed or cooked, such as a margarita cocktail or roasted pineapple.

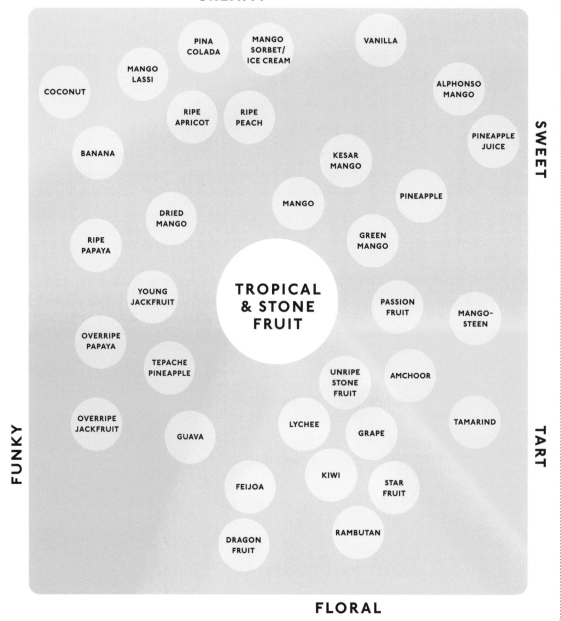

CREAMY

PINA COLADA

MANGO SORBET/ ICE CREAM

VANILLA

MANGO LASSI

COCONUT

ALPHONSO MANGO

RIPE APRICOT

RIPE PEACH

BANANA

KESAR MANGO

SWEET

PINEAPPLE JUICE

PINEAPPLE

MANGO

DRIED MANGO

GREEN MANGO

RIPE PAPAYA

TROPICAL & STONE FRUIT

YOUNG JACKFRUIT

PASSION FRUIT

MANGO-STEEN

OVERRIPE PAPAYA

TEPACHE PINEAPPLE

UNRIPE STONE FRUIT

AMCHOOR

OVERRIPE JACKFRUIT

LYCHEE

GRAPE

TAMARIND

FUNKY

GUAVA

KIWI

STAR FRUIT

TART

FEIJOA

RAMBUTAN

DRAGON FRUIT

FLORAL

CITRUS FRUIT HOP AROMAS

Citrus fruits are another category of common hop aromas, ranging from fresh and complex to floral and herbal and cooked and combined. Citrus fruits, particularly, lend themselves to descriptions of cooked or combined flavors, such as orange cake or roasted citrus. They also include aromas such as ginger, coriander, bergamot, and gin and tonic.

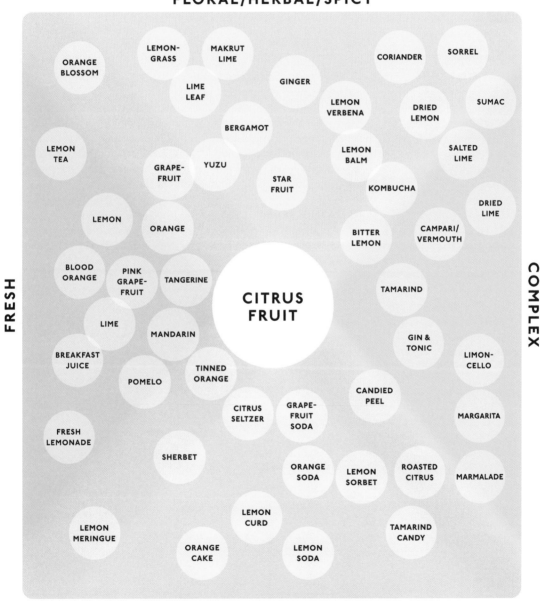

FLORAL/HERBAL/SPICY

ORANGE BLOSSOM
LEMON-GRASS
MAKRUT LIME
CORIANDER
SORREL
LIME LEAF
GINGER
LEMON VERBENA
DRIED LEMON
SUMAC
BERGAMOT
LEMON TEA
LEMON BALM
SALTED LIME
GRAPE-FRUIT
YUZU
STAR FRUIT
KOMBUCHA
DRIED LIME
LEMON
ORANGE
BITTER LEMON
CAMPARI/VERMOUTH
BLOOD ORANGE
PINK GRAPE-FRUIT
TANGERINE
CITRUS FRUIT
TAMARIND
LIME
MANDARIN
GIN & TONIC
LIMON-CELLO
BREAKFAST JUICE
TINNED ORANGE
POMELO
CANDIED PEEL
MARGARITA
CITRUS SELTZER
GRAPE-FRUIT SODA
FRESH LEMONADE
SHERBET
ORANGE SODA
LEMON SORBET
ROASTED CITRUS
MARMALADE
LEMON CURD
LEMON MERINGUE
ORANGE CAKE
LEMON SODA
TAMARIND CANDY

FRESH | **COMPLEX**

CANDY/COOKED/COMBINED

YEAST & FERMENTATION

Without yeast, there's no alcohol. Alcohol and many of beer's underlying flavor compounds are created during fermentation.

BEER, BREAD, WINE, & WHISKEY

S. cerevisiae yeast is also used to ferment bread, wine, and spirits, though bakers, winemakers, and distillers use strains that are different from those that brewers use.

FERMENTATION

Fermentation is the process of yeast converting sugars into alcohol. The process is complex, so this is a simplified overview.

Brewing yeast is added (pitched) into sweet wort in the fermentation vessel. The yeast first takes in oxygen in the wort, which enables it to grow and multiply. It then consumes the sugars, starting with the most basic (glucose), followed by the rest, including the maltose. As the yeast metabolizes the sugars, it creates alcohol, carbon dioxide, and numerous different flavor-active compounds, as well as giving out heat.

While brewers need to add the right amount of yeast to enable the healthiest fermentation, there are many variables in the fermentation process, such as the yeast strain, temperatures, original gravity (see p.67), and tank geometry.

BREWING YEAST

Yeast is a single-cell microorganism, and inside the cell are many different enzymes that catalyze a variety of different chemical reactions. As a living organism, yeast consumes sugars for energy, and as part of its metabolization, it produces alcohol.

Brewers use different species and strains of yeast to make beer. The two main species of beer yeast are *Saccharomyces cerevisiae*, which makes ales, and *Saccharomyces pastorianus*, which makes lagers. Additionally, wild beers are fermented with *Brettanomyces*.

There are different strains within each of those species. Each strain works best in particular environments and gives different characteristics that suit certain beer styles. Typically, a yeast will have been cultured and cultivated to produce a certain beer style, such as for a Hefeweizen or a Hazy IPA.

A TYPICAL FERMENTATION

For both ales and lagers, the temperature rises and is then cooled. It's held for a couple of days as a diacetyl rest, then dropped to 32°F (0°C) to mature and condition until the beer is ready to be packaged.

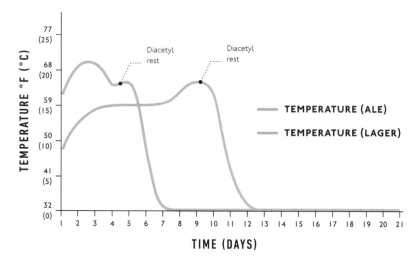

— TEMPERATURE (ALE)

— TEMPERATURE (LAGER)

ALE VS LAGER FERMENTATION

Ale and lager are fermented with different species of yeast, and those species perform optimally in different conditions. Simply put, ale yeast likes to be warm, while lager yeast likes to be cold, and temperature impacts the time fermentation takes. Brewers still use the terms "top-" and "bottom-fermenting," which refer to where they used to collect yeast from the tank near the end of fermentation: ale yeast collected on the top and lager yeast dropped to the bottom. Today, many breweries use temperature-controlled sealed conical tanks, so they all tend to collect the yeast from the bottom of the vessel.

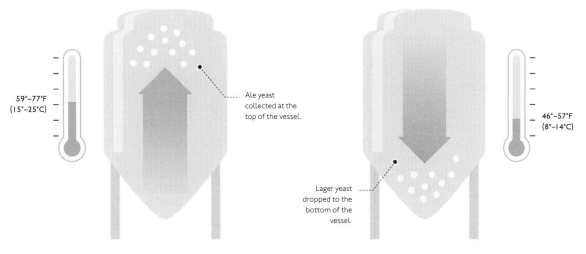

59°–77°F
(15°–25°C)

Ale yeast
collected at the
top of the vessel.

46°–57°F
(8°–14°C)

Lager yeast
dropped to the
bottom of the
vessel.

ALE FERMENTATION
An ale fermentation will typically take place at 59°–68°F (15°–20°C). Styles with a more noticeable yeast flavor, such as Hefeweizen, Witbier, Saison, and other Belgian ales, ferment up to 77°F (25°C). The typical fermentation time is two to five days.

LAGER FERMENTATION
Lager fermentation will typically be at 46°–57°F (8°–14°C). Colder temperatures create a cleaner fermentation profile with less yeast aroma. The typical fermentation time is seven to 10 days.

BREWING WILD & SOUR BEER

There are three distinct types of sour beer: Lambic/spontaneously fermented beers (see pp.182–183); wild/mixed fermentation (see pp.190–191); and "fast sours," like Berliner Weisse and Gose (see pp.192–193).

Wild and mixed fermentation includes the wild yeast *Brettanomyces* in either primary or secondary fermentation, usually alongside regular ale yeast and different bacteria (*Lactobacillus* and *Pediococcus*). The brewing is consistent with a regular ale, with the fermentation and maturation taking much longer to develop the complex flavor profiles of these beers. "Fast sours" are brewed and sold within a few weeks compared to the months or years needed for the "slow sours" like Gueuze and Wild Ale.

All of these beers are soured with lactic bacteria or lactic acid. The most common methods are the sour mash and kettle sour. For both, the base beer is mashed to have a light body and low pH. Then brewers can add *Lactobacillus* straight to the wort (once cooled) in the mash, or transfer the wort to the kettle and then add the *Lactobacillus* there. If using the kettle souring method, brewers can boil the wort before adding the bacteria, which can help control the souring process and eliminate any unwanted bacteria. In all processes, the bacteria will acidify the beer over 12–48 hours, fermenting sugars and creating lactic acid. When brewers are happy with the level of acidity, they boil the beer with a small amount of hops, then they transfer it to a fermenter and ferment it with a regular yeast.

There's also a shortcut to do this for sweeter sours and traditional Gose, which involves adding lactic acid to the fermented beer, simplifying the process and giving more control to brewers.

THE FLAVORS OF FERMENTATION

The fermentation process creates a wide range of different flavor-active chemical compounds, including esters, phenols, and alcohols.

ESTERS

Esters are organic compounds and a natural byproduct of fermentation. They are integral to the flavor of every beer style, providing an underlying fruitiness and the distinctive flavor of fermentation.

Yeast creates alcohol, primarily ethanol but also other "higher" alcohols. When the alcohol and organic acids in the yeast combine, esters are formed. Acetic acid is a common acid, and when it reacts with ethanol, it produces ethyl acetate, which is the most common ester and responsible for a light fruity aroma.

All beers contain a complex mix of different esters, with each ester present in different volumes—some below the flavor threshold and others above it. Sometimes a beer is very distinctive with a single ester, like Hefeweizen with its banana-like aroma from the ester isoamyl acetate; other times there is a fruity mix of aromas. Esters also work synergistically to produce entirely new flavor profiles based on how they mix, and they can combine with hop compounds to produce even more new aromas.

Some yeasts produce more esters than others. A classic California ale yeast, used for American Pale Ales, is low in esters.

Many British ale yeasts have a fruitiness to them. Belgian ale yeasts have expressive ester profiles and sometimes some phenols. The yeasts used in Hazy IPAs produce a broad range of fruity esters like stone fruit, vanilla, and tropical fruit, which are often a significant part of the aroma profile.

Several factors influence ester production, including the specific yeast strain, the fermentation temperature, the gravity (sweetness) of the wort, and even the shape or type of fermenter—shallow and wide fermenters produce more esters and these are found more often in Belgium and traditional British ale breweries.

COMMON ESTERS

Common ester aromas include red apple, green apple candy, plum, anise, banana, strawberry, tropical fruit, pear, bubble gum, vanilla, rose, honey, and more.

ISOAMYL ACETATE
Banana, banana candy

PHENYLETHYL ACETATE
Rose, floral, honey

ETHYL ACETATE
The most common beer ester but not necessarily the most flavor active: light fruity, solvent

ETHYL BUTYRATE
Tropical fruit, pineapple, juicy fruit

Gravity in a beer is a measure of dissolved sugar content in solution. The higher the number, the denser the sweetness. Brewers measure the gravity of the wort before fermentation begins (original gravity) and again at the end of fermentation (final gravity). They can use those numbers to calculate the alcohol content.

Water is measured at 1.000. Mid-strength beers have an original gravity of 1.048–1.052. Their final gravity, or the sweetness left after fermentation, is 1.008–1.020, depending on the beer's sweetness—all beer has some residual sweetness.

Alcohol by volume (ABV) shows how much of the beer is alcohol: 5% ABV means 5 percent of the liquid is alcohol. Central European brewers often use degrees Plato (°P) to measure alcohol content. It's a percentage measure of sugar to water, where water is 0°P and sugar is 100°P. So a 10°P beer is 10 percent sugar and 90 percent water—that's a measure of the original gravity; the final gravity might be 2°P.

PHENOLS

Certain yeast strains naturally produce phenols, which smell and taste like clove, medicines, plasters, or smoky whiskey. In some styles, such as Witbier and Wild Ales, they can be important parts of the flavor profile. The main phenols are 4-vinyl guaiacol (clove), often in Witbier, 4-ethylphenol (medicinal, barnyard), and 4-ethylguaiacol (smoke and clove), both in Wild and *Brett* beers.

ALCOHOL, ALDEHYDES, KETONES, & SULFUR

Alcohols have their own flavors, often a light fruitiness and sometimes a vinous quality, but in high volumes, they can be harsh and smell like acetone (nail-polish remover) or just pure alcohol—the stronger the beer, the more common it is to find higher alcohols. Aldehydes, primarily acetaldehyde, are produced in the early stages of fermentation. They are like a tart green apple candy aroma and often considered an off flavor if present in high volumes. Ketones, primarily diacetyl, can have a butter or butterscotch flavor. Aldehydes and ketones are given out by the yeast and reabsorbed and further broken down by it if given the time. Sulfur is in all beers, but it's often more prominent in lagers.

HOP OR YEAST?

Esters have a generally fruity flavor, but so do hops. The best way to identify an ester is to think of them as having a candied or artificial fruitiness, or a solvent-like quality (think markers). Isoamyl acetate smells like banana candy (circus peanuts) but doesn't smell exactly like a fresh, ripe banana. We often find pear drops or bubble gum as ester aromas, and these are candied flavors. At high levels, they can become unpalatable, whereas the fruitiness from hops, which presents as more natural fruitiness, can continue to be delicious in very high volumes.

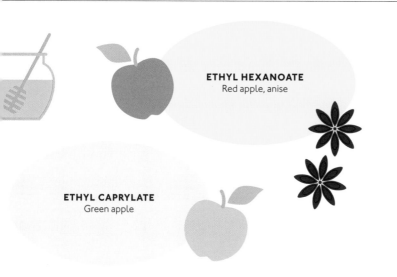

ETHYL HEXANOATE
Red apple, anise

ETHYL CAPRYLATE
Green apple

MATURATION & FINISHING BEER

All beer undergoes a period of maturation to develop its final flavor and finished qualities before it's packaged.

MATURATION & CONDITIONING

When fermentation has finished, the beer is cooled to around 32°F (0°C). It might be held there for a few days or even a few months, depending on the beer. This helps round out the flavors, allow any residual yeast to drop through the beer, and let the beer develop its carbonation.

Wild beer and barrel-aged beer work a little differently and are typically stored at ambient temperatures for months or even years as the flavor evolves. More of these beers will then undergo their own "finishing" process, such as blending barrels and finalizing the carbonation.

BRIGHT OR HAZY BEERS

Before a beer is packaged, brewers have to decide whether it's going to be bright or hazy. There are several ways to remove haziness.

Filtration removes the yeast and other particles, leaving a clear beer. By removing the yeast, the beer becomes crisper to drink, but it also tends to take some flavor and texture with it. Filtered beer is not necessarily a bad thing, and some beers are much better this way. Filters work by passing the beer through a fine filter plate or sheet, which catches the solids and lets the clear liquid pass through.

A centrifuge rapidly spins the beer, sending denser yeast particles out of suspension. It can be a gentler way of creating a clear beer while retaining a little more character. Centrifuges can also ensure a consistent level of haziness in intentionally cloudy beers.

Processing aids like finings can be added into the beer in tank. These work essentially by grabbing ahold of the solid matter and pulling it to the bottom of the vessel, leaving a clear beer. There are different types of fining, including animal-derived ones like isinglass (fish) and gelatin (cow or pig), plus vegan-friendly ones.

COLD BEER IS FIZZY BEER

The colder a beer is, the more it will absorb and hold on to its carbonation. As a beer warms, more CO_2 escapes from the beer and it becomes flat.

CARBONATION

All beer has bubbles. Sometimes the carbonation level is low, like in British cask ales, while other beers have a very high carbonation, like Belgian Tripel. Carbon dioxide (CO_2) is the main bubble in beer, though nitrogen is also used. There are several ways to get bubbles into beer.

Brewers measure and adjust the final carbonation level.

NATURALLY CARBONATED IN TANK
When beer is cooled down to condition and mature, there's still active yeast in the tank and it's still producing CO_2. If the tank is sealed and under pressure, then the bubbles will be absorbed into the beer and create the carbonation.

FORCED CARBONATION
Instead of letting CO_2 naturally carbonate the beer, brewers can force it into the beer when the beer's in tank, either at the end of its conditioning or after filtration and before packaging.

PASTEURIZATION

Pasteurization destroys any bacteria that might be in a beer. It's used mostly by large breweries or brewers in hot climates to ensure stability and consistency of flavor. It works by heating the beer, usually at or after packaging, which kills the bacteria and stops any more yeast activity. It's usually done between 140° and 162°F (60° and 72°C). Some very good beer is pasteurized, so it's not necessarily a bad thing, though it does dull flavors and it's not common in small breweries.

140°–162°F/
60°–72°C

CARBONATION LEVELS IN BEER

A beer's carbonation is measured by brewers in volumes of CO_2, and it's a specific measurement. If a pint of beer has 2 volumes of CO_2, that means there are 2 pints of CO_2 in the pint of beer. Different styles have different expected volumes, and knowing the specific level in draft beer is important for pubs and bars to ensure they serve the beer properly.

STYLE	VOLUMES OF CO_2
Lambic	0.5–1.5
Cask ale	1–1.5
Imperial Stout	1.5–2.3
Kellerbier	1.7–2.2
American IPA	2–2.5
Hazy IPA	1.8–2.3
Most ales	1.5–2.5
Most lagers	2.2–2.7
Hefeweizen	3.5–4.5
Dubbel/Tripel/Quad	3–4
Gueuze	3–4.5
Soda	3–4
Champagne	4–6

EXPECTED VOLUMES
Some beers, such as Lambic, contain little carbonation, while others, such as Gueuze, contain as much as Champagne.

WHAT IS HAZE IN BEER?

Different types of haziness occur in beer. Permanent (or "colloidal") haze, found in Hazy IPAs and wheat beers, comes from using high-protein grains like wheat and oats and from polyphenols in hops (especially if the beer is heavily dry hopped). Yeast haze is from residual yeast in a beer, and if the beer is left for long enough, the yeast will drop out of suspension. Some haze is known as "chill haze," which occurs as a beer gets very cold and proteins in the grain cling to polyphenols in the hops. As the beer warms, this haze disappears.

BOTTLE CONDITIONED
Uncarbonated and unfiltered beer is put into bottles, and as the yeast consumes any residual sweetness, it produces CO_2, which is absorbed into the beer. It can take a few weeks or a few months until the beer is appropriately carbonated.

CASK CONDITIONED
Much like bottle conditioning, flat beer is filled into casks that are sealed, then the beer undergoes a secondary fermentation and produces a low level of carbonation in the beer, which is often misunderstood as being "flat."

NITRO BEERS
Nitrogen gas is dissolved into the beer in tank to the desired level. CO_2 is also in there at a lower level. Nitrogen bubbles are smaller than CO_2, and they appear to cascade to the top of the glass when the beer is served (see p.83).

BARREL AGING & OTHER INGREDIENTS

Beyond the main processes and ingredients used to brew beer, many beers today are barrel aged, and others contain a wide variety of additional ingredients.

WHICH WOOD?

While barrels that previously held whiskey and wine are the most common in breweries, wood that has aged all sorts of different drinks, like rum, sherry, Cognac, tequila, gin, or regional spirits such as cachaça in Brazil, is also used.

A HISTORY OF BEER & WOOD

For at least 2,000 years, beer has come into contact with wood at every stage of production. A few hundred years ago, beer in a typical brewery was fermented in open-top wooden vessels, then stored in large barrels before being put into smaller barrels for transportation and serving. Oak was most common, and for almost all of that time, flavor derived from the barrel was deemed to be a negative attribute.

From the late 19th century, wood began to be replaced with different materials (glass- and enamel-lined tanks, concrete, steel, aluminum), before stainless steel became the industry standard from the 1960s.

BARRELS FOR FLAVOR

The first use of barrels to impart new character in beer is often assigned to Goose Island Beer Company in the United States and its Bourbon County Stout. Brewed in 1992, it was intended to be a strong Stout aged in bourbon barrels, taking character and flavor from the wood and the whiskey that had previously matured in the barrel.

By the 2000s, bourbon barrel aging was increasingly common for strong beers, while Scottish brewers began using local whisky barrels. Both bourbon and Scottish whisky barrel beers are typically intended to be "clean" and not sour. The main flavors from whiskey casks include vanilla, coconut, caramel, wood, char, sweet spices, smoke and salt (in Scottish whisky), a boozy warmth, and oak tannins.

Wine barrels became common in breweries based in wine regions, especially California, where brewers used them to intentionally turn their beers sour and draw wine-like character from the barrels, while also utilizing any resident bacteria and microflora.

THE SCIENCE OF BARREL AGING

The barrels are slightly porous so they "breathe." As ambient temperatures rise, the barrels expand, and beer is absorbed into the wood grain. As the wood cools and contracts, the beer is squeezed back out, taking flavors and tannins with it. Barrels all age differently and take on different qualities, so barrels are often blended together to create the best finished beer. Beers may spend any time from two months to two years in the barrels.

BARREL-AGED FLAVORS
Ex-alcohol (wine, whiskey)

Oaky/wood

Tannin (dryness)

Aniseed/clove

Fruity (lemon/berry/stone fruit)

Coconut/toasted coconut

Vanilla/vanillin

Caramel/toffee

Smoke (wood or peat)

Umami/soy sauce
(positive autolysis)

OTHER INGREDIENTS IN BEER

In addition to water, grains, hops, and yeast, beer can be brewed with virtually any other ingredients. Sometimes these ingredients are for a subtle and complementary flavor, like grapefruit in an IPA, while other times, they are the dominant flavor, especially in modern Fruit Sours and Pastry Stouts.

FRUITS & VEGETABLES

The most common fruits used are cherries and raspberries, added into Lambic, and other berries are now also popular. Grapefruit and other citrus fruits are often used in IPAs; tropical fruits like mango, guava, and passion fruit are common in sweeter sour beers; grapes can give flavor or their juice can be a cofermentable in some beers; and watermelon and cucumber give a light freshness to low-alcohol beers. Fruits can be added in numerous ways, including fresh fruit, fruit puree, dried fruits, fruit peels, juice, or syrups. Brewers might add them on the hot side of brewing or infuse them during or after fermentation.

Pumpkin Beer is a major seasonal brew, especially in North America. Pumpkin can be added to the mash or kettle as a puree or as cooked pieces. It's often used alongside spices such as cinnamon and nutmeg.

HERBS & SPICES

Coriander is a classic spice in Witbier and Gose. Other spices often used are: peppercorns, grains of paradise, cinnamon, cardamom, nutmeg, and ginger. They are usually added as whole spices into the mash tun or whirlpool, or steeped like tea during conditioning. Chile peppers are common, where they range in warmth from a gentle and fruity tingle to lip-burning. Vanilla seeds or tonka beans are popular additions in a range of styles, adding a luxurious creaminess. Fresh herbs and flowers like juniper, rosemary, bay leaves, hibiscus, elderflower, and teas can be used like hops to infuse flavor.

CHOCOLATE & COFFEE

Coffee can be added at any stage as beans or as espresso. The best coffee flavor often comes from the addition of lots of fresh, cooled espresso.

Chocolate can be added as cacao or cocoa powder, nibs, extract, essence, or as bars. It's sometimes added as a flavor addition after fermentation or it might be part of the mash or boil.

NUTS

Coconut is very common in beer, often dried and toasted. Nuts such as peanut (and peanut butter), hazelnut, pecan, and almond are also used. Fat can diminish a beer's foam, so nuts are sometimes added as powders or extract.

SUGARS

Lactose (milk sugar) is usually added toward the end of the mash or boil and gives a smooth, sweet, and creamy quality. Brown sugar, table sugar, candi sugar, molasses, maple syrup, and honey give both fermentable sugars and flavor. Sometimes cakes and candy are added give flavor and sugar.

FRESH VS. AGED BEER

Most beer is designed to be drunk within a few months of being packaged, especially hop-forward styles, but some beers can improve like fine wine if they're left to mature.

WHY FRESH IS (USUALLY) BEST

A lot of beers' flavors are delicate and volatile, so will change over time. When a beer is packaged and sold, it's typically ready to be drunk right away before those changes occur. That's particularly true for beers with high hop aromas, which can diminish within a few weeks.

Every beer has a window of freshness, and it changes according to the style and how it's served—most British cask ale, for example, has to be drunk younger than a bottle of Belgian Quadrupel.

Most beers will stay fresh for a month or two after being packaged, after which they may begin to change negatively.

There are certain beers that can be left for months or years, and they may even improve as they get older. Very few beers genuinely improve beyond one to three years, although there are some exceptions (see right).

HOW TO STORE BEER

The enemies of beer are oxygen, heat, and light. Oxygen can turn it stale, heat can speed up the aging process, and light can change the flavor (see light-struck beer on p.80). Hopefully, the brewery was diligent in keeping out oxygen, but drinkers can control heat and light.

Temperature can have a big impact on freshness. The ideal temperature to store beer is a cool 50°–54°F (10°–12°C). Not many people have the luxury of a cellar for storing beer, so a cool, dark place with consistent temperatures, such as the fridge or the back of a cupboard in the coolest part of the home, is a good option. A beer stored above room temperature (68°F/20°C) for three weeks might taste as if it's three to six months old, whereas a beer kept in the fridge that whole time should taste brewery fresh.

STAND UP STRAIGHT
Unlike wine, beer should be stored upright. You can lay corked bottles down, but before opening, stand them upright for a day or two to allow yeast to settle in the bottom of the bottle.

THE BEST BEERS TO AGE

The best beers to age are strong (7% ABV and above), dark—although some pale beers can age well—and bottle-conditioned beers.

BELGIAN QUADRUPEL

Belgian Quadrupels are usually bottle conditioned so are good options for aging, but they typically peak within a year or two.

IMPERIAL STOUT

Imperial Stouts can be "hot" when released (intense with alcohol and not quite balanced), so a few months or longer can help. Barrel-aged versions will be better drunk sooner. The best to age have been brewed and packaged to be matured and are bottle conditioned.

BARLEY WINE AND VINTAGE ALE

These are high in alcohol, malt, and hop, and those characteristics can mellow and mature nicely to develop into beers that are similar to their fresh versions but also taste distinctly new.

GUEUZE

Some drinkers love how this style can last for many years, whereas others prefer to drink it soon after it's released— remember this beer has already been matured for years by the brewery. It's bottle conditioned so can develop in the bottle.

Good flavors:
More interesting malt flavor, more complexity of grain and yeast, more fig- or prune-like notes, lower bitterness and spice, a greater expression of flavor and depth with more interesting yeast character, and a softer texture overall.

1–3 YEARS

Bad flavors:
Thinner body, low carbonation, too much sherry character, a muddy/muddled quality instead of a vibrant flavor profile.

Good flavors:
Richer malts in the middle, a sweeter balance with less roast and more chocolate, integrated alcohol, and new yeast flavors develop.

1–5 YEARS

Bad flavors:
Intense autolysis/soy sauce, too sweet and unbalanced, thinner body, and sherry-like flavors.

Good flavors:
Malt amplifies, pleasant dried fruit (fig, prune, port) and sherried notes develop, complexity increases, bitterness mellows, and hop aroma integrates more flavor into the beer.

1–10 YEARS

Bad flavors:
Carbonation decreases, oxidized notes and autolytic soy sauce increase, and it loses expressiveness of flavor and becomes thin.

Good flavors:
Maintains acidity and brightness of flavor, some malt sweetness adds richness, more complexity grows within the beer, and more fruity aromas with the funkier yeast notes diminishing.

1–15+ YEARS

Bad flavors:
No carbonation and too much sweet sherry flavor instead of a bright acidity.

BEST-BEFORE DATES

Most craft breweries put 6–12 months as best-before dates. In reality, most beer should be drunk within three months. Packaged-on dates can be more useful, as you know exactly how old the beer is.

SOME CANS OR BOTTLES MIGHT HAVE A LABEL SAYING: "KEEP IN FRIDGE! HOPS FADE FAST!" THAT'S GOOD ADVICE: THE COLD TEMPERATURE HELPS PRESERVE THE HOP FLAVOR LONGER.

THE TASTE OF AGED BEER

How does a great aged beer taste? Overall, there might be some positive oxidation flavors such as sherry or dried fruits, which are in overall balance with the beer, adding complexity and not tasting as if the beer is lacking something.

- Hop flavors tend to become more integrated, with much aroma lost or changed, while bitterness lowers. Hoppiness can be more like marmalade, oily citrus, woody, or resinous.

- Pale beers can develop more nutty, almond, brioche, or honey flavors, with more yeast flavor coming through.
- A richer and mellow malt flavor develops, with roastiness becoming more chocolaty, caramelized, or with more nutty or vinous flavors.
- Alcohol flavor can be harsh and noticeable in young strong beers. With age, however, alcohol flavor mellows and integrates, adding more complexity and some perceived sweetness.

- An expressive yeast such as a British Barley Wine or strong Belgian ale will often lose some of its fresher fruitiness or spice, but it will develop more complexity with vanilla, tea, and vinous notes.
- Acidity can last for a long time, but after many years, it can reduce as sherry notes increase and acidity becomes more vinous.
- Barrel-aged beers can become more integrated overall, but watch out for autolysis, which tastes like soy sauce.

TASTING OLD BEER THAT'S NOT SUPPOSED TO BE OLD

It's good to taste old beer to really understand what it's like, so look in the back of the cupboard or search supermarket shelves for any out-of-date beers. It's a distinctive flavor once you know what to look for.

- **Old hoppy beers** taste like chewy caramel, raisins, berries, and stale citrus fruit, plus they have lost their fresh hop aroma and have a drying quality on the palate.
- **Old lagers** have a honey-like or sherry flavor and also a drying quality, like licking paper or cardboard.

- **Old dark ales** tend to get sweeter but also thinner, as if some of the flavor has disappeared, with raisin or sherry flavors developing and roasted flavors diminishing.
- **Pale beers** can change color and darken as they oxidize, similar to the browning of a half-eaten apple or banana.

WHAT'S ACTUALLY HAPPENING AS BEER GETS OLDER?

Oxygen slowly changes the beer, and compounds break down and become new ones. Some good flavors are produced and others not so good. Yeast in the beer can synthesize the new flavor compounds, but over time the yeast can also give negative qualities, like an autolyzed soy-sauce flavor.

IS MY BEER TOO OLD?

Signs of a beer that's past its best include a strong sherry or raisin-like flavor, a drying mouthfeel, a quality that seems as if the beer is missing some of its flavor, a savory soy sauce–like flavor, and a lack of condition and carbonation.

WHAT IF MY AGED BEER TASTES BAD?

Bad luck! There's no way to know if a beer— even one known to age well—will taste good after a few years in the bottle, and it won't age in any predictable way. The risk of deliberately aging beer is knowing that sometimes it won't taste good. You can always use it in a cake or stew.

CAN OLD BEER MAKE ME SICK?

No, there's nothing in beer that will do you any harm, apart from alcohol or the result of an exceptionally rare brewery mishap. Lager that's been in the back of a cupboard for a few years might not taste great, but it's safe to drink, and is a good way to know what old beer really tastes like.

DOES TEMPERATURE CHANGE MATTER?

If you buy a beer from the bottle-shop fridge and it gets warm on the way home before you refrigerate it again, it probably won't affect the flavor unless it got very warm. Constant high to low temperature fluctuation might have more of an impact.

MY BEER GUSHED EVERYWHERE AND IT'S SOUR!

Is it supposed to be sour? If not, then the beer picked up a bacterial infection somewhere and is probably undrinkable. If it's supposed to be sour but still gushed, then the brewery didn't package it properly. Either way, you could let the brewery know with a polite private message.

BEER OFF FLAVORS

Not every beer tastes great. Here, we're not thinking about styles that you might not personally like, but the introduction of particular chemical compounds that are not always considered to be good.

SOMETHING'S A BIT OFF

As much as we want to celebrate beer as being a wonderful and delicious drink, the simple truth is that a considerable amount of beer shows what can be considered off flavors (see pp.78–81). Sometimes they're only minor faults or at levels so low that only an off-flavor detective could find them, but other times they can be offensive and make a beer undrinkable. A lot of the time, however, we aren't aware that something isn't quite right; we just sense that the beer isn't excellent without knowing why. If you drink a beer that you think is a bit strange and unbalanced but aren't quite sure why, it probably has a brewing fault.

There are a few things to consider here. Some flavors are negatives in certain styles but positives in others (see below). Many of these chemical compounds are in most beers at low levels and only become negative when they are above a certain flavor threshold. We can be "nose blind" to some of these compounds, being unable to smell them unless present in very high volumes. And some people can be extra-sensitive to certain aromas, particularly diacetyl and clove/phenols.

WHAT DO YOU DO WITH BAD BEER?

If you don't mind the flavor of a beer with a fault, it's fine to carry on drinking it. If not, you might want to pour it out and open something else. You can always politely and privately message the brewery to let them know, or return the beer if you're in a pub or bar. It's better to return a beer only if it's a certain off flavor associated with the venue, such as unintentional sourness, which could be a sign that the lines are dirty or the beer has been on for too long.

Beer that has gone sour, has oxidized, or has unusual flavors isn't harmful to drink—unless the brewery has done something very wrong—it's just not as delicious as it should be.

NEGATIVE AND POSITIVE FLAVORS

Most beer flavors have a level of appropriateness depending on the type of beer. A flavor could be a positive in one style, and a negative in another.

PHENOLS
Yeast phenols are great in a Witbier but would leave a harsh taste against the hops in an IPA.

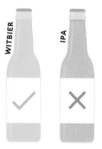

OXIDATION
Oxidation can add complexity to a Barley Wine but can strip hop flavor from a Pale Ale.

ISOAMYL ACETATE
A banana-like aroma is great in a Hefeweizen but would unbalance the crisp bitterness of a Pilsner.

TRAIN YOUR PALATE

It's possible to learn to detect specific flavors in beer, and the more we practice, the better we get at identifying them.

OFF-FLAVOR TRAINING

The best way to learn about off flavors is to take part in off-flavor training—it can be expensive but it's worthwhile. You'll be presented with numerous samples of beer spiked with different chemical compounds and you'll learn exactly what those chemical compounds taste like, making it much easier to taste them in your beer. It's only with experiencing off flavors that we can train ourselves to recognize those exact compounds.

You can replicate the experience at home by tasting beers that are known to have specific flavor compounds: for example, try a German Hefeweizen for isoamyl acetate, a Belgian Witbier for phenols, a Czech Pilsner (such as Pilsner Urquell) sometimes has a butter-like quality, a lager in a green bottle might be light-struck (see p.80), and an out-of-date beer will likely be oxidized.

GOOD-FLAVOR TRAINING

Training to find singular negative flavors is useful, but beer contains many more positive aroma and flavor compounds, and being able to identify those is a very rewarding experience—it's also surprisingly challenging to blind-smell common food aromas. The best way to become a better flavor detective is simply to be more curious about foods: smell everything properly; every time you use a spice in cooking, smell it; every time you eat fruit, smell the skin and the flesh, and taste them both; buy fruits that you've never tasted before.

Another idea is to wear a blindfold and have someone put pieces of fruit in different glasses and then see if you can identify them by smell—it's a real challenge. By smelling and tasting more foods and consciously thinking about them, we can become much better beer tasters.

COMMON OFF FLAVORS

There could be numerous reasons why a beer
tastes odd or unbalanced. Here are some of
the most common off flavors in beer.

OFF FLAVOR	DIACETYL	ACETALDEHYDE
SMELLS/ TASTES LIKE	Butter, butterscotch, margarine, buttered popcorn. It can have a slick, fatty mouthfeel. It can be acceptable in low levels in some English ales and Czech lagers, but not in Pale Ales and IPAs, where it will negatively affect the overall balance.	Apple candy, chemical apple scent, cider, pumpkin, emulsion/latex paint. It can be fine in low levels and add a hint of fruitiness but quickly goes from fruity to unpleasant if present in high volumes.
WHY?	Diacetyl is produced by all yeast during fermentation, but the yeast will also reabsorb it if it's given the right conditions and enough time. It can be present if the brewer has rushed the beer or not performed a "diacetyl rest" (slightly increasing the temperature of beer toward the end of fermentation, which reactivates the yeast and encourages it to absorb the diacetyl). It can also be a byproduct of a lactic fermentation or a sign of dirty lines.	Acetaldehyde is a natural byproduct of fermentation and a compound created as malt sugars convert to alcohol (it's also the compound our bodies metabolize alcohol into as it's processed inside us, and it's often thought of as a culprit for hangovers). It's a sign that the beer is too fresh or green, or that the yeast has been stressed in production. It's most common to find this in English cask ales, and you might find it alongside diacetyl.

DIMETHYL SULFIDE (DMS)	SULFUR	OXIDIZED OR OLD BEER
Sweetcorn, creamed corn, cornflakes, stewed cabbage, strawberry jam, or **cooked tomatoes**. It can add a pleasant complexity in low volumes but can be unpleasant in high amounts. It's usually only found in lagers or very pale ales.	**Eggy, struck match, burned rubber, cooked vegetables, skunk spray**. Sulfur can give mineral-like and even fresh notes in some lagers and ales, which is often not a negative. All sulfur tends to be volatile, so if it's present, it'll quickly evaporate.	**Sherry, old honey, dried fruits, unsweet caramel,** a drying quality like licking **paper** or **cardboard**. Often this comes with a thinner mouthfeel and a general sense that some flavor is missing from the beer.
DMS comes from a compound found in malt. When malt is kilned, the compound typically isn't present, so this is something found most often in pale lager malts. It's driven out during the mashing process, then typically boiled away in the kettle. If it's in the beer, then it could be a sign that the boil wasn't strong or long enough.	Eggy hydrogen sulfide is usually produced either during fermentation or from beers brewed with high mineral content in their water, particularly calcium sulfate. It's associated with the hard waters of Burton on Trent, giving a sulfur character known as "Burton snatch," but it's not found often. Sulfur dioxide is like a struck match, and you'll find this sulfitic quality in lager yeasts. It can have a fresh, even sweet, aroma in small quantities.	Oxidized beer is stale and often old. Oxygen creates new flavor compounds and changes the balance, often making a beer feel like it's lost complexity, depth, or freshness. Old hoppy beers might be more caramel-like with a much-reduced hop character, often developing black currant or dried, stale citrus in place of the fresh hop notes. A small amount of oxidation can add character and complexity in some aged beers (see p.74).

OFF FLAVOR	UNINTENTIONAL SOUR BEER	LIGHT-STRUCK OR "SKUNKED" BEER
SMELLS/ TASTES LIKE	Sour milk or yogurt (even goatlike or "sweaty"), citric-like, lemon, cidery, vinegary (malt or balsamic). This sour taste might come with additional unwelcome esters or other aroma compounds.	Ever opened a bottle of lager or drunk a pint outside on a sunny day and it has an aroma like rotting vegetables, garlic, marijuana, or even skunk spray? That's light-struck beer, also colloquially known as "skunked" beer.
WHY?	A sour taste can mean the beer has suffered a bacterial contamination, often from the same bacteria that contribute acidity to intentional sour beers. As the beer gets older, the sourness becomes more prominent. It could also be caused by dirty lines in a pub or bar, and the solution there is for the venue to properly clean the lines before serving more beer through them.	Ultraviolet (UV) rays break down some hop molecules, creating a sulfurous reaction and producing chemicals that are the same as a skunk spray (3-methyl-2-butene-1-thiol, or MBT). A beer should never smell light-struck, but many consumers have got used to it as part of the flavor of bottled lagers. Brown bottles can block UV rays better than clear or green glasses. Beer can get light-struck quickly, so keep your pint in the shade if you're drinking outside.

PHENOLS	ESTERS	AND THE REST ...
Clove, pepper, black cardamom, smoke, medicinal, bandages, vanilla, smoky whiskey, even **animal-like aromas** often described as "horse blanket."	**Fruity flavors**, like a **chemical, artificial**, or **candied fruitiness**: banana, pear, pear drop, apple, aniseed, honey, rose, strawberry, plum, pineapple, vanilla, grape, bubble gum.	**Soy sauce, yeast extract, burned tires, blue cheese rind.** It's likely that the yeast has autolyzed (died and ruptured). A small amount can add complexity to aged beers, but too much can be undrinkable.
		Alcohol, acetone (nail-polish remover). There are a lot of higher alcohols in the beer.
		Cheesy, sweaty socks. The brewery probably used old hops.
Phenols develop with fermentation. If they are not intentional, they are considered negative compounds, often due to poor temperature control during fermentation or a bacterial infection. They are intentional in Hefeweizen, Witbiers, Belgian ales, and some *Brettanomyces* beers, but can be unpleasant in high volumes. Certain drinkers are highly sensitive to this flavor (like some people dislike fresh cilantro).	These yeast-derived aromatic compounds are an underlying flavor in every beer and are fundamental to the profiles of lots of different beer styles (see pp.66–67), but they can become unpleasant if in high volumes or if they are inappropriate to the beer style. They are a byproduct of fermentation and typically the warmer the fermentation, the more esters there will be.	**Metallic** like **tin foil, coins,** or **blood.** It's usually due to an issue with water or a contaminant in the brewery vessels. If you're drinking direct from the can and taste metal, you're tasting the can itself, not a metallic note in the beer—all cans are lined inside so beer should never be touching aluminum.

BEER IN THE BAR

When you order a beer in a pub or bar, the way it is delivered to your glass depends on whether you've ordered a cask ale, a kegged lager, or a pint of creamy nitro Stout.

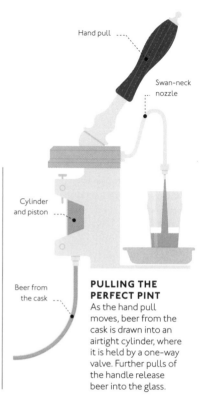

Hand pull

Swan-neck nozzle

Cylinder and piston

Beer from the cask

PULLING THE PERFECT PINT
As the hand pull moves, beer from the cask is drawn into an airtight cylinder, where it is held by a one-way valve. Further pulls of the handle release beer into the glass.

WHAT IS CASK ALE?

Cask ale, or real ale, is a British institution, and drinking a freshly poured and perfectly kept pint of it is a wonderful experience. Cask ale is a format for serving beer, and any beer style can be served this way. Historically, all beer was delivered to pubs in wooden casks, and beer was served directly from the cask. Today, the casks are stainless steel and usually stored in the pub's cellar, where they are connected to a hand pull at the bar.

A beer brewed for cask finishes its primary fermentation and then has a few days of maturation in tank before being filled (racked) into casks along with a fining agent—to draw yeast to the bottom of the cask—and possibly a mix of yeast and priming sugar. The beer undergoes a secondary fermentation inside the cask and develops a light carbonation. All cask ale is reliant on the pub or bar to store and serve the beer properly in order for it to taste as it should.

PREPARING THE CASK TO SERVE

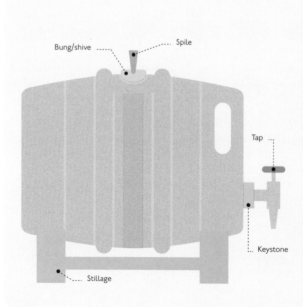

Bung/shive

Spile

Tap

Keystone

Stillage

Once filled with beer, the cask is sealed with a bung/shive. Within a few days, the cask arrives in a pub cellar, where it's put onto a framework (stillage). Here, it undergoes a secondary fermentation (conditioning period) for a couple of days, when the yeast converts some residual sugars in the beer into carbon dioxide, giving the beer a gentle carbonation. Any yeast or sediment drops to the bottom of the cask to leave a bright beer.

When the beer is nearly ready, a peg is hit into the bung, knocking a plastic shive into the cask and releasing excess pressure. A soft, porous spile is put into the bung, venting the cask, and the tap is inserted through the keystone. The beer is then left for 24 hours, after which it's checked and tasted. If it's ready, the soft spile is replaced by a hard spile (to hold the carbonation in place) and the cask is connected to the line that draws beer up to the bar. There may be an ingress of oxygen into the cask once it's been tapped, so it's important to serve the beer within a few days to avoid it turning stale or sour.

KEG BEER

The most common kind of draft beer has a fairly complicated set-up. There are numerous ways to serve kegged beer, but all of them have gas, usually carbon dioxide (CO_2), at one end and a gas line connecting the gas to the keg via a coupler connector. The gas line pushes CO_2 into the keg, while the beer line pushes the beer out of the keg, with the gas filling the space left by the beer and preventing oxidation. The beer line runs through a cooling unit, which chills the beer in-line on its way to the tap at the other end of the line.

The speed at which beer pours can be controlled with the tap, and regulator valves attached to the gas help control flow pressure. The key to any keg draft system is balancing the temperature of the beer with the gas pressure—the pressure increases with warmer temperatures. Creating this balance requires a complex understanding of the interaction of temperature, pressure, and the length and diameter of the beer line. A craft-beer bar cellar might have more than 20 kegs attached, with each needing to be individually balanced based on its carbonation.

SERVING KEG BEER

Most systems for serving keg beer include a gas cylinder and line, beer line, and cooling equipment.

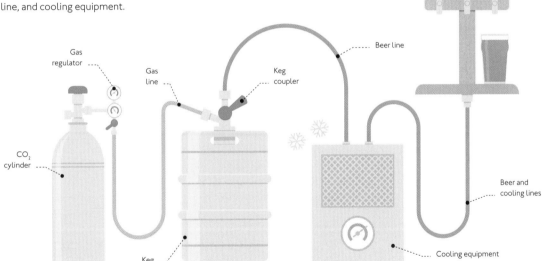

Gas regulator

Gas line

Keg coupler

Beer line

Tap

CO_2 cylinder

Keg

Cooling equipment

Beer and cooling lines

NITRO BEER

A perfect pint of Guinness has upwardly cascading bubbles and distinctive creamy foam. Unlike regular beers, it's infused with nitrogen. In the brewery, the beer is in a pressurized tank with a low level of CO_2, and nitrogen is dissolved into the tank. Nitrogen doesn't dissolve well in beer, so it tries to escape when the beer's served, carrying the CO_2 with it and creating that cascade of bubbles. Nitro beers are poured through a tap nozzle with small holes that help knock more gas out of suspension. Nitro kegs are connected to mixed gas (nitrogen and CO_2) in the cellar.

BEER & FOOD

Whether you want to understand what beers might taste best with your food and what to avoid, or whether you're planning a beer-led feast, a flavor-focused approach can help with finding a good match.

WHY BEER & FOOD?

While wine is seen as the fancier fine-dining choice, beer has become the casual partner for pizzas and burgers. That's not necessarily a bad thing, and there are many amazing and simple combinations that can be put together. But anything wine can do, beer can do, too, and because beer has important characteristics that help it taste great with food, we could even argue that beer can do more. Here we're trying to simplify the approach to beer and food and focus on finding great flavor matches. Here are some reasons why beer and food can work so well together.

CARBONATION

The carbonation is refreshing with heavier or rich high-fat foods (Dubbel with pork chops), while bitterness can refresh and balance very salty foods, which is why chips and beer taste so good together.

MALT FLAVOR & GRAINS

The pale malt flavor has an underlying cooked and bread-like quality, which naturally aligns it to most food, like bread on the side of the plate.

Some grains that give beer an amber to brown color have a Maillard caramelization to them, making them good matches for grilled and caramelized foods—such as Amber Lager with a hot dog topped with grilled onions.

ROASTED FLAVORS

Most dark beers have a roasted flavor that works with other roasted flavors, such as Stout and brisket.

FERMENTATION & ACIDITY

Beer's fermentation profile naturally makes it work well with all sorts of different fermented foods, especially bread, pickled vegetables, sausages, cheese, and chocolate.

Some beers are refreshingly acidic, so have a mouthwatering quality similar to wine.

AROMATIC HOPS

Aromatic hops link more to a dish's aroma or top notes, such as fresh seasoning, herbs, citrus, or even the sauce used, so think about those on top of the underlying food flavors.

FINDING BALANCE

Beers paired with the right dishes can be revelatory, but that doesn't mean it will always be an amazing match. Most of the time, we want to find a simple balance of flavors, and sometimes certain beers and food just don't work well.

Flavor matches are personal, and the only way to understand what you like is to try lots of different foods with various beers. The more you do, the more you'll see how different flavors, intensities, and characteristics all interact. Don't worry about finding perfect pairings. Keep it simple and focus on flavor.

DRINK LOCAL

The world knows how to match beer and food, and wherever you go, locals eat certain foods while drinking. In Germany, people eat schnitzels with malt-forward lagers. In Britain, Australia, and New Zealand, it's pints of ale with pub food: pies, roast dinners, and sandwiches. In North America, it's burgers, wings, and tacos. In Southeast Asia, refreshing lager goes with noodle dishes, and in Brazil, it's fried bar snacks.

MATCHING FLAVOR INTENSITY

The number one tip with pairing beer and food is to match the intensity and find beers and foods with a similar strength of flavor. There are some exceptions, where we're trying to refresh particular heavy flavors, such as pale lagers with very strong Indian curries, Pilsner with spicy pork belly, or Schwarzbier with ramen.

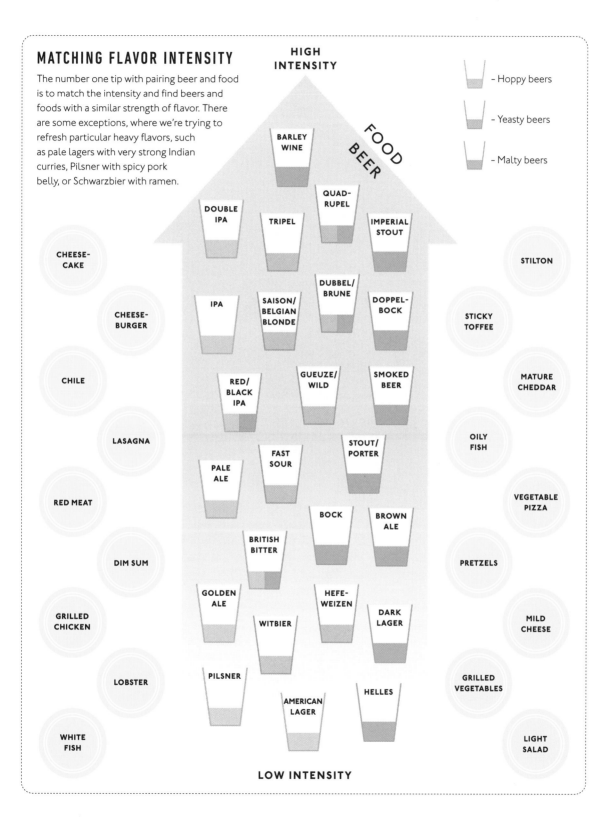

HIGH INTENSITY

FOOD
BEER

- Hoppy beers
- Yeasty beers
- Malty beers

BARLEY WINE

QUAD-RUPEL

DOUBLE IPA

TRIPEL

IMPERIAL STOUT

CHEESE-CAKE

STILTON

DUBBEL/BRUNE

IPA

SAISON/BELGIAN BLONDE

DOPPEL-BOCK

CHEESE-BURGER

STICKY TOFFEE

RED/BLACK IPA

GUEUZE/WILD

SMOKED BEER

CHILE

MATURE CHEDDAR

FAST SOUR

STOUT/PORTER

LASAGNA

OILY FISH

PALE ALE

RED MEAT

BOCK

BROWN ALE

VEGETABLE PIZZA

BRITISH BITTER

DIM SUM

PRETZELS

GOLDEN ALE

HEFE-WEIZEN

GRILLED CHICKEN

WITBIER

DARK LAGER

MILD CHEESE

PILSNER

LOBSTER

HELLES

GRILLED VEGETABLES

AMERICAN LAGER

WHITE FISH

LIGHT SALAD

LOW INTENSITY

DIFFERENT APPROACHES TO BEER & FOOD

There's no single way to think about beer and food, and there are many different approaches to finding the best flavor matches.

FIND SHARED FLAVORS & TEXTURES

Here, we want to find something similar in the beer and the food, and often this will be a feature of all matches. If there's a shared flavor, then we naturally create a bridge between beer and food, and it could be pairing a major part of either beer or food or picking out a particular shared quality.

First, identify the hop, malt, or yeast characteristics of the beer, and then match it with foods that go well with those qualities.

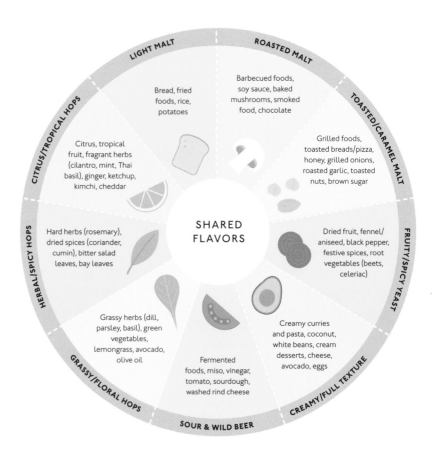

LIGHT MALT

ROASTED MALT

TOASTED/CARAMEL MALT

FRUITY/SPICY YEAST

CREAMY/FULL TEXTURE

SOUR & WILD BEER

GRASSY/FLORAL HOPS

HERBAL/SPICY HOPS

CITRUS/TROPICAL HOPS

SHARED FLAVORS

Bread, fried foods, rice, potatoes

Barbecued foods, soy sauce, baked mushrooms, smoked food, chocolate

Grilled foods, toasted breads/pizza, honey, grilled onions, roasted garlic, toasted nuts, brown sugar

Dried fruit, fennel/aniseed, black pepper, festive spices, root vegetables (beets, celeriac)

Creamy curries and pasta, coconut, white beans, cream desserts, cheese, avocado, eggs

Fermented foods, miso, vinegar, tomato, sourdough, washed rind cheese

Grassy herbs (dill, parsley, basil), green vegetables, lemongrass, avocado, olive oil

Hard herbs (rosemary), dried spices (coriander, cumin), bitter salad leaves, bay leaves

Citrus, tropical fruit, fragrant herbs (cilantro, mint, Thai basil), ginger, ketchup, kimchi, cheddar

PAIRING TECHNIQUES & INTERACTIONS

With any dish, you might be able to find several different beer styles that all complement the food in different ways. A falafel kebab, for example, shares similar spicy flavors with a Belgian Blonde; while a Brown Ale adds some nice toasty malts to the bread, the frying, and the nutty flavors; and a hoppy Pilsner refreshes with citrus and carbonation, finding affinity with the salad.

FIND BALANCE AND HARMONIZE

You'll find the most success with this approach. It might not always give amazing pairings, but you'll rarely be disappointed. Aim to align the flavors, such as a shared match, ensuring neither the beer nor the food is overpowered, creating a tasty balance and harmony (see pp.88–89).

REFRESH HEAVY FOOD FLAVORS

For dishes that are rich or high in fat, a beer can be refreshing, lifting the flavors with high carbonation, acidity, or bitterness. A lighter beer can work with a heavier dish, such as Pilsner with roasted pork belly, but it depends on the side dishes and sauce—it works if the pork is served with rice and salad, for example, but not with gravy and mashed potatoes.

BELGIAN BLONDE with salmon and creamy dill sauce

HOPPY PILSNER with arancini

DUBBEL with beef Wellington

TRIPEL with pork and gratin potatoes

ENHANCE FLAVORS

Consider all the elements of a dish's composition in relation to the beer, or add specific ingredients to get a match just right. Lifting heavier flavors is often a key part of this pairing, but sometimes it works simply by the beer adding a completely new quality to the dish.

HAZY PALE ALE with mushroom fried rice

DUBBEL with lasagna or ragù

SWEET CHERRY BEER with dark chocolate mousse

AMERICAN DOUBLE IPA with carrot cake

HOLD FIRE!

Chile contains capsaicin, which gives a burning sensation when eaten. Certain beers, such as very bitter or high-alcohol ones, can make that burn feel like it's getting hotter. Spicy foods need beers that can cool them down. The best are those with a creamy or malt-forward texture, moderate alcohol, and a small amount of sweetness.

MALTY LOW-BITTER LAGER with tomato-based curries

WITBIER OR HEFEWEIZEN with coconut-based curries

DUNKEL with spicy fried noodles or fried rice

OATMEAL STOUT with buffalo wings or a chili

MATCH THE SAUCE

For dishes served in a sauce, you want a beer that matches the sauce, as that will be in every mouthful. Fish in a cream sauce, for example, needs a pale and creamy-textured beer, while a meaty gravy needs a richer dark ale. You can use this approach with foods that are accompanied by side serves of ketchup (hoppy ales), mayonnaise (Witbier and Hefeweizen), mustard (Dark Lager and Best Bitter), or hot sauce (Porter).

FINDING BALANCE & HARMONY

These are some examples of how different tastes and qualities in food and beer can balance each other. Here, we're also usually looking to find some shared flavors and always thinking about intensity.

SWEETNESS & SPICE

MILK/ OATMEAL STOUT
with chili

PORTER
with peri peri chicken

DUNKELWEIZEN
with tagine

BITTER BEER & SALTY FOOD

PALE ALE
with fried chicken

GERMAN PILSNER
with salt and pepper tofu/squid

TRIPEL with anchovy and caper pizza

HOP BITTERNESS & FAT

BEST BITTER
with sausage roll

AMERICAN IPA
with cheddar and leek risotto

BARLEY WINE
with blue cheese

SWEETER BEER & UMAMI/ SAVORY FOODS

HAZY IPA with mushroom fried rice

DUBBEL with pasta and marinara sauce

PORTER with miso eggplant salmon

ROAST & ACIDITY

OATMEAL STOUT
with buffalo wings

STOUT with salmon and lemon butter sauce

RASPBERRY SOUR
with dark chocolate

ROAST & ROAST/SPICE

BLACK IPA
with brisket or Chinese roast duck

BLACK LAGER
with blackened cod/ cauliflower

IMPERIAL STOUT
with coffee cake

CARBONATION & FAT/CREAM

GUEUZE with goat cheese tart

TRIPEL with roast pork belly

KRIEK with baked cheesecake

CREAMY/SMOOTH & CREAMY, UMAMI, OR SPICY

HEFEWEIZEN with avocado, egg, and chile

WEIZENBOCK with pulled pork and slaw

OATMEAL STOUT with stroganoff

ACIDITY & SALT & FAT

SOUR RED-BROWN with bacon sandwich

GOSE with spiced grilled mackerel

WILD ALE with cured meats

ALCOHOL & FAT, SALT, & SWEETNESS

TRIPEL with herb-roast pork and vegetables

HAZY DIPA with Hawaiian pizza

QUADRUPEL with farmhouse cheese and fruit chutney

BITTER & SWEET

TRIPEL with lemon sponge cake

AMERICAN IPA with sweet potato fries

AMERICAN BARLEY WINE with ginger cake

SWEETNESS & SWEETNESS

DOPPELBOCK with apple cake

BARLEY WINE with fruit cake

FRUIT BEER with jelly doughnut

GREAT BEER & FOOD MATCHES TO TRY

Depending on the food or cuisines, there are some top combinations to try that incorporate the different approaches outlined on the previous pages.

BRUNCH

COFFEE STOUT
with blueberry pancakes

HAZY IPA
with chicken and waffles

DUNKEL
with eggs and bacon/sausage

SUMMER ALE OR HEFEWEIZEN
with avocado on toast

BURGERS & SANDWICHES

AMERICAN PALE ALE
with grilled cheese

AMERICAN IPA
with cheeseburger

AMBER LAGER
with hot dogs

HOPPY LAGER
with banh mi (Vietnamese baguette)

ITALIAN FOOD

DUBBEL
*with lasagna, ragù,
or marinara*

BELGIAN BLONDE
with carbonara

DUNKELWEIZEN
with mushroom risotto

PILSNER
with margherita pizza

SNACKS

HOPPY LAGER
*with guacamole
and nachos*

HELLES
with Bavarian pretzels

**DUNKEL OR
BEST BITTER**
with grilled sausages

HAZY PALE ALE
*with halloumi fries
and sweet chile*

VEGETARIAN/VEGAN DISHES

WITBIER OR SAISON
with falafel wrap

HAZY IPA
with bean burger

OATMEAL STOUT
*with cauliflower
buffalo wings*

**DUNKELWEIZEN OR
OATMEAL STOUT**
with bean chili

MEAT

**HELLES OR
HELLES BOCK**
with roast chicken

SOUR RED-BROWN
with steak and chips

DUBBEL OR PORTER
with beef stew

BELGIAN BLONDE
with lamb kebabs

FISH

ENGLISH PALE ALE
with fish and chips

**AMERICAN
PALE ALE**
with fish tacos

WITBIER
with lobster rolls

BELGIAN BLONDE
*with steamed
mussels in beer*

CURRIES & NOODLES

**WITBIER OR
HEFEWEIZEN**
with laksa curry

HELLES
with Madras curry

HOPPY LAGER
*with Vietnamese
noodle salad*

DUNKELWEIZEN
*with drunken
noodles*

CHEESE

**HAZY PALE ALE
OR HEFEWEIZEN**
with Brie or Camembert

KRIEK OR GUEUZE
with goat's cheese

**IMPERIAL STOUT
OR AMERICAN DIPA**
with strong blue cheese

**AMERICAN IPA OR
ENGLISH BARLEY WINE**
with mature cheddar

DESSERTS

IMPERIAL STOUT
*with chocolate
brownie/cake*

SWEET CHERRY BEER
*with dark chocolate
mousse*

**BARREL-AGED TRIPEL
OR PALE BARLEY WINE**
with crème brûlée

DUNKELWEIZENBOCK
*with sticky toffee
pudding*

FRUIT

**BARREL-AGED
DOPPELBOCK**
with apple strudel

HAZY DIPA
*with pineapple upside-
down cake*

SWEET CHERRY BEER
with cherry cheesecake

**BARREL-AGED
IMPERIAL STOUT**
with banana cake or pudding

NAVIGATING
BEER
BY
STYLE

THIS SECTION EXPLORES MORE than 50 of the world's most popular beer styles, from great lagers, wonderful hoppy IPAs, and delicious dark ales, to sour and fruit beers, wheat beers, and Belgian beer styles. For each style, you'll discover the flavors to expect, how the beers are brewed, and their history. There are four different beers to compare in each, which are considered to be true examples of the style. It's the perfect opportunity to sample these beers and do your own side-by-side tastings.

LAGERS

OFTEN THOUGHT OF AS just one type of refreshing golden beer, lager is in fact a whole family of beer styles, all brewed with lager yeast (as opposed to ale yeast). The lager family gives a wide range of flavors and drinking qualities, with everything from crisp American Lagers to rich and strong Doppelbocks, and from bitter German Pilsners and toasty Ambers and Dunkels to roasty Schwarzbiers and celebratory Festbiers. The family includes some modern hop-forward brews, extending the range to new generations of lager lovers.

GERMAN-STYLE PILSNER

These bitter, golden lagers originate from Germany and are now popular all around the world.

WILLIBECHER   TALL FLUTED

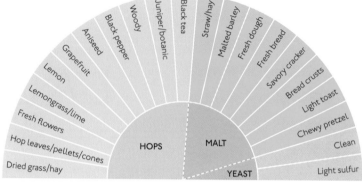

FLAVOR WHEEL

FLAVOR, PROCESS, & STORY

German Pilsners are bitter, hop-forward lagers and often bright in appearance, though some are unfiltered and lightly hazy. They should always be served with a crown of white foam. German hops such as Hallertau Mittelfrüh, Hallertau Tradition, Spalter Select, and Hersbrucker are key to this style's flavor profile. Hop character is noticeable—though not always aromatic—with a firm and lasting bitterness, and herbal, spicy, citrus, and grassy flavors. American and New World hops produce a different overall character but can still be excellent in a Pilsner. Fermentation aromas are minimal and carbonation levels are medium to high.

Often, only Pilsner malt is used, adding a light malt body and subtle malt flavor without sweetness. Classic German versions may use a decoction mash for upfront body and a drier finish.

First brewed in the Czech city of Pilsen in 1842, Pilsner became the first beer style to be brewed outside of its home region, taking on different local characteristics: lighter in North America, drier in Asia, and less sweet and more bitter in northern Europe—it was this Pilsner that truly became the global brew. Today, classic German Pilsner has come to be the archetypal beer and arguably the world's most-drunk style.

BEER STATS				
Color	Clarity	Ferment	ABV	Bitterness
Straw to gold	Bright	Clean/neutral	4.6%–5.2%	25–45 IBU (medium–high)

ROTHAUS TANNENZÄPFLE PILS

5.1% ABV	BREWED: GRAFENHAUSEN, GERMANY

This has arguably become the world's defining example of a German Pilsner. The beer is perfectly structured: hop aromatics to invite you in, with citrus (think pithy, candied peel) and hop flowers. Malt brings a little sweetness at first before elegantly dispersing to a dryness and a lasting, peppery bitterness that makes you want another sip to restore the initial sweetness.

ALDER BEER CO. HERING

5.2% ABV	BREWED: SEREGNO, ITALY

Think of an Italian garden with its beauty, symmetry, and Mediterranean plants in warm sunshine. That's the kind of evocation that Alder's Hering brings. It's a balanced and yet striking example of a German-style Pilsner, both wonderfully aromatic, thanks to a light dry hopping, and also deeply bitter. Some of the world's great Pilsners are found in Italy.

JEVER PILSENER

4.9% ABV	BREWED: JEVER, GERMANY

The first time you taste Jever, it's probably going to be a surprise, even a shock. It's a remarkably bitter beer (40 IBU), herbal and citrus-pithy, with a spicy and woody depth. The base malt for the beer is subtly in the background, adding structure but not much flavor. The hops are oily in the glass and become bracing and assertive in the best of ways. This is one of the more intense examples of the style.

DURATION BREWING DOSES PILSNER

5.1% ABV	BREWED: WEST ACRE, ENGLAND

Most German-style Pilsners have a precision to them, being crisp, snappy, and bright. With Duration Doses, you get something with a little more rusticity. It has grain up front giving some toasted maltiness. It's unfiltered so there's naturally more texture, which holds on to more of the hops (Hallertau Mittelfrüh, Saphir, Saaz). The hop flavors are bitter lemon, orange pith, blossom, and bitter herbs, with an oily lemon richness.

OTHER EXAMPLES TO TRY

LOST & GROUNDED KELLER PILS: floral, herbal, fragrant German hops.

THREES BREWING VLIET: dried lemon, herbal hops, pithy bitterness.

BELLWOODS BELLWEISER: floral hop, light citrus, cracker malt, crisp.

CZECH PALE LAGER

First brewed in the Czech city of Pilsen in 1842, this is the original pale lager style, notable for having sweet, caramelized malts and bitter Czech hops.

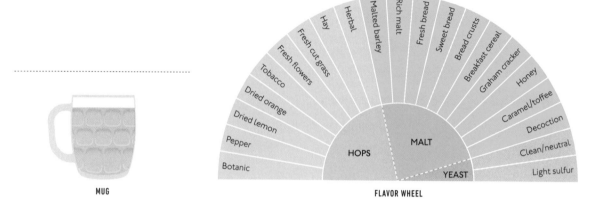

MUG

FLAVOR WHEEL

Hay · Herbal · Malted barley · Rich malt · Fresh bread · Sweet bread · Bread crusts · Breakfast cereal · Graham cracker · Honey · Fresh cut grass · Fresh flowers · Tobacco · Dried orange · Dried lemon · Pepper · Botanic · Caramel/toffee · Decoction · Clean/neutral · Light sulfur

HOPS · MALT · YEAST

FLAVOR, PROCESS, & STORY

Characteristics vary from lightly malty and low in bitterness to richly bittersweet, with the two best-known examples—Budweiser Budvar and Pilsner Urquell— at either end of that scale. Unlike a German Pilsner, these typically have a pronounced caramelized malt depth from a decoction mash and a soft texture from a low carbonation and the use of very soft water, which enhances the sweeter malt flavors. Czech Saaz hops are a defining quality, giving a firm bitterness and aromas that are floral and grassy like hay, tobacco, and some dried lemon. A creamy, thick layer of foam is important when serving these beers.

Usually made with just Pilsner malt, the beer's richness comes from a decoction process, which gives flavor and color. Most are filtered, but it's increasingly common to find unfiltered versions.

While commonly called Pilsner, there's only one true Czech Pilsner: Pilsner Urquell. When it was first brewed, it used a then-new combination of processes and ingredients: soft Pilsen water; British indirect malting to make pale malts from Moravian barley, which became known as Pilsner malt; hops from Žatec; German lager yeast; and German lager-brewing techniques. Compared to German Pils, these are more malt rich, caramelized, softer bodied, and hop aromatic.

BEER STATS				
Color	Clarity	Ferment	ABV	Bitterness
Pale gold to dark gold	Bright to light haze	Clean/neutral	4%–5%	20–40 IBU (medium)

PILSNER URQUELL

4.4% ABV	BREWED: PILSEN, CZECH REPUBLIC

Much of the beer's nuance is lost to pasteurization and packaging, so drink it fresh in the Czech Republic to understand it properly. Malt is richly caramelized, toasty, honeyed, rounded, and slightly sweet, with a distinctive Maillard flavor of triple decoction. Saaz hops are aromatic—floral, herbal, dried lemon—and high in bitterness (38 IBU), with a bittersweet overall balance. The texture is soft with noticeable residual sweetness.

BUDWEISER BUDVAR

5% ABV	BREWED: ČESKÉ BUDĚJOVICE, CZECH REPUBLIC

Where Pilsner Urquell is rounded and bitter, Budvar is leaner in malt sweetness and low in bitterness (22 IBU). The grain flavor is Czech and of double decoctions, with restrained toasted malt, honey, bread crust, and graham cracker. The whole flower Saaz hops are floral and fragrant, with a balanced elegance and a light herbal bitterness, but not the grip of other more bitter lagers. The yeast gives a hint of light fruitiness.

NOTCH BREWING THE STANDARD

4.5% ABV	BREWED: SALEM, MA, USA

Brewed in the style of Czech classics, the Standard is double decocted, open fermented, and long lagered. It uses Czech floor malt and, in an American twist, it's brewed with Sterling hops. Brilliant gold in color with a thick, white foam, it's rounded with the moreish richness of grain flavor amplified by its decoction. The fermentation gives a light yeast fruitiness, the hoppiness is distinct, firm, and floral with a note of dried lemon and herbs.

GODSPEED BREWERY SVĚTLÝ LEŽÁK 12°

5% ABV	BREWED: TORONTO, CANADA

Brewed with Czech ingredients to achieve a classic flavor profile, this is a rich golden-amber color with the round mouthfeel that comes from a decoction mash. The brewery uses special Czech malt that benefits from this kind of mash, giving caramel, toast, bread dough, and some sweetness. The bitterness is high—similar to Pilsner Urquell—and there are layers of floral and herbal hoppiness all the way through it.

OTHER EXAMPLES TO TRY

ÚNĚTICKÉ PIVO 12°: toasted malt, floral hops, dry, crisp.

MATUŠKA DESÍTKA 10°: bread crusts, rich malt, lasting herbal bitterness.

HEATER ALLEN PILS: toasty malts, floral hops, crisp bitterness.

AMERICAN LAGER & PILSNER

These crisp lagers are the United States' most popular mainstream beer, with craft brewers now making their own interpretations.

SHAKER

WILLIBECHER

FLAVOR WHEEL

Grassy · Straw · Corn · Rice · Barley tea · White bread · Savory cracker · Honey · Light citrus · Graham cracker · Fruity · Clean · Light esters · Light citrus · Woody · Light herbal · Light spice · Tobacco · Dried lemon · Light floral · Dried grass/hay

MALT · HOPS · YEAST

FLAVOR, PROCESS, & STORY

Crisply refreshing, filtered, well carbonated, and unchallenging, and appealing to a large audience, American Lager is characterized more by an absence of flavor than a noticeable presence. Pilsner or lager malt are the base grain. Rice or corn might be used and could be up to 40 percent of the grain bill. Hops (any variety) are for a light bitterness and not typically

for flavor, although modern examples might shoot for something more aromatic and bitter. There might be a small amount of fermentation character (light fruity esters, acetaldehyde, DMS), which is found in most mainstream lagers and is sometimes a result of high-gravity brewing.

The first North American lagers were brewed in the 1840s, and they were dark, sweet, and low alcohol, made by German émigrés and drunk by their compatriots.

By the 1870s, more Americans were drinking beer and they wanted something lighter, so rice or corn was added to recipes. These new American Lagers were brewed in large volumes, heavily marketed, and nationally distributed, and their consistency and filtered clarity made them popular. Today, craft brewers may try to make more characterful versions of well-known American or Mexican lagers, or they may look at older and more traditional recipes.

BEER STATS				
Color	Clarity	Ferment	ABV	Bitterness
Straw to pale gold	Bright	Clean to light fruitiness	4%–5%	10–25 IBU (low–medium)

BUDWEISER

| 5% ABV | BREWED: ST. LOUIS, MO, USA |

Knowing how brands such as Budweiser, Miller, or Coors taste is important to understand their place in the beer world. Budweiser is very pale in color and has little to no lasting foam. It's brewed with rice, is dry and drying on the palate, but has a light barley tea sweetness, and often has an apple ester aroma or acetaldehyde. Bitterness is almost absent, so refreshment comes from dryness and carbonation.

LIVE OAK BREWING PRE-WAR PILS

| 5% ABV | BREWED: AUSTIN, TX, USA |

Based on a recipe from 1912, this beer uses one-third corn grits. It's a very pale straw color with a light haze, and it's crispy, light, and maximally refreshing. There is an interesting light lemony-floral hop note, a fuller malt flavor with an enhanced creaminess of corn, some crackers, and a bit of honey, then it dries out with a nice bitterness and uplifting carbonation. It's a taste of what American Lager was like before it was lightened.

GREEN BENCH BREWING CO. POSTCARD PILS

| 4.7% ABV | BREWED: ST. PETERSBURG, FL, USA |

An old-school American Lager recipe updated for modern drinkers, it's brewed with German malt and six-row barley and corn, and undergoes a decoction mash, which brings out more of the corn flavor and aroma. It's reminiscent of a classic German Pils in its depth of flavor, while it has a distinct American accent from the corn, some yeast fruitiness, light citrus hoppiness, and 35 IBU of herbal bitterness.

21ST AMENDMENT EL SULLY

| 4.8% ABV | BREWED: SAN LEANDRO, CA, USA |

Mexican Lager has grown in popularity in the US, inspired by the light refreshment of famous Mexican lager brands. El Sully uses corn and Vienna malt in the grain bill, with the corn giving the dryness that defines the style, and the Vienna and Pilsner malt adding a touch of color, toastiness, some honey, and bread. There's a lightly floral hoppiness and a hint of dried citrus. There's no need for a slice of lime to enjoy this one.

OTHER EXAMPLES TO TRY

YUENGLING TRADITIONAL LAGER: light toasted malt, floral hops, crisp.

LITTLE HARPETH CHICKEN SCRATCH: creamy malts, smooth texture, light herbal hops.

FIRESTONE WALKER 805 CERVEZA: light lime, bread crusts, crisply refreshing.

MODERN PILSNER

The pale lager is updated by craft beer's love for aromatic and flavorful hops, including Pilsners for Italy and New Zealand, and the stronger India Pale Lager (IPL), which is Pilsner meets India Pale Ale (IPA).

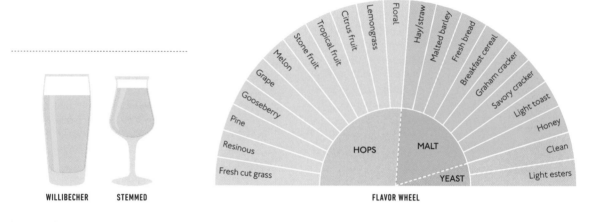

WILLIBECHER **STEMMED**

FLAVOR WHEEL

FLAVOR, PROCESS, & STORY

Imagine a pale lager with aromatic hops, whether an elegant dry hop with German varieties or a Pale Ale or IPA-like hop hit. Regardless of hop intensity or alcohol content, these beers should remain crisp and dry with a snappy bitterness, retaining the essential balance of any great lager. Malt depth is often slight but can add complexity and a sweetness that enhances hop flavor. They are typically unfiltered but rarely fully hazy.

Most have very simple Pilsner malt base brews, perhaps also with some Munich or cara for color and some extra body or sweetness. Italian Pilsner uses German hops as a dry hop. New Zealand Pils uses Kiwi hops and often has richer and more toasty malt. A Hoppy Pilsner or a stronger IPL are like a dry-hopped Pils or lager/IPA hybrid, typically using American and other New World hops.

"Hoppy Lager" is a catch-all term for lagers with a strong accent of hops. The Italian Pilsner and New Zealand Pilsner began as local beer styles, grew nationally, and then became renowned internationally. They show how craft beer has sought to evolve the classic base of a quality lager, and they've reimagined what a "lager" can be for many drinkers.

BEER STATS				
Color	Clarity	Ferment	ABV	Bitterness
Straw to gold	Bright to light haze	Clean to light esters	4%–7%+	20–50+ IBU (medium–high)

BIRRIFICIO ITALIANO TIPOPILS

5.2% ABV	BREWED: LIMIDO COMASCO, ITALY

Tipopils is the original Italian Pilsner, first brewed in 1996. It took a classic base of a German Pilsner with light malts, a little malt sweetness, and a lasting herbal German hop bitterness. What made it different was being unfiltered and dry hopping it like a British ale to add more aroma. It's not a massive IPA-like dry hop, just a small extra seasoning of hops, which gives herbal, lemon, lemongrass, and floral aromas.

LIBERTY BREWING HALO PILSNER

5% ABV	BREWED: HELENSVILLE, NEW ZEALAND

Halo Pilsner immediately hits with the passion fruit, lychee, grape, gooseberry, and mandarin aromas of New Zealand hops. Some brewers take this style toward a Golden Ale (even using an ale yeast), but the style is at its best with a spritzy, wine-like aroma; a slightly sweet and juicy malt base, with some bread and toffee; and the expected refreshing finish. Halo Pilsner is a perfect example of tropical hoppiness and Pilsner together.

HIGHLAND PARK TIMBO PILS

5.8% ABV	BREWED: LOS ANGELES, CA, USA

This is a modern evolution of the American Lager, combining the aromatic hoppiness of a West Coast Pale with the crisp and elegant bitterness of German-style Pilsner. It's unfiltered and has higher alcohol than a standard Pilsner, so it's got more body and texture but remains light. The bitterness is pithy, herbal, and clean, with Citra and Mosaic hops giving stone fruits, tropical fruits, orange zest, pine and floral notes, and a general oily hoppiness.

JACK'S ABBY HOPONIUS UNION

6.5% ABV	BREWED: FRAMINGHAM, MA, USA

IPL is the perfect combination of IPA and Pilsner. It's a lightly hazy gold with a lasting foam and a cereal-like sweetness in the malt that helps to enhance the hop flavor and a jammy fruit sweetness. The hops have pulpy and pithy citrus, with marmalade, grapefruit, mango, and pineapple. The lager yeast and cool fermentation, plus the smoothing effects of a longer conditioning time, create a lovely balance and a dry crispness at the end.

OTHER EXAMPLES TO TRY

OXBOW LUPPOLO: floral hops, citrus peel, herbal, light cracker malt.

EMERSON'S PILSNER: tropical, grape, gooseberry, light toffee.

LOST AND GROUNDED RUNNING WITH SCEPTRES: citrus, piney, light toasty malt.

HELLES

Helles means bright or pale, a contrast to the dark Dunkel lagers, and these highly drinkable golden lagers are the most popular beers in Bavaria, especially Munich, where the style originated.

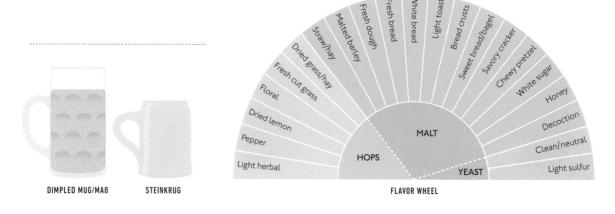

DIMPLED MUG/MAß   STEINKRUG

FLAVOR WHEEL

Flavor wheel segments: Light herbal, Pepper, Dried lemon, Floral, Fresh cut grass, Dried grass/hay, Straw/hay, Malted barley, Fresh dough, Fresh bread, White bread, Light toast, Bread crusts, Sweet bread/bagel, Savory cracker, Chewy pretzel, White sugar, Honey, Decoction, Clean/neutral, Light sulfur — grouped into HOPS, MALT, YEAST.

FLAVOR, PROCESS, & STORY

Bright golden Helles is often described as malty, but that's more as a comparison to the hop-forwardness of a Pilsner. While the malt is a distinct flavor, it's a beer to celebrate for always being interesting without commanding attention. A sulfur yeast note is common in fresh versions. Hop bitterness is low but balanced, with delicate floral or grassy flavors. Carbonation is lower than a Pils and the texture is smooth.

It's often brewed with just Pilsner malt and German noble hops, but sometimes with colored malts such as Vienna or Carapils. Water gives a slightly snappy, dry finish. Most German brewers use a decoction mash to increase malt flavor. They're classically filtered. The precision in a Helles is difficult to achieve in the brewery, and it will reveal even the smallest flaws or imbalances.

The first true Munich Helles is credited to Munich's Spaten brewery in 1894. There was resistance to start, with some local brewers concerned that the new type of beer detracted from Munich's famous dark lagers. But drinkers wanted paler beers, and bright Helles arrived alongside dark Dunkel. It's now the most-drunk beer style in Bavaria.

BEER STATS				
Color	Clarity	Ferment	ABV	Bitterness
Gold	Bright	Clean/neutral	4.8%–5.2%	15–30 IBU (low–medium)

AUGUSTINER LAGERBIER HELL

| 5.2% ABV | BREWED: MUNICH, GERMANY |

This textbook-defining Munich Helles is bright gold with thick, white foam. There's sometimes a little sulfur, which can smell like fresh lemon. The malt is robust and round, yet light and gentle, with a fresh bread crust depth but without any lasting heaviness before it heads into an impeccably clean, refreshing finish and a little floral, herbal hop depth. It's a great beer that reveals itself further the more you drink it.

SCHÖNRAMER HELL

| 5% ABV | BREWED: SCHÖNRAM, GERMANY |

Beautiful and brilliant gold in color, it's got the expected light toasty malt flavor, with a quality of pure pale malts that are enhanced as it's brewed using a decoction. There's a floral hop quality, some dried citrus peel, and a light peppery spiciness, but that bitterness is all perfectly restrained, as if peeking out from behind the malt. This beer stands out because it has a great overall depth, complexity, and volume of flavor.

BIERSTADT HELLES

| 5% ABV | BREWED: DENVER, CO, USA |

Bierstadt describe this as walking the line between bland and sublime. It's a wonderful description for the style. This Helles is bright yellow-gold, the malt is pronounced in a whispering way, with decocted enriched bread crusts and fresh bread, and the hops give an oily or grassy depth. It's long lagered and filtered, which gives it a polished and elegantly clean finish. It's one of the truest and best Helles brewed outside Bavaria.

STIEGL GOLDBRÄU

| 5% ABV | BREWED: SALZBURG, AUSTRIA |

This is an Austrian Märzen, a style with a distinct name that is really the same as a Bavarian Helles (a few outlier Austrian examples express an older style of Märzen). Goldbräu is bright gold; has an inviting pale malt aroma and flavor; a pleasing soft smoothness and slight sweetness to its body; with some honey, cracker, and graham cracker depth, a delicate hop quality of dried lemon peel, and a peppery, drying bitterness.

OTHER EXAMPLES TO TRY

TEGERNSEER HELL: pale malt, cracker, light sulfur, peppery hops.

WEIHENSTEPHANER HELLES: biscuit malts, decoction depth, crisp.

UTOPIAN BRITISH LAGER: fresh bread dough, toast, citrus pith.

FRANCONIAN LAGER & KELLERBIER

Commonly found around Franconia, these unfiltered lagers have a rustic quality to them compared to the refined character of a Bavarian Helles.

MUG

WILLIBECHER

Flavor wheel labels: Spicy, Herbal, Cut grass, Floral, Dried citrus, Pepper, Malted barley, Bread dough, Fresh bread, Breakfast cereal, Graham cracker, Bread crusts, Toast, Toasted nuts, Chewy pretzel, Honey, Light caramel, Decoction, Clean, Light sulfur, Light esters

HOPS, MALT, YEAST

FLAVOR WHEEL

FLAVOR, PROCESS, & STORY

These beers can range from unfiltered Helles-like lagers to rustic and richly malty Amber Lagers. They share a soft carbonation and a smooth, unfiltered drinkability, where malt is typically the dominant flavor: toasted, bread crust, brown bread, graham crackers, and honey. Traditional German hops are more for bitterness and flavor, which can vary in intensity and are floral, spicy, and herbal. They're usually very fresh when served on draft. There's usually some residual sweetness, which gives the beers a comforting quality.

Pilsner, Munich, and Vienna are the main malts, giving color and their distinctive malt flavors and richness, with a decoction mash increasing that malt flavor and adding a Maillard caramelization.

Recipes for these beers are often passed down through generations of small family brewers, reflecting old-style lager brewing before Pilsner took over. Maintaining traditional qualities is important, so beers in Franconian brewpubs will all differ but also all share a similar amber color, some malt sweetness and flavor, and a soft carbonation. Kellerbier (cellar beer)—an unfiltered lager drunk straight from the cellars—is now synonymous with Franconia but not exclusive to it. You might find Helles-like Kellerbier or just a Keller version of a hoppier Pilsner.

BEER STATS

Color	Clarity	Ferment	ABV	Bitterness
Gold to amber	Bright to light haze	Clean to light esters	4.4%–5.2%	15–35 IBU (low–medium)

MAHRS BRÄU AU

5.2% ABV	BREWED: BAMBERG, GERMANY

This famous Franconian amber lager is a comforting and joyful glass of German malts, with fresh toast, fresh bread, light caramel, and sweet crackers, with the sweetness pleasing on the lips to begin, then restrained at the end (a decoction mash helps that). The hops are floral and herbal and nicely bittersweet. Carbonation is low, especially on draft, and overall, it's a wonderful moreish beer.

ST. GEORGENBRÄU BUTTENHEIMER KELLERBIER

4.7% ABV	BREWED: BUTTENHEIM, GERMANY

A deep amber color, it's unfiltered and pours with a rich foam. There's light fermentation character and a little yeast fruitiness that mixes with the honey, fresh dough, and toasty malts. The texture is soft and smooth, carrying the malt flavor and some residual sweetness, and the finish is light on bitterness, leaving some pepper and grassiness. In this part of Germany, order a lager and this is the typical type of beer you'll get.

SUAREZ FAMILY BREWERY MS. FRANK

4.7% ABV	BREWED: HUDSON, NY, USA

You can taste when an American brewer has visited Franconia, because without having drunk numerous fresh glasses of its beer, it's impossible to nail the nuance. Ms. Frank is orange-amber with a light haze. Toast, honey, and graham crackers impress first; with a fullness of body like true Franconian beers; before a lasting crisp, herbal, and floral hoppiness. One Suarez Family update is a fine and uplifting carbonation.

BRAYBROOKE HELLES

4.2% ABV	BREWED: MARKET HARBOROUGH, ENGLAND

Braybrooke was founded with Franconian inspiration. This Helles is a Franconian-style Helles and not like one you'd find in Munich. Deep gold and lightly hazy, there are some toasted brioche bread, frangipane or almond, malt toastiness, and moreish malts (and more malt richness than a Munich brew), then an herbal spiciness like pepper from the Hallertau Tradition hops.

OTHER EXAMPLES TO TRY

MÖNCHSAMBACHER LAGERBIER: toasted, rich sweet malts, spicy hops.

FOX FARM GATHER: cracker and toasty malts, herbal hops, light citrus.

FÄSSLA LAGERBIER: toasted malts, brown bread crusts, herbal hops.

VIENNA LAGER & AMERICAN AMBER LAGER

These amber-colored lagers vary from classic European lagers to modern American Amber Lagers.

SHAKER   WILLIBECHER

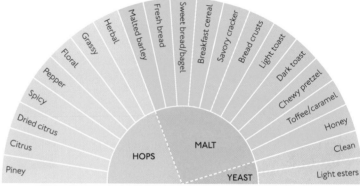

FLAVOR WHEEL

FLAVOR, PROCESS, & STORY

The best versions of these beers achieve a perfect intersection of malt flavor and sweetness, hop bitterness, dryness, and alcohol content. Some Vienna Lagers only use Vienna malts, while other brews might also use Pilsner, Munich, caramalts, or some roasted malt. Traditional Vienna Lagers might use a decoction to enhance the malt depth and richness.

Vienna Lager hoppiness is usually moderate—spicy, floral, and herbal—while American Ambers are typically American hopped, sometimes highly aromatic and citrusy or piney; other times delicate and peppery. A clean lager yeast fermentation and extended lagering give a smooth, easy-drinking quality.

Viennese brewer Anton Dreher used British malting technology to produce a new, paler type of malt, which he used in a recipe for new lager-brewing techniques he'd

learned in Munich. His Vienna Lager, first brewed in 1841, became one of the world's first great modern lager styles, notable for its amber color alongside the dark lagers, before it was superseded by golden Pilsners. It was then largely forgotten but has since been revived by craft brewers and returned to Vienna. American Amber was one of the original craft beer styles of the 1980s, notable for its richer malt flavor and higher hoppiness compared to standard American Lager.

BEER STATS				
Color	Clarity	Ferment	ABV	Bitterness
Light amber to deep amber	Bright to light haze	Clean/neutral	4.5%–6%	20–35 IBU (medium)

BRAUEREI SCHWECHAT WIENER LAGER

5.5% ABV	BREWED: VIENNA, AUSTRIA

This was Anton Dreher's brewery. The beer disappeared until it was resurrected for the brewery's 175th anniversary in 2016. The recipe feels more like a modern construct than a historical recreation. Regardless of that, it's deep amber colored, made with Pilsner and Vienna malt, rich and caramelly, quite sweet, and toasty with lots of malt depth. Saaz hops give a floral quality through it and a lasting bitterness.

DOVETAIL BREWERY VIENNA-STYLE LAGER

5.1% ABV	BREWED: CHICAGO, IL, USA

Brewed with 100 percent Vienna malt, it's a copper-amber color with a light haze and a thick, lasting foam. Toasted and caramel-like, there are bread crusts and bagels, a moreish Maillard depth, and lots of lovely malt flavors. There's a softness to the body, with a light herbal hoppiness leading to a dry finish, but not a bitter one, keeping a comforting malt-forward quality and a lasting toasted bread finish.

BROOKLYN BREWERY BROOKLYN LAGER

5.2% ABV	BREWED: BROOKLYN, NY, USA

This is a modern classic and one of the first American Amber Lagers, effectively creating or championing this new style. It's the color of a shiny old penny and bright and clear. It's dry hopped, so a lightly citrus and floral aroma is noticeable at first, with grapefruit zest, fresh hops, and an herbal-piney quality. The malt is like toasted bread, bread crusts, vanilla, and graham crackers, with a little sweet caramel before it gets dry and crisply bitter.

GREAT LAKES ELIOT NESS AMBER LAGER

6.1% ABV	BREWED: CLEVELAND, OH, USA

This American classic is deep amber, and the Munich and caramalts give bread, toasted bread crusts, and some light caramel flavors. It's pleasingly malt forward without being sweet, with the higher alcohol adding more oomph and a little fruity yeast character. Mount Hood hops give it an herbal, floral, and orange-peel quality, but the bitterness is mostly smoothed out by the maltiness. It has an American fizz and crispness.

OTHER EXAMPLES TO TRY

OTTAKRINGER WIENER ORIGINAL: bread crusts, toffee sweetness, peppery hops.

SAMUEL ADAMS BOSTON LAGER: toffee, buttered brown toast, dried citrus peel.

CHUCKANUT VIENNA LAGER: Vienna malt, nutty, dark toast, fragrant, floral hops.

MÄRZEN & FESTBIER

These are celebration lagers. Märzen celebrates the shifting brewing seasons, while Festbier is brewed for a festival, mostly famously for Munich's annual Oktoberfest and the many celebrations inspired by it around the world.

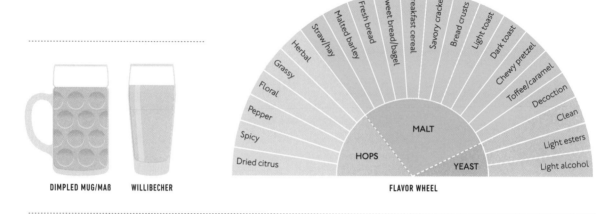

DIMPLED MUG/MAß   **WILLIBECHER**

FLAVOR WHEEL

FLAVOR, PROCESS, & STORY

Märzen and Festbier tend to be long lagered, low in carbonation, relatively low in malt and hop character, and filtered, which increases their smooth, crisp, and easy drinkability and gives them a unique kind of revelrous quality. Most Munich-brewed versions are like strong golden Helles, while craft-brewed versions cross over into a broader Märzen-Festbier-Oktoberfest group, which are amber and maltier. No single ingredient or quality should impress more than any other.

Märzen was originally a beer brewed in March, lagered during summer, and served in September or October. At some point, it came to be brewed with Munich malt and was lighter in color than the standard dark lagers. In the 1870s, a Märzenbier was served at the Oktoberfest for the first time and a new tradition began. Since then, Oktoberfestbiers have become stronger versions of Munich Helles.

In Germany, Märzen is now more a reference of strength than style, and is rarely seen. In the wider craft beer world, Märzen means an amber-hued, stronger lager, with Fest-Märzen sitting in between. An Oktoberfest beer—unless served at the actual Oktoberfest—could be golden or amber. In the brewery, Festbier is basically brewed like a stronger Helles, while Märzen is similar with some Munich malt.

BEER STATS				
Color	Clarity	Ferment	ABV	Bitterness
Straw to deep amber	Bright to light haze	Clean/neutral	5.5%–6.5%	20–35 IBU (medium)

AUGUSTINER OKTOBERFESTBIER

6.3% ABV	BREWED: MUNICH, GERMANY

Munich-brewed Oktoberfestbiers are brilliant gold in color with a rich, white foam. Like a Helles but stronger, there are more lightly toasted malts, more richness from the decoction, some bread crusts and pale malt, a smoother and softer texture, and lightly quenching hops, which intersect with dryness and alcohol. Bottled versions never quite give the same experience (flavor, carbonation, social spirit) as beer drunk at the festival.

WAYFINDER BEER FREIHEIT!

5.7% ABV	BREWED: PORTLAND, OR, USA

Traditionally brewed, Freiheit! is in the style of a Munich Festbier. It's a deep brilliant golden color and pours with a lot of foam. It's soft bodied with rounded toasty malts of soft white bread and chewy pretzels, while what keeps the interest is the gentle carbonation that is cut with dryness and a crisp bitterness. The herbal and floral quality throughout gives more hop character than is typically found in Munich.

HOFBRÄU OKTOBERFESTBIER

6.3% ABV	BREWED: MUNICH, GERMANY

Made by one of Munich's "Big Six" brewers, this is a classic Oktoberfestbier. Bright gold with a huge pillow of white foam, there's a depth of toasted and slightly sweet pale malt, almost brioche or challah bread, with a richness of alcohol that feels hearty and celebratory but still refreshing. It's supremely drinkable, as these beers are designed to be, with a very clean finish and a cut of bitter and slightly herbal German hops.

DONZOKO FESTBIER

5.8% ABV	BREWED: LEITH, SCOTLAND

A deep golden lager, it straddles old style and new with added hoppiness. It uses mostly Pilsner malt, with some Munich and Vienna adding color and some extra toastiness. A decoction mash gives an amplified malt flavor and some more texture, and leads to a drier finish. The hops give a moderate bitterness, the carbonation is bright, and it has uplifting aromas of dried lemon, woody herbs, and peppery spice.

OTHER EXAMPLES TO TRY

HACKER-PSCHORR OKTOBERFEST MÄRZEN: bready, brown toast, spicy hops.

GREAT LAKES OKTOBERFEST: toasted malts, smooth toffee, spicy hops.

SIERRA NEVADA OKTOBERFEST: honey, bread crusts, crackers, peppery hops.

CZECH-STYLE AMBER & DARK LAGER

With rich malt profiles and Saaz hops, these Czech-style lagers range from Polotmavý (amber) and Tmavý (brown) to Černé (black).

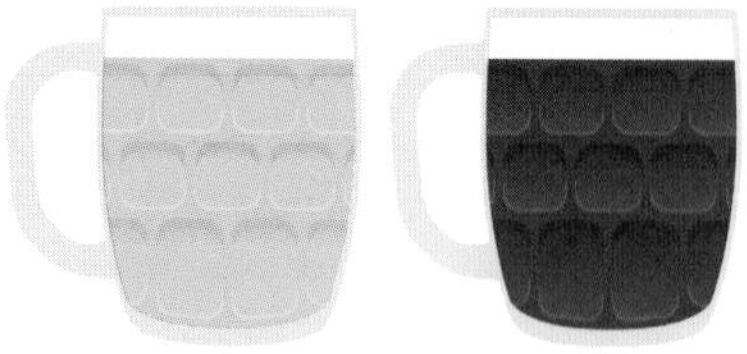

MUG

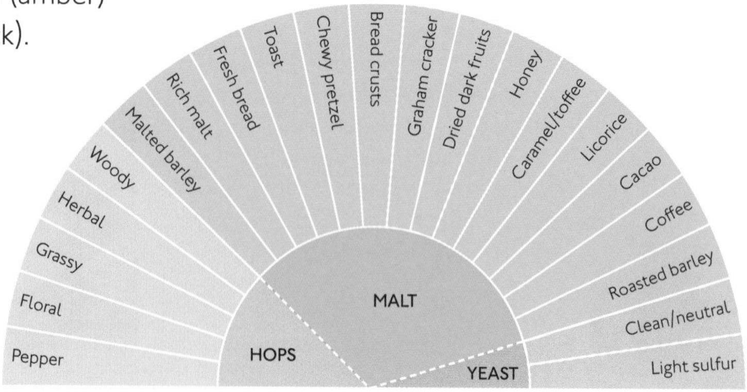

FLAVOR WHEEL

FLAVOR, PROCESS, & STORY

Aromas in these beers are evocative of bakeries and coffee shops: bread, toast, and graham cracker in ambers; chocolate, toffee, and coffee in the darker ones. The foam should be thick and carbonation is often low, giving a smooth drinkability. Most use only Czech hops and have a moderate bitterness to balance higher residual sweetness, but they are malt-forward beers. They could have notable residual sweetness.

Ambers are richer in malt character than Franconian Lagers, Vienna Lagers, and American Amber Lagers, while the dark beers have a much fuller quality compared to Dunkel or Schwarzbier. Pilsner malt is the majority of the grain bill. Amber versions use Vienna, Munich, and perhaps some caramalt, while Dark and Black versions use more Dark Munich and perhaps some Carafa or black malt. Soft brewing water helps the soft mouthfeel, while cold lagering and conditioning give a round, smooth texture.

Until the late 2010s, these beers were distinctively Czech and rarely drunk elsewhere, but they've grown in popularity since then. They are not as common as Czech Pale Lagers and are typically slightly stronger—13°–14°P is common for darker lagers.

BEER STATS				
Color	Clarity	Ferment	ABV	Bitterness
Amber to black	Bright to light haze	Clean/neutral	4.5%–6%	25–40 IBU (medium)

VINOHRADSKÝ PIVOVAR JANTAROVÁ 13

4.9% ABV	BREWED: PRAGUE, CZECH REPUBLIC

This amber-colored Polotmavý is a 13°P beer that finishes at 4.9% ABV, so there's some sweetness here, but it's not sticky on the lips. It's robustly malty, with typical caramelized malt flavors, bread crusts, toast, and graham cracker with a hint of malt bitterness. A strong hop bitterness, with herbal and spicy notes, adds balance to the beer's residual sweetness. A thick, sweet foam adds wonderful texture to the drinking experience.

U FLEKŮ FLEKOVSKÝ TMAVÝ LEŽÁK

5% ABV	BREWED: PRAGUE, CZECH REPUBLIC

Many brewers have tasted this classic Czech Tmavý Ležák and tried to replicate it. The beer begins as 13°P, so the 5% ABV comes with residual sweetness. It's a very dark brown beer with a tan-colored foam. There's a lot of malt flavor and depth: cacao, chocolate, dried fruit, roasted malt, a toffee-like sweetness, licorice, and berries. It finishes with a clear snap of dryness and herbal Becherovka-like bitterness.

SCHILLING BEER CO. MODERNISM

4.8% ABV	BREWED: LITTLETON, NH, USA

This Czech-style Dark Lager has a lift of Saaz hops, with floral and herbal aromas drawing you into the sweet foam. The malt is dark toffee, cola, dark toast, and chocolate cookies. It's a leaner body than some sweeter Czech versions, although authentic to others, like Budweiser Budvar's Tmavý Ležák, and the herbal hop bitterness is more prominent. Schilling also makes Augustin 13°, a Polotmavý.

UTOPIAN BREWING ČERNÉ SPECIÁLNÍ

5.9% ABV	BREWED: CREDITON, ENGLAND

This stronger black lager is brewed in the Czech way but with English ingredients. Dark brown with a lasting creamy foam, the texture is soft, with carbonation lower than usual British-brewed lagers. There's bitter dark chocolate; roasted malts; aniseed; some boozy dark fruits; and a spicy, herbal, almost minty finish. The high bitterness is more noticeable than most Czech examples. It achieves that Czech magic trick of finishing light.

OTHER EXAMPLES TO TRY

STRAHOV SVATÝ NORBERT JANTAR 13°: caramel, toasted malts, graham crackers, herbal hops.

PIVOVAR SOLNICE POLOTMAVÁ 11°: biscuit malts, creamy malt, toasty, spicy.

BUDWEISER BUDVAR TMAVÝ LEŽÁK: dark malt, dark dried fruits, light caramel, crisp.

DUNKEL & SCHWARZBIER

These dark German-style lagers range from amber-brown Dunkel to brown-black Schwarzbier and have a distinct flavor from darker malts.

MUG

WILLIBECHER

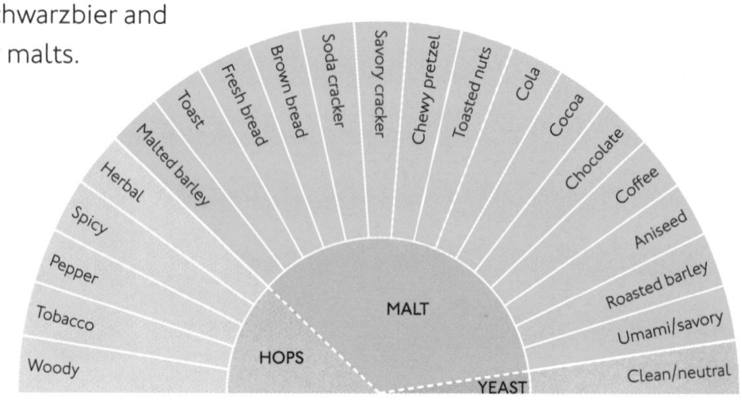

FLAVOR WHEEL

FLAVOR, PROCESS, & STORY

Dunkels tend toward Munich malt flavor, with toast, bread crusts, and light cocoa flavors. Schwarzbier (black beer) more often has a roastiness to its flavor. Dunkels are reminiscent of dark Helles, and Schwarzbier is closer to a black Pilsner with less hop bitterness. While malt forward, the malt character should never be out of balance, and they seldom have a strong dark malt flavor.

Dunkels may be brewed entirely with Munich malt, or with some Pilsner malt or other cara or dark malts added. A decoction mash in classic recipes enhances the mouthfeel, malt flavor, and complexity, leaving a dryness that stops the beer being heavy.

Schwarzbier uses Pilsner malts with roasted malts, unhusked dark malts, or even Sinamar, a natural liquid malt extract to add color without flavor. Schwarzbier is drier and has a higher carbonation than a typical Dunkel.

Dunkel recalls the earliest lagers, brewed over 600 years ago using roasted malts. Over time, the grain bill changed to Munich malts and later some pale malts, but the richer malt flavor profile remains. Schwarzbier has heritage in the German regions of Franconia, Saxony, and Thuringia. It was possibly a top-fermented beer that came to be brewed as a lager.

BEER STATS				
Color	Clarity	Ferment	ABV	Bitterness
Dark amber to black	Bright to light haze	Clean/neutral	4.5%–5.9%	15–25 IBU (low–medium)

AYINGER ALTBAIRISCH DUNKEL

5% ABV	BREWED: AYING, GERMANY

An old-style Bavarian Dunkel, it's a clear, deep red-brown color with a billowing, off-white foam. The malt is rounded and layered through the beer, giving toast, bread crusts, dark dried fruits, toffee apple, just a hint of cocoa, and dark malt, and it's fuller and moreish in flavor thanks to the decoction mashing process. The hops are light, but this is a beer that celebrates the comforting depths and flavors of German malt.

KC BIER CO. DUNKEL

5% ABV	BREWED: KANSAS CITY, MO, USA

A bright copper-brown color with a lasting tan foam, this is a glassful of Munich malts, giving their characteristic bread crusts, chewy pretzels, dark toast, and caramel cookies, but all subtle. The body has a pleasing malt smoothness, carrying all the malt flavors without making them sweet, and leading to dryness at the end. Bitterness is low, as expected, and it has a crisper finish than many Munich versions.

KÖSTRITZER SCHWARZBIER

4.8% ABV	BREWED: BAD KÖSTRITZ, GERMANY

The most famous German Schwarzbier is a dark red-black color. The aroma is mild, with dried fruit, aniseed, bread, cocoa, toasted nuts, and a very light roastiness, almost like cocoa-seltzer or the smell of chocolate malt, and all that carries through to the flavor. Some herbal hops run through it, complementing the malt bitterness. The carbonation refreshes and it has a quick-finishing dryness.

SUAREZ FAMILY BREWERY BONES SHIRT

4.9% ABV	BREWED: HUDSON, NY, USA

Dark brown in appearance, it's got an elegant and tight body of malt, much like a Pilsner, with just a little cocoa powder, some dark rye bread, and the distant flavor of roasted malts, but all with a layered depth of flavor. The hops bring a snap of bitterness, floral tobacco, and tea, and a lasting spiciness. The fine carbonation gives it a lovely lightness and it's a great modern take on the style.

OTHER EXAMPLES TO TRY

AUGUSTINER DUNKEL: light toast, bread crusts, dark toffee, floral hops.

BIERSTADT DUNKEL: bread crusts, cocoa, chewy pretzels, spicy hops.

KLOSTERBRÄU SCHWÄRZLA: sweet black tea, dark malts, cola, herbal hops.

BOCK & DOPPELBOCK

Originating in Bavaria, these strong and special lagers are released annually to celebrate the changing seasons, with pale Maibocks, dark Bocks, and stronger Doppelbocks the most common types.

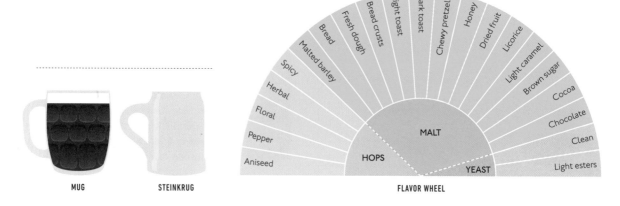

MUG   **STEINKRUG**

Spicy · Herbal · Floral · Pepper · Aniseed · Malted barley · Bread · Fresh dough · Bread crusts · Light toast · Dark toast · Chewy pretzels · Honey · Dried fruit · Licorice · Light caramel · Brown sugar · Cocoa · Chocolate · Clean · Light esters

MALT · HOPS · YEAST

FLAVOR WHEEL

FLAVOR, PROCESS, & STORY

These stronger lagers are smooth and malt forward, rarely with much hop character or bitterness. Pale Bocks (Maibock, Heller Bock) have bready and toasty flavors, while darker Bocks and Doppelbocks have more caramel, Maillard, dark toast, and, possibly, roasted flavors. They may have residual sweetness, but they're designed to be drunk in great volumes. Bitterness is usually low, as is

carbonation. The Dutch have their own Bockbier traditions, with beers more reminiscent of a Dubbel in flavor.

German versions are brewed like any traditional lager, so mostly pale malts with darker versions using different additional grains—Munich, Vienna, caramalts, and even darker, more roasted malts in small amounts. They often have a full malt flavor, especially sweet Doppelbocks, which is enhanced by a decoction mash or the use of sweeter malts. German hops are

typical. They are long-lagered for a smooth depth.

These beers originally signified the shifts in Bavarian brewing seasons, with long-matured beers opened as a celebration. They still reflect changing seasons today and are often associated with a festival or special event. Pale Bocks are more common in the spring (Maibocks, or May bocks), while dark Bocks are brewed for fall and winter. Doppelbocks have a link to Easter and were originally brewed by Munich monks.

BEER STATS				
Color	Clarity	Ferment	ABV	Bitterness
Pale gold to dark brown	Bright to light haze	Clean to light ester	6%–8%	20–50 IBU (low–medium)

MAHRS BRÄU HELLER BOCK

6.8% ABV	BREWED: BAMBERG, GERMANY

Released in October, this Bock is deep gold in color with a light haze. There's lots of pale malt depth in this, along with overlapping hints of yeast: light toffee, brioche, white bread, vanilla, honey, marzipan, and toast. It's very smooth to drink, pleasingly rich but not lip-sticking sweet, with a pronounced hop bitterness and floral, herbal hop flavor running through it. It's robust yet drinks like a Helles.

SCHELL'S BOCK

6.5% ABV	BREWED: NEW ULM, MN, USA

An early-year seasonal brew, this bright amber-brown Bock is a comforting glass of smooth malts: toasted, light toffee, molasses, brown bread toast, fruitcake, and pretzels. It's got some sweetness but not too much, and overall, it's a leaner beer than many German versions. It's more characteristic of American-brewed Bocks, where the brisk carbonation keeps it relatively light and crisp, with just a little bit of bitterness at the end.

LA TRAPPE TRAPPIST BOCKBIER

7% ABV	BREWED: BERKEL-ENSCHOT, NETHERLANDS

Released in the fall, Dutch Bock comes from the same traditions as German Bock, but it's a little different in flavor. Typically dark red-brown, 6.5%–7% ABV, sometimes top fermented, with more yeast and hop flavor than a German Bock. This top-fermented Bock has burned toast, caramel, brown sugar, licorice, aniseed, Dubbel-like dried dark fruits, chocolate, some alcohol warmth, yeast ester fruitiness in the aroma, and a spicy bitterness.

AYINGER CELEBRATOR

6.7% ABV	BREWED: AYING, GERMANY

This classic Doppelbock is at the low strength range of the style but at the upper end of the complexity range. Dark red-black with a creamy off-white foam, there are layers of bread, caramel, bitter chestnut honey, molasses, licorice, raisins, fruitcake (with burned dried fruit pieces), some roastiness, and a coffee herbal liqueur finish. All those layers of flavor come individually, not as one big jumbled bundle.

OTHER EXAMPLES TO TRY

PAULANER SALVATOR: tea cake, caramel, toasted malt.

UTOPIAN RAINBOCK: sweet malts, honey, sponge cake, spicy hops.

SCHLOSS EGGENBERG SAMICHLAUS: boozy, rich sherry-like malt, cherry.

KÖLSCH

Famously associated with the German city of Cologne, these pale beers are bright, crisp, hop accented, and brewed with an ale yeast.

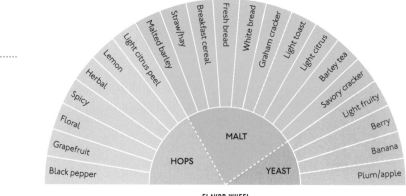

STANGE

FLAVOR WHEEL

FLAVOR, PROCESS, & STORY

Kölsch has a bright, filtered yellow appearance, a light malt flavor similar to a Pilsner but with less carbonation, a lean and dry body, a crisp and sharp bitterness, and a mineral-water quality. Variety typically comes with the aromas, often led by a light yeast ester fruitiness or with some gentle hoppiness. Many versions brewed outside Cologne fail to get the correct flavor profile.

True Cologne-brewed Kölsch is made according to the Kölsch Convention, which defines the beer as: pale, filtered, hop accented, top fermented, around 4.5% ABV, and brewed in the Cologne area. Recipes have a simple base of Pilsner malt, perhaps with some Munich malt for more color and maltiness. German hops give a snappy, herbal, spicy bitterness, sometimes a little floral and herbal flavor. The use of an ale yeast and warm fermentation creates some fruity

esters, and the longer conditioning time creates a clean flavor profile.

As Pilsners spread across Europe, Cologne's brewers appreciated their popularity while also maintaining their own well-hopped ale traditions, creating a golden idiosyncrasy of a style that locals celebrate heartily. Technically, only Cologne-based brewers can use the name "Kölsch." Düsseldorf has a similar ale tradition, only its beer (Altbier) is dark, and there are fierce city rivalries over which beer is best.

		BEER STATS		
Color	Clarity	Ferment	ABV	Bitterness
Yellow	Bright	Clean to light esters	4.4%–4.9%	15–35 IBU (low–medium)

FRÜH KÖLSCH

4.8% ABV	BREWED: COLOGNE, GERMANY

This Kölsch is a perfectly bright, very pale straw-yellow color with creamy white foam. There's a little light yeast fruitiness in the aroma. The body is light and clean, with a little toasted malt flavor, leading to a crisp, dry, and gently bitter finish with a lemon seltzer snap at the end. It's not a complex beer, but it's wonderful for its balance, freshness, crispness, and drinkability, though some of that subtlety is lost in bottles or cans.

GAFFEL KÖLSCH

4.8% ABV	BREWED: COLOGNE, GERMANY

There's an underlying, appealing fruitiness in this beer, which is a nice mix of hop and yeast giving a hint of grape, apple, and some lemon, but it's all subtle. The malt is richer than Früh's, a touch bready and cracker-like. A crisp carbonation crosses over perfectly with a mineral dryness and a firm hop bitterness. It's a precise, simple, yet interesting beer that you can drink several small glasses of without ever getting bored.

THORNBRIDGE BREWERY TZARA

4.8% ABV	BREWED: BAKEWELL, ENGLAND

Tzara is a true-tasting Kölsch. Brilliant pale gold in color, there's a hint of lemon and floral hops in the aroma, plus a background note of yeast and fermentation. The recipe has some wheat and Carapils, which add a good amount of texture to the body and a toastier flavor to the pale malts. Crisply refreshing with a lasting peppery hop finish, Tzara shows how a great Kölsch sits so neatly between Blonde Ales and Pilsners.

DOVETAIL BREWERY KÖLSCH

4.6% ABV	BREWED: CHICAGO, IL, USA

Dovetail brewery serves its Kölsch in branded 7 fl oz (200 ml) *Stange* glasses. It's unfiltered so could be considered a Weiß, which is what an unfiltered Kölsch would be in Cologne. The beer has a traditional character but there's a sense it has picked up a hint of local inflection: there are fruit esters and lemon in the aroma; a fuller body and creamy texture; some cracker-like malts and a bit of breakfast cereal; and an herbal, pithy bitterness.

OTHER EXAMPLES TO TRY

REISSDORF KÖLSCH: honeyed malts, light peppery hops, balanced.

PÄFFGEN KÖLSCH: lemon and herbal bitterness, cracker, pale malt.

CHUCKANUT KÖLSCH: classic, light malt, light citrus, floral hops.

ALTBIER

Altbier is a dark and bitter "old-style" top-fermented brown beer, which is famously associated with the German city of Düsseldorf.

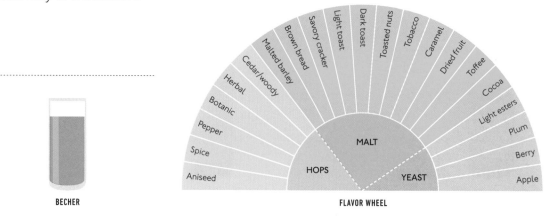

BECHER

FLAVOR WHEEL

FLAVOR, PROCESS, & STORY

These are clear, brown beers with tan foam, and the flavor is a mix of toasted malts, herbal-bitter hops, and fruity esters. The malt evokes toasted nuts, dark toast, light caramel, dried fruit, and a little roast. They are moderate to high in bitterness and there are herbal, peppery, and spicy German hop flavors. Yeast esters vary between beers, with some very fruity and others more neutral. Dark Munich malts give flavor and color. Herbal German hops are true to the style. An ale yeast and a higher-than-usual fermentation temperature encourage some fruity esters.

It's cool conditioned like a lager, smoothing some of the rougher edges of dark malt, high bitterness, and yeast esters. A harder-water profile gives a dry and mineral-like depth, which adds a snappy quality to the malt and hop bitterness.

"Altbier" means "old beer," but it's a reference to an old style, not a long-aged beer. Bitter brown ales were common around northwest Germany, and as new kinds of lagers spread that way, the old beer took on a new name and significance. It's Düsseldorf's city-defining beer and, like Kölsch in Cologne, to truly understand its character you need to drink it fresh from the tap in its hometown.

BEER STATS				
Color	Clarity	Ferment	ABV	Bitterness
Copper-brown	Bright	Clean/light esters	4.5%–5%	25–50 IBU (medium–high)

UERIGE ALTBIER

4.7% ABV	BREWED: DÜSSELDORF, GERMANY

This bright chestnut-brown beer leads with light, fruity esters. The malt is toasted and caramelized, there's brown bread, brown sugar, and dried fruit, and it's robust and yet gentle, with a mineral dryness. Its 50 IBUs are a defining quality of Uerige's beer, and it has a firm and lasting herbal bite at the end, gripping with bitterness, while a floral note (it uses whole flower hops) freshens it up throughout as it combines with fruity esters.

HAUSBRAUEREI ZUM SCHLÜSSEL ORIGINAL ALT

5% ABV	BREWED: DÜSSELDORF, GERMANY

Düsseldorf's Altbiers vary more than Cologne's Kölsches. Füchschen has quinine-like bitterness and extra malt sweetness, Kürzer is like cherry jam on brown toast, while Schlüssel is perfectly in the middle. Nuanced and well integrated between malt and hop, with a gentle malt depth, some Munich malt toastiness, and a fuller body than others, the hop flavor and bitterness eases through the beer to a spicy and peppery finish.

CERVEJARIA BAMBERG ALTBIER

4.8% ABV	BREWED: VOTORANTIM, BRAZIL

This is a classically brewed Altbier made by a Brazilian brewery that specializes in German beer styles. At 48 IBU, it's high in bitterness, but it's balanced by some sweeter caramel, brown bread toast, brown sugar, and a little roasted malt. That roast malt bitterness meets the hop bitterness—herbal, spicy, and prominent—while the yeast gives some cherry and apple. It's crisp, bitter, and a little fruity, just how a good Altbier should be.

ENEGREN BREWING CO. VALKYRIE

6.2% ABV	BREWED: MOORPARK, CA, USA

You could call this one a Sticke Alt, a stronger version of a typical recipe. It's bright and deep amber. There's a lot of Munich malt, giving brown bread toast, bread crusts, and a caramelized depth (it uses melanoidin malt, which gives a decoction-ish flavor), plus some dark fruits and dried fruits. The hoppiness is herbal, woody, and firm beneath the malt sweetness, and there's a touch of fruitiness in the aroma.

OTHER EXAMPLES TO TRY

SCHUMACHER ALT: nutty, caramel, spicy and herbal hops.

ALASKAN AMBER: toasted malts, bread, crisp, floral hops.

UERIGE STICKE: richer caramel, stronger, herbal hops, dried fruit.

RAUCHBIER & SMOKED BEER

These beers continue the tradition
of brewing beer with smoked malt,
which gives a smoky aroma and flavor.

MUG

WILLIBECHER

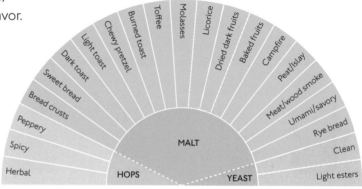

FLAVOR WHEEL

FLAVOR, PROCESS, & STORY

Smoked beers are usually
immediately obvious in their
smokiness, which could be like
smoked meat, bonfires, peat, or
Islay whisky. Rauchbier is the
main style of smoked beer and
is a malty German lager with a
distinct smoked meat aroma.
Any other beer styles can use
smoked malt, though it's most
common in dark ales.

The underlying style will
determine the brewing process
and base flavor. Most smoked
malts (barley or wheat) are pale,
so brewers add colored or roasted
malts depending on the color of
beer they want. Some beers are
all-smoked malt; others use a
smaller percentage for a lighter
flavor addition. Hops are usually
low and rarely aromatic.

Before indirect heat took
fires and smoke away from the
malthouse, much of the malt used

in beer probably had a smokiness
to it as well as a dark color. As
the smoke flavor left more beers,
and beer generally got paler and
more refreshing, a couple of
outlier breweries in Bamberg—
the home of Rauchbier—continued
to use wood to fuel their malt
kilns. Bamberg's brewers use
beechwood, which gives a smoked
sausage and bacon aroma, and
elsewhere, brewers might use
cherry wood, oak, and other woods.

BEER STATS				
Color	Clarity	Ferment	ABV	Bitterness
Gold to dark brown	Bright to light haze	Clean to light esters	4.5%–6.5%	15–25 IBU (low–medium)

SCHLENKERLA MÄRZEN RAUCHBIER

5.1% ABV	BREWED: BAMBERG, GERMANY

Considered *the* Rauchbier and made by a brewery that produces its own smoked malt over beechwood fires, it's a deep violet-brown Märzen (a stronger lager). The smoke immediately saturates the senses with an evocative mix of wood smoke, warm ashes, smoked meat, and smoked cheese. Beneath that there are sweet malts, dried fruits, and burned toast, and it has a satiating, umami-like depth, ending with a grip of peppery bitterness.

SPEZIAL RAUCHBIER LAGER

4.9% ABV	BREWED: BAMBERG, GERMANY

Spezial is Bamberg's other Rauchbier brewer, and its main smoked lager is a deep amber color. The smoke is softer than Schlenkerla's, but still beechwood's smoked sausage smell. There's toasted malt, a smooth texture, honey sweetness in the middle, with a cracker-like dryness and a peppery hop bitterness at the end. Spezial brews an intriguing Smoked Hefeweizen, which combines light smoke with fruity banana esters.

ALASKAN SMOKED PORTER

6.5% ABV	BREWED: JUNEAU, AK, USA

Released every November 1, this American classic has the smokiness of a campfire—the sort you sit around with marshmallows on sticks. It has an elegant smoke aroma, sweetly smoky like cherry wood, with dark chocolate, light roasted barley, treacle, cocoa, and a little smoked whiskey character, perfectly balancing the smoke with the underlying rich Porter flavors, and leaving a light but lasting smoked quality.

JACK'S ABBY SMOKE & DAGGER

5.6% ABV	BREWED: FRAMINGHAM, MA, USA

This is an elegantly smoked dark lager, with the smoke swirling in the back and playing the trick of making the other ingredients taste richer and fuller. There's dark chocolate, light roastiness, smoky bacon and beechwood, fruity coffee, and spicy hops at the end. It's fairly light and crisp overall, drinking between a Porter, Schwarzbier, and Rauchbier, where it's the flavor enhancement of smoke that's most noticeable here.

OTHER EXAMPLES TO TRY

YAZOO SUE: dark chocolate, wood smoke, dark fruit.

BAMBERG BIER RAUCHBIER: smoked meats, honey, toast, dried fruit, herbal.

SCHLENKERLA EICHE DOPPELBOCK: rich sweet malts, deep oak smoke, woody.

PALE ALES, IPAS, & HOP-FORWARD ALES

IF THERE'S ONE CHARACTERISTIC that has come to define modern beer, it's the aroma and flavor of hops: citrus, stone and tropical fruits, herbs, flowers, and spices. Hop-forward styles include refreshing Session IPAs, juicy Hazy Pale Ales, bitter West Coast IPAs, impactful Double IPAs, classic English IPAs, summery Pacific Pale Ales, and beers ranging in color from Blonde and Golden Ales to Ambers, Reds, and Black IPAs. While these beers all have different recipes, they share a wonderful aroma and flavor of hops.

AMERICAN-INFLUENCED IPA

By the early 2000s, IPAs had become the flagship style of American craft beer. They represented everything a light lager wasn't: high bitterness, impactful hop aroma, a rich body of malt, and more alcohol strength.

FOUR TYPES OF IPA

It's possible to distinguish four types of American-influenced IPAs: West Coast, American, Hazy, and New England IPA.

WEST COAST IPA
West Coast IPA is often bright/clear, pale gold to amber, and with a citrus, floral, pine, and dank hop profile from varieties such as Cascade, Centennial, Chinook, and Simcoe, plus some tropical qualities in certain modern versions. It could have clean and crisp malt with a caramel-like depth and should be noticeably bitter.

AMERICAN IPA
With a bright or light haze, American IPA is gold to pale amber with a classic citrus, floral (more prominent than in West Coast), and pine hop profile from Cascade, Centennial, Columbus, Amarillo, Simcoe, and others. It has some toasted or light caramel sweetness and moderate to high bitterness.

HAZY IPA
Light to medium hazy and yellow to orange, Hazy IPA has citrus, tropical, melon, and juicy aromas from hops such as Mosaic, Citra, and El Dorado, plus the addition of other varieties. Bitterness is medium, and mouthfeel has some fullness and smoothness but also finishes dry. Oats and/or wheat make up some of the grain base. Fruity esters are mild.

NEW ENGLAND IPA
Medium hazy to cloudy and yellow to orange, New England IPA has strong citrus, tropical, melon, and juicy aromas from new hop varieties such as Citra, Mosaic, Azacca, Idaho 7, and Ekuanot. Bitterness is low to medium, texture is medium to full. Oats and/or wheat make up a large part of the grain base. Fruity and/or sweet-smelling esters might be strong.

WEST COAST VS AMERICAN

West Coast will typically be leaner in malt and more perceptibly bitter, with dank and resinous hops alongside the citrus, while an American IPA might have more of a caramel or sweeter malt flavor and more toward floral and citrusy (often grapefruit) hops.

NEW ENGLAND VS HAZY

There's not exactly a distinction between these two, more of a continuum of flavor, with Hazy at the lighter end. New England is thicker in mouthfeel and texture, cloudier in appearance, and often more aromatic overall.

HAZY WEST COAST

There's overlap between all of these styles, so you might see Hazy West Coast IPAs or New England IPAs using more classic American hops (like Cascade) and having a higher bitterness. IPA is a style that's constantly evolving and taking new inspirations.

FLAVOR PROFILES

There's some overlap between the flavor profiles and characteristics of the different American-influenced IPAs.

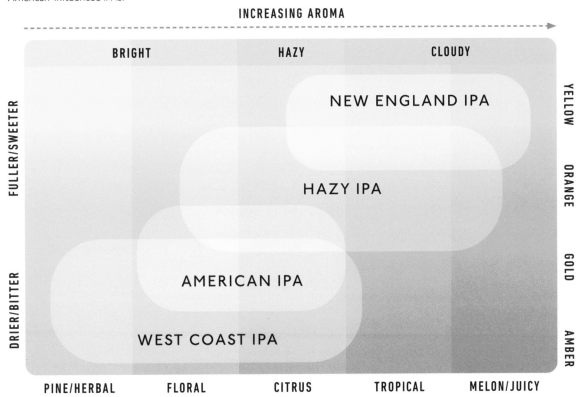

INCREASING AROMA

BRIGHT   HAZY   CLOUDY

FULLER/SWEETER

DRIER/BITTER

NEW ENGLAND IPA

HAZY IPA

AMERICAN IPA

WEST COAST IPA

YELLOW   ORANGE   GOLD   AMBER

PINE/HERBAL   FLORAL   CITRUS   TROPICAL   MELON/JUICY

THE FAMILY OF IPA

IPA has become a broader family of beers, with distinct sub-types. You'll find Session, Double, or Imperial (or even Triple) versions of most IPAs. It's common for these to be abbreviated, so Double IPA becomes DIPA, pronounced "dipper." Strong Pale Ales overlap between Pale Ale and IPA, although that's more of a competition standard than a style you'll see listed on labels.

GOLDEN ALE
4%–5% ABV
20–45 IBU

PALE ALE
4.5%–6% ABV
20–50 IBU

SESSION IPA
3.5%–5% ABV
20–55 IBU

IPA
6%–7.5% ABV
30–70 IBU

DOUBLE IPA
7–9% ABV
40–100 IBU

AMERICAN PALE ALE

The original craft beer style, American Pale Ale is a refreshing mix of citrusy hops, some lightly sweet malts, and a lasting bitter finish.

SHAKER   PINT

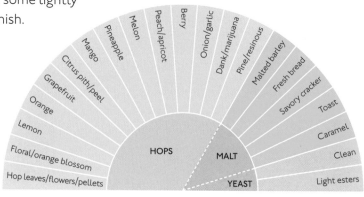

FLAVOR WHEEL

FLAVOR, PROCESS, & STORY

American and other New World hops create a distinctive and inviting aroma with a wide range of citrus flavors, tropical fruits, pine, and floral aromas. Hops like Cascade, Centennial, Chinook, Simcoe, and Amarillo define an older flavor profile, while newer varieties like Citra and Mosaic give a more tropical quality. They are typically hopped throughout the

boil and also dry hopped. The mostly (or solely) pale ale malt flavor has some sweetness to it, with bread, toasted malt, and light caramel flavors.

The style varies from under 4% to over 6% ABV, with some more caramelized and malty, and others leaner and more bitter. Compared to IPA, Pale Ale may have more malt character and is lower in alcohol, bitterness, and hop aroma. Some are filtered and bright, while others are lightly hazy. Hazy Pales differ with

the use of wheat and oats in their body and more tropical aromas.

The original American craft-beer style took a recipe for an English Pale Ale, added more malts, and used American hop varieties to produce a stronger, more bitter, and more aromatic beer compared to English versions. Now American-style Pale Ale (sometimes written as APA) is brewed all around the world. Hazy Pales have developed into their own style.

		BEER STATS		
Color	Clarity	Ferment	ABV	Bitterness
Yellow to amber	Bright to light haze	Clean to light esters	4%–6.5%	30–50 IBU (medium–high)

SIERRA NEVADA PALE ALE

5.6% ABV	BREWED: CHICO, CA, USA

The quintessential American Pale Ale, it's bright deep gold. The Cascade hop aroma is elegant but not intense, with grapefruit zest and peel, candied grapefruit, and bittersweet citrus, and a freshness from the smell of hop flowers. The body has a malt richness without sweetness, giving some toasted flavors, balancing a pithy, peppery, and lasting bitterness. Some Pales are more bitter or more aromatic; this sits perfectly in the middle.

THREE FLOYDS BREWING ALPHA KING

6.66% ABV	BREWED: MUNSTER, IN, USA

This is a big Pale Ale that's almost at IPA intensity, with an old-school character, being deep amber in color and having some sticky caramelized malt sweetness. The hops are pithy, piney, and powerful, with citrus peel, dried stone fruit, grapefruit, some dank and resinous notes, and a spicy rye bread quality. Its 68 IBU gives a robustly bitter finish, and that kind of bittersweet balance has defined American Pale Ales for decades.

TRACK SONOMA

3.8% ABV	BREWED: MANCHESTER, ENGLAND

This modern British American Pale Ale shows how the style can be influenced by different drinking cultures. Sonoma is hopped with Mosaic, Citra, and Centennial, giving tropical fruit, lemon zest, and grapefruit. High bitterness combines with mineral dryness at the end, and it's all balanced with toasty malts. On cask, Sonoma has a softer texture and a creamier stone-fruit quality compared to the sharper hoppiness from keg or can.

MATUŠKA APOLLO GALAXY

5.5% ABV	BREWED: BROUMY, CZECH REPUBLIC

Hopped with Apollo, Galaxy, and Citra, this lightly hazy golden beer pours with a thick and lasting foam, which holds on to all the finer hop aromas and gives them an elegance: juicy tropical fruits, peaches, apricots, florals, mango, pineapple, oranges. That American aroma meets classic Czech balance: the base beer is brewed with lager malts, giving a soft texture, a little sweetness, and a Pilsner-like lasting herbal bitterness.

OTHER EXAMPLES TO TRY

HALF ACRE DAISY CUTTER: fresh citrus, light resinous, balanced.

LIBERTY BREWING YAKIMA MONSTER: grapefruit, mandarin, bitter pine.

THE KERNEL PALE ALE: floral and fruity, smooth malt, lasting bitter.

AMERICAN IPA & WEST COAST IPA

American-style IPA, with its high citrus hop aroma and strong bitterness, has come to define the flavor of craft beer.

SHAKER   PINT

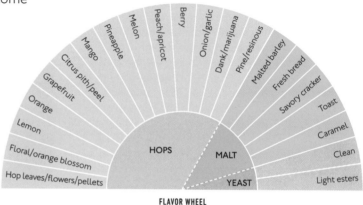

FLAVOR WHEEL

FLAVOR, PROCESS, & STORY

American IPA and West Coast IPA share similar hop profiles, with classic American varieties like Cascade, Centennial, and Simcoe, and many brews also including juicier hop varieties like Citra, Mosaic, and Ekuanot. Hops give citrus, pine, stone fruit, and floral aromas. They have a high bitter hop addition, then are hopped throughout the boil with a large dry hop for aroma, with a strong and lasting bitterness and a moderately high alcohol content (around 7% ABV).

Grain is mostly pale ale malt with some specialty malts. American IPA has more malt flavor and sweetness and more floral hop aromas. West Coast tends to be leaner in malt, more bitter, drier, and with more citrus aromas. Both captivate with their aromas, flavors, and bitterness.

The American IPA developed from the mid- to late 1990s, taking the old idea of an English IPA and Americanizing it with lighter malts and more aromatic American hops. The American IPA has shifted over the years, going from richer caramelly malts and grapefruity hops to being intensely bitter to then becoming more balanced and aromatic. Now it has shifted to more juicy and tropical aromas. There's huge love for this great style, with its impactful hop flavor.

BEER STATS				
Color	Clarity	Ferment	ABV	Bitterness
Yellow to amber	Bright to light haze	Clean to light esters	5.5%–7.5%	40–70 IBU (medium–high)

BELL'S BREWERY TWO HEARTED ALE

7% ABV	BREWED: COMSTOCK, MI, USA

Two Hearted Ale is a classic American IPA. Deep gold in color, it's brewed with Centennial hops and smells like orange zest, orange blossom, orange cake, orange gummy bears, tangerine, and bitter orange peel, plus grapefruit soda, floral hops, and sweetly bready malts. It ends with an herbal, resinous bitterness (60 IBU) that seems to grow as you drink. The light sweetness and floral-orangey hops define the American IPA.

RUSSIAN RIVER BREWING CO. BLIND PIG

6.25% ABV	BREWED: WINDSOR, CA, USA

Blind Pig is the archetypal West Coast IPA. Bright yellow-gold, there's a classic American hop aroma with orange pith, peel, and flesh; grapefruit zest, oily citrus, apricot jam, and a hint of resinous pine, with a Campari-like herbal bitterness and a dry, snappy minerality to the finish. Defining qualities are its lean body and how it's impeccably balanced at an extreme of hoppiness, leaving a very clean and crisp character.

EPIC ARMAGEDDON IPA

6.66% ABV	BREWED: AUCKLAND, NEW ZEALAND

A deep golden-amber color with a light haze, Armageddon is brewed with pale ale malt and caramalt, and a classic combo of Cascade, Centennial, Columbus, and Simcoe hops. There's canned mandarin, sweet ruby grapefruit, dried lemon, some resin, and pine—all the things we expect in an IPA. The body has some slight juicy malt sweetness, which plumps up the fruitiness and gives balance to the 66 IBUs, which last for a long time.

THORNBRIDGE JAIPUR IPA

5.9% ABV	BREWED: BAKEWELL, ENGLAND

Brewed with only low-color Maris Otter malt, Jaipur is very pale gold with a light yet sturdy body, capable of holding onto lots of hops without giving sweetness—a quality of the best American IPAs. Chinook, Centennial, Ahtanum, Simcoe, Columbus, and Cascade hops give orange blossom, orange candy, bitter apricot, floral notes, grapefruit bitters, and a lasting herbal bitterness.

OTHER EXAMPLES TO TRY

DRIFTWOOD FAT TUG IPA: grapefruit, resinous, crisp bitterness.

BENTSPOKE CRANKSHAFT: juicy orange, fresh tropical, light caramel.

PASTEUR STREET JASMINE IPA: floral, grapefruit, refreshing bitterness.

AMERICAN DOUBLE IPA & WEST COAST DOUBLE IPA

Highly hopped, high alcohol, and high impact, Double IPA is the most intensely hopped style you'll find in the craft-beer world.

SHAKER

PINT

FLAVOR WHEEL

Mango
Pineapple
Melon
Peach/apricot
Papaya
Onion/garlic
Dank/marijuana
Pine/resinous
Malted barley
Fresh bread
Toast
Caramel
Light esters
Warming alcohol
Citrus pith/peel
Grapefruit
Orange/tangerine
Lemon
Marmalade
Floral/orange blossom
Hop leaves/flowers/pellets

HOPS
MALT
YEAST

FLAVOR, PROCESS, & STORY

Expect an intense hop experience, with full-on aromas and strong bitterness. Double IPAs are much like IPAs but with more of everything: more pale malts, more hops for bitterness, more dry hops for more aroma, and more alcohol. Hops are greatly intensified and enhanced by the additional malt and alcohol, which both amplify flavor. We expect hops like Chinook, Columbus, and Simcoe but also find modern tropical-scented varieties.

Aromas are the typical range of citrus, tropical fruit, stone fruit, pine, and some dank and herbal qualities. Bitterness is high to very high, and there may be some yeast esters or warming alcohol. Some might use sugar as an adjunct to keep the body lighter, and some might use a bitter hop extract to give a cleaner hop bitterness. West Coast beers are brighter, drier, more bitter, and have more pithy citrus aroma.

These beers emerged in the mid-1990s and grew in popularity in the early 2000s. Since the 2010s, they've become a favorite style of many drinkers who love the impact of the hop aromas and flavors. Hazy versions have adopted "DIPA" as their name, whereas we might still see West Coast as Double or Imperial IPA (IIPA).

BEER STATS

Color	Clarity	Ferment	ABV	Bitterness
Yellow to amber	Bright to light haze	Light esters to warming	7.5%–10%	60–100 IBU (medium–high)

RUSSIAN RIVER BREWING CO. PLINY THE ELDER

8% ABV	BREWED: WINDSOR, CA, USA

The quintessential West Coast Double IPA, Pliny the Elder is a brilliant deep gold beer. It's hopped with Amarillo, Centennial, CTZ, and Simcoe, giving grapefruit, orange pith, bitter apricot, sweet tangerine, and some light pine. It's superb for being so clean and lean in the body, so wonderfully refined, with low malt flavor still giving enough balance for the strong, piney, pithy, and resinous bitterness with a mineral dry finish.

LAWSON'S FINEST LIQUIDS SIP OF SUNSHINE

8% ABV	BREWED: WAITSFIELD, VT, USA

Sip of Sunshine is a juicy fruit salad kind of American Double IPA, and a nice modern expression of the style. Deep gold and lightly hazy (but not fully Hazy DIPA), there's tropical fruit, sweet orange and orange soda, mango, floral honey, and apricot. The malt gives some sponge/pound cake flavor and a nice smooth texture. It has less perceived bitterness than a West Coast, and the hop character is more juicy than citrusy.

FOREST ROAD JUPITER DOUBLE IPA

8.7% ABV	BREWED: LONDON, ENGLAND

It's in a West Coast Double IPA like Jupiter that you get a sense that hops contain oils—they are almost visible, dancing through the beer, rich on the palate. With Centennial, Citra, Mosaic, and Amarillo, it's both juicy and pithy, with papaya, pineapple, peach schnapps, fruit candy, creamy mango, bitter lemon, orange peel, and a high bitterness. It's wonderfully bright, impeccably clean, and a perfect example of the style.

PIRATE LIFE BREWING IIPA

8.8% ABV	BREWED: ADELAIDE, AUSTRALIA

Golden in color with a lasting white foam, it's hopped with Centennial, CTZ, Simcoe, and Mosaic, giving aromas of fleshy citrus, tangerine, orange candy, mango, bitter orange peel, and resinous herbal pine. It has the kind of malt depth that gets almost sticky with a combination of hop oils and sweeter malts, which is a great quality of the style, and with a lower perceived bitterness, it gives something more Australian than American.

OTHER EXAMPLES TO TRY

STONE RUINATION DOUBLE IPA: grapefruit, tropical, pithy bitter.

BELL'S BREWERY HOPSLAM: sweet orange, resinous, bitter honey.

CLOUDWATER CRYSTALLOGRAPHY IIPA: pithy citrus, piney, herbal bitterness.

HAZY PALE ALE

These hazy-looking Pale Ales have a juicy hop aroma with citrus, tropical, and stone fruits and a smooth texture.

SHAKER   PINT

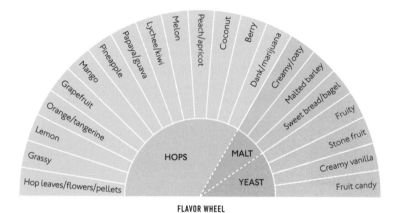

FLAVOR WHEEL

FLAVOR, PROCESS, & STORY

These are dominated by fruity, juicy, and tropical-scented hops like Citra, Mosaic, Azacca, Idaho 7, El Dorado, Mandarina Bavaria, and Galaxy, giving aromas of mango, passion fruit, pineapple, lychee, guava, and coconut alongside oranges and stone fruits. While they are very aromatic, they tend to be lower in bitterness—they have low bitter hop additions and

are heavily late hopped and dry hopped. Oats and wheat give proteins that make it hazy and help to give a smooth texture. Water is higher in chlorides, which help the soft, smooth mouthfeel and perceived fullness. They're low in carbonation with a balanced and refreshing, or juice-like, finish. We expect them to have a prominent yeast ester, adding its own fruitiness.

As more brewers sought to make very cloudy beers, so the

Hazy styles separated themselves from the American Pale and IPA styles. The Hazy styles are often interchangeably called Hazy, New England (NEPA/NEIPA), or Juicy. "Juicy" refers mostly to aromas such as melon, papaya, or guava, or to a juice-like quality in the flavor or texture. Hazy tends to be lighter-bodied than the creamier New Englands. The difference between Hazy Pales and DIPA is the strength and volume of ingredients.

		BEER STATS		
Color	Clarity	Ferment	ABV	Bitterness
Yellow to orange	Light haze to opaque	Fruity esters	4%–6%	20–40 IBU (medium)

TRILLIUM FORT POINT PALE

6.6% ABV	BREWED: CANTON, MA, USA

An orange juice appearance is a visual cue to the fruitiness that follows, with mango, sweet orange and tangerine, papaya, grapefruit, and some melon notes. The texture is light for its ABV, soft and silky smooth (so more New England than Hazy), making it easy-drinking as it carries a zesty and juicy fruitiness, and leading to an herbal bitterness and freshness at the end. Hop fruitiness and a lush texture are the dominant characteristics.

CLOUDWATER DDH PALE

5% ABV	BREWED: MANCHESTER, ENGLAND

Expect each Cloudwater DDH Pale to vary, with an evolving combination of hops (which are typically listed on the can). Those hops are always brightly and freshly aromatic, and thanks to the double dry hop, they have an intensity to them that is always compelling but never overpowering. The base beer is soft-textured but more crisp than creamy, with a lasting and mineral finish—it's a great combo of juicy hops and clean, dry bitterness.

TOPPLING GOLIATH PSEUDO SUE

5.8% ABV	BREWED: DECORAH, IA, USA

Brewed with only Citra hops, it's a singular showcase of North America's most popular aromatic hop variety. It pours hazy yellow like pineapple juice. There's sweet mandarin, ripe pineapple, creamy mango, tangy citrus, grassy myrcene hop oil, and slightly sweaty, sticky, dank hops in the back. It's dry and crisp, with a bright carbonation and lasting bitterness, placing this between American and Hazy Pales.

GARAGE PROJECT HAZY DAZE

5.8% ABV	BREWED: WELLINGTON, NEW ZEALAND

With lager malt, oats, and wheat, the base beer here is creamy and smooth, with the characteristic softness that's so good about this style. Every brew of Hazy Daze contains a different mix of hops, so each time you try one, you get to experience different varieties and the aromas and flavors they bring. The beer has nice flow to the drinking experience, from upfront malt and juicy hops into a dry, refreshing bitterness.

OTHER EXAMPLES TO TRY

BELLWOODS BREWERY JUTSU: stone fruits, juicy melon, dry finish.

HILL FARMSTEAD EDWARD: grapefruit, orange soda, resinous pine.

DEYA STEADY ROLLING MAN: citrus pith, light tropical, clean bitterness.

HAZY IPA

Hazy IPAs have become one of the most popular beer styles in the world, loved for their juicy tropical aromas and smooth, creamy textures.

SHAKER   PINT

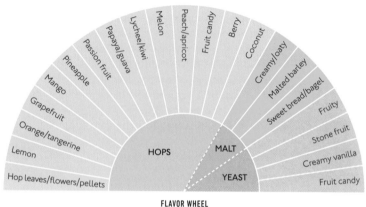

FLAVOR WHEEL

FLAVOR, PROCESS, & STORY

Four main qualities combine in most Hazy IPAs and New England IPAs: abundant hop fruitiness, prominent yeast esters, a smooth mouthfeel, and a relatively low perceived bitterness. Hop aromas from modern hops like Citra, Mosaic, Ekuanot, Azacca, Idaho 7, and Sabro are mostly tropical, stone fruit, sweet citrus, melon, and coconut, with yeast esters

giving a sweet creaminess. Hops are mostly added at the end of the boil and as dry hops. Hop and yeast aromas merge seamlessly. They could be lightly cloudy or fully opaque, and most of the haze comes from higher-protein grains like oats and wheat, which also contribute to the silky texture. Polyphenols in the hops also combine with the grain proteins to add to the haze.

Pleasing to drink with their smooth textures and low

carbonation, many have a quality of alcoholic fruit juice. Hazy tends to be lighter bodied than New England style.

Within a decade, Hazy IPAs have gone from an anomaly to a style brewed all over the world. They began as soft-bodied, unfiltered, smooth-textured, and extra-fruity IPAs, and have evolved to be more full bodied and even juicier and fruitier. It's the bold fruity flavors and low bitterness that have made these beers so popular.

BEER STATS				
Color	Clarity	Ferment	ABV	Bitterness
Yellow to orange	Hazy to opaque	Fruity esters	5.5%–7.5%	30–60 IBU (medium)

TREE HOUSE BREWING CO. JULIUS

6.8% ABV	BREWED: CHARLTON, MA, USA

Tree House arguably created the prototypical New England IPA. Julius pours a hazy orange with a lasting creamy white foam. There's hop and yeast combining in the aroma, with some creamy mango, vanilla, fruit candy, peach, apricot, orange, lemon sherbet, and zesty citrus. It's soft-textured, low in carbonation, and super fruity with some sweet bagel-like malt, and it has a crisp bitterness to finish—it's New England IPA at its finest.

SIERRA NEVADA HAZY LITTLE THING IPA

6.7% ABV	BREWED: CHICO, CA, USA

Hopped with a juicy mix of Citra, Magnum, Simcoe, Comet, Mosaic, and El Dorado, Hazy Little Thing has an elegance to it rather than the intensity of some New England–style IPAs. Lightly hazy yellow-orange, the aroma is of sweet oranges, candied citrus, pineapple, lemon peel, a light juicy tropical quality, and some floral hoppiness. It's dry at the end and lighter overall than other examples, making it easy-drinking.

VERDANT BREWING EVEN SHARKS NEED WATER

6.5% ABV	BREWED: PENRYN, ENGLAND

Verdant's Hazy IPAs have a prominent yeast character, giving a vanilla custard and sweet peach aroma that makes the hops smell sweeter and juicier. Even Sharks Need Water is brewed with wheat and oats, plus Citra and Galaxy hops. You get juicy peaches and cream, orange flesh, sweet mandarin, tepache, citrus candy, and mango, with a smooth texture and a drying, herbal bitterness at the end.

MOUNTAIN CULTURE BE KIND REWIND

7.3% ABV	BREWED: KATOOMBA, AUSTRALIA

This one pours like breakfast juice and smells just like it, too. Aussie Vic Secret and American Citra hops combine to give lots of juicy citrus, tangerine, pineapple, papaya, mango, some light coconut, and candied watermelon. It's got a soft and velvety texture, with a ripe tropical fruit kind of sweetness and a gentle bitterness at the end. It has the ideal balance of hop flavor, soft yet light texture, and refreshing finish.

OTHER EXAMPLES TO TRY

STRANGE BREW JASMINE IPA: mango, melon, juicy citrus.

WELDWERKS JUICY BITS: pulpy citrus, melon, zesty citrus.

O/O BREWING NARANGI: mango, pungent tropical, pithy.

HAZY DIPA

These silky smooth, strong, and wonderfully aromatic Double IPAs—or DIPAs as hazy versions are typically called—are juicy with the flavors of hops and are one of the world's most popular modern beer styles.

SHAKER   STEMMED

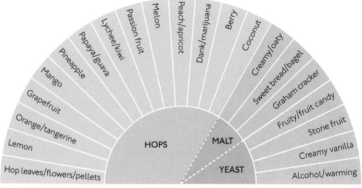

FLAVOR WHEEL

FLAVOR, PROCESS, & STORY

Hop aromas of exotic tropical fruits, sweet and zesty citrus, ripe stone fruit, and melon combine with a strong fruity ester character (stone fruit, vanilla), often being suggestive of creaminess that adds to the perception of sweeter fruits. Hops will mostly be modern varieties (Citra, Mosaic, and so on), and added mostly as late and dry

hops. Some are full-bodied, soft, and silky (or "juicy") to drink with higher perceived sweetness (using lots of oat and wheat for haze and that textural experience), while others have a lighter haze and body to them, showing a little more bitterness. Carbonation is often low. Yeast will be a noticeable aroma in most beers, adding to the perception of fruitiness. Alcohol might be present in flavor.

The aromas of bold juicy fruits, and a new textural experience of soft, smooth, almost creamy IPAs, and a low bitterness, led to this style going from nonexistent to one of the most prevalent craft-beer styles in the world, all within a decade—it's been such a seismic shift that many drinkers now expect IPAs to be hazy and juicy, not clear and citrusy. Now Hazy DIPAs are a standard style for brewers to make all around the world.

BEER STATS				
Color	Clarity	Ferment	ABV	Bitterness
Yellow to orange	Light haze to opaque	Fruity	7.5%–10+%	40–80 IBU (medium–high)

THE ALCHEMIST HEADY TOPPER

8% ABV	BREWED: STOWE, VT, USA

This is arguably the beer that set in motion the Hazy IPA craze, inspiring the fuller-bodied New England IPAs that followed. It's easy to see why: Heady Topper has glorious ripe and juicy peaches and apricots, soft and sweet fruitiness, pineapple cake, and boozy mango juice. The haze is light and the texture is soft but not thick, with a refreshing carbonation, a dry finish, and strong and thrilling bitterness.

OTHER HALF ALL CITRA EVERYTHING

8.5% ABV	BREWED: BROOKLYN, NY, USA

This one pours a distinctive cloudy yellow color. It's all Citra in the recipe, exotic with guava, tropical citrus, fresh mandarin, orange soda, vanilla sponge cake, peach schnapps, and dried tropical fruits, plus some herbal notes at the end, and it's all enhanced by the alcohol and some sweetness. It's medium-bodied with a light carbonation, so you could drink this one dangerously fast, especially as it has a zingy kind of dryness.

DEYA BREWING CO. SATURATED

8% ABV	BREWED: CHELTENHAM, ENGLAND

Deya's Saturated is a rotating DIPA that is brewed with a new hop each time, so it might be Saturated in Mosaic or Saturated in Strata. It's great to try as a showcase of a single hop, giving an intense experience of that variety, in which it reveals a wide range of qualities thanks to being used in high amounts. Expect pungent tropical fruit, citrus, something herbal or spicy, some underlying malt sweetness, and a juicy texture.

BISSELL BROTHERS SWISH

8% ABV	BREWED: PORTLAND, ME, USA

Citra, Mosaic, and Simcoe are the hops in this juicy orange-colored DIPA. It's great for its full-bodied silkiness with some sweeter malts, but also remains quite soft and dry on the palate. You can smell it at arm's length, and there's citrus, overripe papaya, peach, creamy jackfruit, grapefruit, lemon, orange, and some herbal spiciness. It's got a complexity and depth that give you new characteristics with each taste.

OTHER EXAMPLES TO TRY

TREE HOUSE HAZE: strong stone fruit, mango, creamy texture.

PARISH GHOST IN THE MACHINE: pungent tropical, citrus, resinous.

HOCUS POCUS OVERDRIVE: creamy mango, pineapple, dried lemon.

SESSION IPA

These IPAs give all the aromas and flavors we expect in a heavily hopped beer, just with a lower alcohol content.

SHAKER   WILLIBECHER

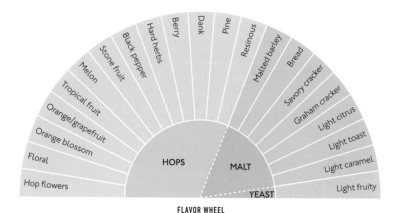

FLAVOR WHEEL

FLAVOR, PROCESS, & STORY

American and New World hops dominate the aromas, with citrus, tropical, stone fruit, melon, and resinous qualities. Some have very pale and light bodies of malt, others have more toasted malt and caramelized flavors. Some are in the Hazy style with a juicier quality. They typically differ from Pale Ales by being lighter in malt flavor, more bitter, and more hop aromatic.

Some malt bills are pale ale malts, others add wheat or oats for body, while some have kilned and character malts to give richer malt flavors. Hop additions are made throughout the boil and then they are dry hopped for aroma. Some aim for all-day drinkability, while others shoot for maximum hop impact and minimal alcohol.

The term "session" comes from the British idea of a "drinking session," where numerous pints of the same low-alcohol beer are drunk over several hours. Session IPA has come to mean lower alcohol than a regular IPA, and it delivers the flavor of an IPA at 4%–5% ABV—the strong flavors make them hard to actually "session," but that's not the intention with most of these beers. Low-calorie/low-carb IPA is an adjacent style, being lighter in body and malt flavor. Australian Extra Pale Ale (XPA) also fits here.

BEER STATS				
Color	Clarity	Ferment	ABV	Bitterness
Yellow to deep gold	Bright to hazy	Neutral to light fruity	4%–5%	30–60 IBU (medium–high)

FAT HEAD'S BREWERY SUNSHINE DAYDREAM

| 4.9% ABV | BREWED: MIDDLEBURG HEIGHTS, OH, USA |

Citra, Azacca, Mosaic, and Chinook are the hops in this bright golden-orange beer, giving a wonderful fresh aroma with grapefruit, orange zest, dried mango, stone fruit, and some tropical notes. The grain gives some toasted malt and a nice bit of sweetness up front that helps balance the 50 IBU of bitterness, which grips like bitter citrus and pepper. It's an impressively hoppy beer that tastes like a full-strength IPA.

BEAVERTOWN NECK OIL

| 4.3% ABV | BREWED: LONDON, ENGLAND |

One of the most widely available hoppy beers in the UK, Neck Oil is very pale yellow, lightly hazy, and crisply carbonated, with an inviting aroma coming from a mix of American and Australian hops. There's light citrus flesh and zest, light passion fruit, stone fruits, sweet melon, and a peppery bitterness, with the malt just a light background flavor. It's light and quenching, making this a refreshing and genuine "session beer."

BALTER BREWING XPA

| 5% ABV | BREWED: CURRUMBIN, AUSTRALIA |

XPA has become a common Australian style. Designed for easy-drinking refreshment on warm days, it's similar to Session IPA, sitting between a Pale and an IPA, usually with a lighter body of malt, a balanced bitterness, and a fresh fruity hop aroma. Balter's XPA is a lightly hazy yellow-gold with a delicate aroma that's like orange blossom, grapefruit soda, pineapple, and lemon. It's light, quenching, and crisply bitter.

WHIPLASH ROLLOVER

| 3.8% ABV | BREWED: DUBLIN, IRELAND |

This Hazy Session IPA is hopped with Simcoe, Ekuanot, Citra, and Mosaic. It's a luminous hazy orange and has a burstingly ripe fruity aroma with mandarin, grapefruit, pineapple, and lemon sherbet, with some fruity peach and apricot esters also coming through. The body is soft and smooth, there's some light bready and doughy malt flavor, with just a little sweetness, with a fuller texture carrying all those juicy tropical hops.

OTHER EXAMPLES TO TRY

FOUNDERS ALL DAY IPA: grapefruit, floral, toasty malt.

BELL'S LIGHT HEARTED: light citrus, tropical, crisp.

KIRKSTALL VIRTUOUS: citrus pith, light tropical, bitter finish.

PACIFIC PALE ALE & IPA

Brewed with mostly Australian and New Zealand hops, these Pale Ales and IPAs are dominated by tropical and citrus fruit aromas.

SHAKER   PINT

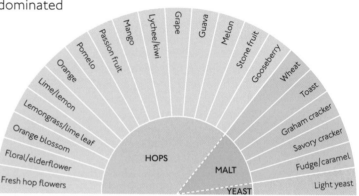

FLAVOR WHEEL

FLAVOR, PROCESS, & STORY

Expect citrus and tropical fruits from Australian or New Zealand hops, with distinct passion fruit, mango, gooseberry, grape, tangerine, and lychee, and an underlying grassy and herbal quality. Pacific Pales and IPAs have a fudgy malt sweetness compared to the hard caramel notes of American Pales and IPAs, with lower overall bitterness and gentler aroma hops. Pacific Ales and Summer Ales are a sub-style and are lower strength, very pale, very fruity, very refreshing, and with low bitterness.

Australian and New Zealand hops are essential, but American and other fruit-forward hops are additionally used. Most of the hops are added late as dry hops. Malt gives a light sweetness, softened by typically being unfiltered. Pacific Ales and Summer Ales are designed for warm-weather refreshment. They use wheat and Pilsner malt as the base.

The earliest Pale Ales took inspiration from the United States with adjustments to suit a volume-drinking, warm-weather country, meaning lower alcohol, fewer hops, and a crisper finish. Pacific Ales and Summer Ales are the lightest of these beers. Using all Australian or New Zealand hops doesn't technically make an IPA a Pacific IPA; it's the body and the lower hop content that separates it from other similar brews.

BEER STATS				
Color	Clarity	Ferment	ABV	Bitterness
Straw to deep gold	Bright to light haze	Neutral to light fruity	3.5%–7%	20–60 IBU (medium)

LITTLE CREATURES PALE ALE

5.2% ABV	BREWED: FREMANTLE, AUSTRALIA

An original Aussie Pale Ale, it uses Australian and US hops. It has an elegant aroma of peach, nectarine, light orange, and grapefruit, and a floral note with some toffee-like malt in the background. The base beer is pale gold, smooth, and soft bodied, with a distinctive fudge-like and graham flavor and a clean, crisp, light bitterness. Led by stone fruit instead of citrus and with a softer malt flavor, it stands apart from American Pale Ale.

STONE & WOOD PACIFIC ALE

4.4% ABV	BREWED: BYRON BAY, AUSTRALIA

This beer is so popular it created the Pacific Ale or Summer Ale as a distinct Australian style. It uses all-Australian ingredients: pale malt, wheat, and Galaxy hops. Hazy with a light lemony-straw color, it has a fresh aroma of passion fruit; ripe, sweet tangerine; honeydew melon; and is lightly floral. Next to the tropical aroma, a hazy, smooth, and light body, gentle bitterness, low alcohol, and high refreshment define the Pacific Ale.

GARAGE PROJECT HĀPI DAZE

4.6% ABV	BREWED: WELLINGTON, NEW ZEALAND

Brewed using New Zealand–grown barley and Nelson Sauvin, Wai-iti, and Motueka hops, it's a lightly hazy golden beer. Hops are fruity and tropical with grape, tangerine, pineapple, pomelo, tangy berry, and a distinct hop-flower aroma. The malt and light haze give it a subtle sweetness. Bitterness is light to keep it easy drinking, while aroma is moderate, not intense— Pacific Pales have a more subtle balance than American versions.

8 WIRED HOPWIRED

7.3% ABV	BREWED: WARKWORTH, NEW ZEALAND

One of the first IPAs to be brewed with only New Zealand ingredients, it's a showcase of the aromas of NZ varieties: lemon and grapefruit, gooseberry and grape, green mango, and a grassy and zesty quality at the end. In this deep golden beer, the NZ malt is light for the strength and low in sweetness, with some fudgy cookie depth and toasted malt. The bitterness is clean and relatively light, giving the style its characteristic easy-drinking quality.

OTHER EXAMPLES TO TRY

BEHEMOTH BREWING CHUR: tropical fruits, toasty malt, citrus pith.

YOUNG HENRYS NEWTOWNER: juicy fruits, stone fruit, crisp malt.

4 PINES INDIAN SUMMER ALE: passion fruit, melon, biscuit malt.

ENGLISH PALE ALE

English hops and malt dominate the flavor of these robust ales. They are high in bitterness but balanced overall.

MUG   PINT

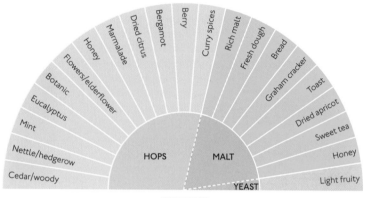

FLAVOR WHEEL

FLAVOR, PROCESS, & STORY

Pale Ales and Best Bitters are essentially the same family of beers and share similar drinking qualities: a fine balance of toasty English malt and fruity-spicy English hops. They vary in bitterness, but they all have low alcohol content and a balance that's designed to be drunk pint after pint. IPAs increase the malt and the hops, with a richer body of toasted, caramelized, and bready malts, a strong bitterness, and hop flavors like dried citrus, woody spice, berries, stone fruit, and a warming and honeyed complexity.

We expect contemporary English Pales and IPAs to use mostly pale base malts, sometimes with character varieties like Maris Otter or heritage grains such as Chevallier or Plumage Archer. They may also include some caramalt or crystal malt for extra color, body, and sweetness. English hops are most typical and usually dry hopped. Most will be bright and without haze, giving them a more refined bitterness.

Whereas the original English-brewed IPAs were made to be drunk months after being brewed, the contemporary version is designed to be drunk fresh. The use of new and fruity English hop varieties is progressing this style with a new aroma profile and often a lighter body of malts.

BEER STATS				
Color	Clarity	Ferment	ABV	Bitterness
Gold to deep amber	Bright to light haze	Light fruity	4%–7%	30–60 IBU (medium–high)

FULLER'S INDIA PALE ALE

5.3% ABV	BREWED: LONDON, ENGLAND

Pale ale malt and crystal malt combine with Fuggle and Golding hops in this all-English IPA. An amber-colored ale, Fuller's house yeast combines with the hops to be like dried orange and pepper. The hops give some honey, light citrus, woody spice, camphor, and a fresher more green or grassy note. The malt has a toasted and light caramel flavor, with the hops leaving a lasting and robust bitterness.

DRAFT BASS

4.4% ABV	BREWED: BURTON, ENGLAND

Bass Brewery's main beer came to be their eponymous Pale Ale, and it's now a brand brewed under the ownership of AB InBev. It's a copper-color pint with a smooth, almost fudgy malt quality to it, with a relatively high sweetness and a floral, spicy, earthy hop character leading to a mineral and peppery bitterness—it's that sweet-bitter balance that defines Burton pales. In bottle it's called Bass Pale Ale and is 5.1% ABV.

ALLSOPP'S INDIA PALE ALE

5.6% ABV	BREWED: SHEFFIELD, ENGLAND

This modern remastering feels authentically like an old style of IPA. It's brewed with Maris Otter and the heritage malt Chevallier, and hopped with Bramling Cross, Fuggle, and Challenger. It's amber colored and overall more malty than hoppy—there's bread crusts and graham crackers, toffee, raisins, roasted apples, plus some hay and bitter marmalade, with a decent body of malt and a snappy dry bitterness that lasts a long time.

ST. AUSTELL TRIBUTE

4.2% ABV	BREWED: ST. AUSTELL, ENGLAND

This golden Cornish Pale Ale is brewed with Maris Otter malt, which gives its distinctive flavors of toast and graham crackers and a moreish depth. It's hopped with English Fuggle, Slovenian Celeia (Fuggle grown in Slovenia), and American Willamette (bred from Fuggle). That hop combination gives a modern accent with zesty orange, grapefruit, orange blossom, and a fresh zesty bitterness with classic English balance.

OTHER EXAMPLES TO TRY

RAMSGATE BREWERY GADDS' NO. 3: honey, lemon, peppery bitterness.

MARSTON'S PEDIGREE: graham cracker, toast, stone fruit.

SCHLAFLY PALE ALE: toasty malts, floral, light orange.

RED IPA & BLACK IPA

Brewed with kilned and roasted malts, Red IPAs and Black IPAs combine deeper malt flavors with aromatic and bitter hops.

SHAKER

STEMMED

Grapefruit
Orange
Marmalade
Dank
Resinous
Pine
Dried citrus
Citrus pith
Berry
Pepper
Ginger
Toast
Caramel
Dried fruit
Sweet berry/açai
Rye bread
Molasses
Cocoa/cacao
Umami/miso
Coffee
Light fruity

HOPS

MALT

YEAST

FLAVOR WHEEL

FLAVOR, PROCESS, & STORY

These are essentially American IPAs brewed with additional kilned and darker malts. Thanks to those grains, the hop flavors present in new ways: grapefruit juice becomes grapefruit marmalade, pineapple tastes grilled, and pine is more resinous. Red IPAs tend to have a more caramelized sweetness, with light dried fruits and nutty notes.

Black IPAs have fruity cacao, a savory depth, and some sweeter maltiness. Both are typically bitter at the end.

Red IPAs use pale base malts plus light and dark crystal malts and even a little chocolate malt or rye, which all give flavor, body, and sweetness. Black IPAs use pale base malts for body and underlying flavor, some caramalt for texture, and dehusked Carafa malts for dark color. In both, hops could be any

variety, such as Centennial, Cascade, Mosaic, or Ekuanot.

Reds became common in the early 2000s. In Australia, hoppy reds are a common category. Black IPA had notoriety in the early 2010s with its oxymoronic name—a Black India *Pale* Ale—while drinkers came to love the mix of dark malt with intense hoppiness. Both styles have lost favor to Hazy IPAs but are returning to bars, often as a seasonal brew.

BEER STATS				
Color	Clarity	Ferment	ABV	Bitterness
Amber red to black	Bright to light haze	Light fruity	5%–8+%	40–70 IBU (medium–high)

SIERRA NEVADA CELEBRATION IPA

6.8% ABV	BREWED: CHICO, CA, & MILLS RIVER, NC, USA

It's not technically a Red IPA, but there are few better red-colored IPAs in the world. It's a winter seasonal brewed with freshly harvested Cascade and Centennial hops. The malts are rich and caramelized, with some roasted bitterness, a red jellybean sweetness, bitter honey, and some burned vanilla raisin cookie. The hops are tangy, grapefruity, herbal, and floral and overall reminiscent of Campari's bitter-sweet balance.

BENTSPOKE BREWING CO. RED NUT

7% ABV	BREWED: CANBERRA, AUSTRALIA

Red Nut is a great example of the Australian take on the hoppy red. It is deep red-brown and packed with lots of juicy malts, giving dark soft caramel, caramelized dark fruits, dark fruity chocolate, toast, and tea cake, with a smoother sweetness than American versions. On top come the hops, which bring a mix of baked orange, orange peel, marmalade, pine, resinous herbs, and pepper, with roasted malt notes meeting bitter hops at the end.

PIVOVAR MATUŠKA ČERNÁ RAKETA

7% ABV	BREWED: BROUMY, CZECH REPUBLIC

The Czechs are masters at getting malt flavor and hop balance in their lagers, and that translates perfectly into hop-forward ales, especially so in this Black IPA. Dark with creamy white foam, there's bitter orange chocolate in the aroma, peach skin, fruity coffee beans, dusty cacao, dried citrus peel, and roasted and candied tropical fruit. There's a smooth almost creamy fullness to the texture before a lasting herbal bitterness.

STONE SUBLIMELY SELF-RIGHTEOUS

8.7% ABV	BREWED: ESCONDIDO, CA, USA

This is one of the original Black IPAs. Hops come first, with Chinook, Simcoe, and Amarillo bringing a range of citrus, pine, berry, and spice. The body of the beer has a rich smoothness to it, with luscious dark chocolate, chocolate oatmeal cookies, some cacao, and toast. There's sweetness in the beer that carries the citrusy oiliness of the hops and tempers the bitterness, which is powerful and lasting.

OTHER EXAMPLES TO TRY

TRÖEGS NUGGET NECTAR: grapefruit, sponge cake, dried mango.

MODUS OPERANDI FORMER TENANT: baked citrus, caramel malt, pithy bitter.

ST. AUSTELL PROPER BLACK: cacao, chocolate orange, light roast.

BLONDE ALE & GOLDEN ALE

These are refreshing and moderately strong pale beers with a light bitterness and inviting hop aroma alongside a smooth body of malts.

SHAKER

PINT

Straw
Hop flowers
Honey
Woody spice
Stone fruit
Light tropical
Light citrus
Floral
Malted barley
Wheat
Fresh dough
Fresh bread
Sweet bread
Breakfast cereal
Graham cracker
Savory cracker
Light toast
Honey
Dried apricot
Light caramel/fudge
Light fruity

MALT

HOPS

YEAST

FLAVOR WHEEL

FLAVOR, PROCESS, & STORY

These easy-drinking pale beers find a gentle balance between fragrant fruity hops and a satisfying pale malt richness. Blondes are typically lighter in malt and body than Golden Ales and perhaps a little more aromatic. Hops are lightly fruity and lean toward floral aromas. Malt flavor is like toasty grains, bread, and savory crackers. Bitterness is low, refreshing, and unchallenging.

They're often made just with Pilsner or pale malt, perhaps with a little caramalt and wheat, which helps to give extra texture. Hops could come from anywhere, with British versions often using Golding for their honey and spice aromas, while US and Australian brewers use their local hop varieties, adding them for light fruity flavors and not for huge aromatic impact. The yeast might add a little fruitiness, which complements the hop. Most will have a small dry hop.

The first modern Golden Ales appeared as lagers were becoming more popular. That lager-like character is consistent with these styles, where they look like lager but have a little more malt body and hop flavor. Australian mid-strength beers fit here and often tend to be more tropical and floral in aroma. Kölsch-style ales often go in this category, especially if they are unfiltered.

BEER STATS				
Color	Clarity	Ferment	ABV	Bitterness
Straw to gold	Bright to light haze	Light fruity	3.5%–5%	15–30 IBU (low–medium)

HOPBACK BREWERY SUMMER LIGHTNING

5% ABV	BREWED: SALISBURY, ENGLAND

One of the original British Golden Ales, it's a bright golden beer that smells like the English countryside on a summer day: warming, hay, honeysuckle, wildflowers, spicy and peppery, plus a little fruity fermented note from the yeast. The malt has a moreish fullness but not sweetness, with the distinctive flavor of Maris Otter. The East Kent Golding hops add flavor, with earthy spice, honey, and dried orange, leading to a clean and bitter finish.

FYNE ALES JARL

3.8% ABV	BREWED: CAIRNDOW, SCOTLAND

This Citra Session Blonde fits right between a Blonde and a Session IPA. The Citra in the name is the first impression you get with Jarl, with the American hop giving enticing aromas of mango, tropical fruits, peach, grapefruit, and a floral citrus aroma. The bright blonde beer adds a little malt flavor but it mostly plays in the background and lets the hops shine. It's nicely bitter at the end to make you want to keep drinking more.

BREAKSIDE TRUE GOLD

5.1% ABV	BREWED: PORTLAND, OR, USA

It's the aroma that makes True Gold so inviting—it's elegant and light, with waves of gentle hop fruitiness (from Galaxy and Mosaic) coming through as you drink. There are new fruits with every sip: peach, grape, elderflower, gooseberry, candied citrus, melon, green papaya, and lychee. The body has the perfect texture for the ABV as it's full enough to be satisfying and light enough to be refreshing.

YOUR MATES BREWING CO. LARRY

4.5% ABV	BREWED: WARANA, AUSTRALIA

This might be called a Pale Ale, but in flavor it sits closer to a Blonde. It's the epitome of an easy-drinking hop-led blonde Australian brew. Light gold, the hops are light and fruity, giving tropical fruit salad, lemon pith, and tangy fruit candy, and those hops stay with the beer throughout, passing through a very light body of beer that barely gives any malt flavor—maybe a little biscuit malt—before a light and crisp finish.

OTHER EXAMPLES TO TRY

TREE HOUSE EUREKA: citrus, tropical juice, refreshing.

VICTORY SUMMER LOVE: fresh citrus, pine, light toast.

CAPITAL BREWING COAST ALE: graham cracker, crisp, light citrus.

AMBER ALE & RED ALE

Malt-forward and moderately hopped, Amber and Red Ales are located in flavor between Golden Ales, Best Bitters, and Pale Ales.

SHAKER

PINT

Grapefruit
Orange
Dried citrus
Floral
Woody
Resinous
Spicy
Peppery
Rich malt
Sweet bread
Breakfast cereal
Graham cracker
Savory cracker
Bread crusts
Toast
Toasted nuts
Dried apricot
Honey
Caramel
Cacao
Light fruity

HOPS

MALT

YEAST

FLAVOR WHEEL

FLAVOR, PROCESS, & STORY

These are generally moderate beers: not too strong or sweet, balanced bitterness, and light hop aromas. They are easy-drinking beers that have enough malt and hop character to remain interesting but never get overpowering. Malt flavor is rich, with the addition of some caramel, toast, and sweeter flavors, or some more dried fruit and nutty notes in darker versions.

Hop bitterness is unobtrusive, while aromas are floral, herbal, and lightly citrusy.

Mostly pale malts are used with additions of Munich, biscuit malt, caramalt, and crystal malts in Ambers, and some dark crystal or a little brown or chocolate malt in Reds. There is a moderate bitter addition, then usually a couple of further hop additions for aroma. Several British Best Bitters have rebranded to be Amber Ales, so those flavors cross over here.

Before Pale Ales and IPAs overtook it, Amber Ale (and Amber Lager) was one of the first craft beer styles to become mainstream. Some became flagship brands, though many have been superseded by more popular hop-led styles. Reds come from a similar place but with a stronger malt flavor. Irish Red is often given its own space in beer style guides, but it's not a style we see much of.

BEER STATS				
Color	Clarity	Ferment	ABV	Bitterness
Amber to red-brown	Bright to light haze	Light fruity	4%–6%	20–40 IBU (low–medium)

NEW BELGIUM FAT TIRE

5.2% ABV	BREWED: FORT COLLINS, CO, USA

A bright amber color and inspired by Belgian Amber Ales, this is one of the best-known craft beers in the US. The aromas are light and of older hop varieties (Willamette, Golding, Nugget), giving herbal, woody, floral, and a little berry or spice, plus some yeast fruitiness. The malt is fuller than a standard lager but still light and refreshing, giving toasted grain and biscuit malts before a clean and crisp bitterness with wonderful overall balance.

ANCHOR STEAM BEER

4.9% ABV	BREWED: SAN FRANCISCO, CA, USA

First brewed in 1971, this Steam Beer is the longest-standing American craft beer. It uses a lager yeast at warmer temperatures, so some light fruity esters mix with an herbal and lightly resinous and peppery hop profile. The malt has bread crust and light toffee flavor, with a lean body, refreshing carbonation, and a crisp bitterness. It's the herbal hop character and fruity esters that separate Steam Beer from an Amber Ale.

MAINE BEER CO. ZOE

7.2% ABV	BREWED: FREEPORT, ME, USA

Zoe is an example of a stronger and hoppier Amber Ale but one that doesn't feel as if it's jumped all the way up to an IPA. That means you get to enjoy all the great flavors of an Amber, just amplified into more toffee and darker toast, plus some dried fruit, berries, and cherries. The hops are piney and pithy, aromatic but not intensely so, and more marmalade than fleshy, with a peppery bitterness at the end.

MOUNTAIN GOAT FANCY PANTS

5.2% ABV	BREWED: MELBOURNE, AUSTRALIA

This deep amber-red beer is a hoppy Australian Amber Ale, a popular style down under. The malt pushes ahead of the hops, with graham cracker, cacao, fruitcake, toffee, and molasses, without being sweet. Above that, Australian hops give a mellow fruitiness like baked pineapple, lemon pith, bergamot, and berry jam, and that leads to a gentle bitterness where darker malts overlap with some spicy and peppery hops.

OTHER EXAMPLES TO TRY

FULLER'S LONDON PRIDE: toasty malts, floral, bitter marmalade.

O'HARA'S IRISH RED: sweet malts, raisin cookie, light fruity.

PIZZA PORT CHRONIC: bread crusts, caramel, peppery hop.

HOPPY BRITISH ALE

These beers combine the easy-drinking balance of classic British ales with the fresh, fruity aromas of modern hops.

PINT   WILLIBECHER

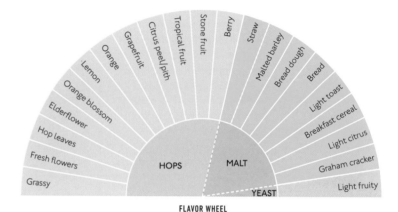

FLAVOR WHEEL

FLAVOR, PROCESS, & STORY

These beers combine the "sessionability" of a pale low-alcohol beer with the aromatic impact of modern hops and have a lasting bitterness to finish. Hops give mostly floral, citrus, tropical, and stone-fruit aromas. Malt flavor is often low, adding some residual sweetness and texture. While these beers might be low in alcohol, the hop flavor makes them taste much more impactful.

Often just pale malt is used as the base, perhaps with a touch of crystal malt or wheat. The yeast has a small amount of fruitiness that complements the hops, which are typically dry hopped. There's a light touch to all these beers and an elegance, which balances big flavors in small packages.

We could argue that this kind of beer inspired the Session IPA.

In the late 1990s, British brewers added citrusy American hops like Cascade to low-alcohol Pale Ales. Recipes got lighter and more aromatic over time and created a distinct new British beer style that most breweries now make a version of. Australian mids-strengths are often similar in their low ABV and high hop aroma. Table Beer has also become a popular derivative of this style, being a light, hoppy ale usually at 3% ABV or less.

BEER STATS				
Color	Clarity	Ferment	ABV	Bitterness
Straw to gold	Bright	Light fruity	3.5%–4.5%	25–40 IBU (medium–high)

OAKHAM ALES CITRA

| 4.2%/4.6% ABV | BREWED: PETERBOROUGH, ENGLAND |

Although it's called a Session IPA, it's an archetypal modern Hoppy Ale. The malt has a richness of graham crackers and toast, but this is all about the Citra hops and their fresh orange pith, mango, and tangy tropical aroma, and peppery bitter. On cask, it's 4.2% ABV, and 4.6% ABV in bottle—both are great, but on cask, it has a soft-bodied elegance and is able to give the Citra hops a more vibrant freshness.

ROOSTER'S BREWING CO. YANKEE

| 4.3% ABV | BREWED: HARROGATE, ENGLAND |

Yankee was one of the first examples of this style and it remains one of the best. It combines American Cascade hops with soft Yorkshire water and lovely British Golden Promise malt. It has an inviting aroma of light grapefruit, lemon pith, fresh flowers, and a general fresh hoppiness. On cask, the texture is smooth and full, almost creamy, while cans have a crisper malt depth, and both end with a strong and lasting hop bitterness.

NEWBARNS TABLE BEER MOSAIC

| 3% ABV | BREWED: LEITH, SCOTLAND |

Table Beer, which can mean any low-alcohol style, has become synonymous in the UK with a 3%-ish ABV pale hoppy beer. Newbarns Table Beer Mosaic is light gold and lightly hazy, the Mosaic hops are wonderfully fresh and elegant, like mango, mandarin, lemon, and young jackfruit, while the malt has a fullness that makes it drink like a stronger beer. The bitterness is high and lasting.

PIRATE LIFE THROWBACK SESSION IPA

| 3.5% ABV | BREWED: ADELAIDE, AUSTRALIA |

Mid-strengths ("middies") are a core category for many Australian brewers, being a low-alcohol, hop-aromatic beer. Throwback is reminiscent of the British brews with more toasty, biscuit malts, which add some sweetness that balances the hops. These are grapefruity, papaya, lychee, and some citrus pith. The carbonation is higher than British brews, and that fizz gives its all-important crisp refreshment.

OTHER EXAMPLES TO TRY

MARBLE BEERS PINT: tangy tropical fruit, biscuit malt, high bitterness.

THE KERNEL TABLE BEER: citrus, fresh hoppiness, crisp bitterness.

BALTER CAPTAIN SENSIBLE: crisp malt, light body, juicy hops.

MALT-FORWARD ALES

WHETHER IT'S TOASTY AND raisin-like British Best Bitters, nutty Brown Ales, chocolaty Porters, creamy or roasted Stouts, vinous Barley Wines, or dessert-like Imperial Stouts, these beers are all connected by their underlying grain flavors from different types of malt. With flavors that remind us of the bakery and coffee shop, some styles are elegant and low in alcohol, others have a high hop flavor alongside the malt, and some are rich and strong, but they all celebrate the amazing range and depth that grain gives to beer.

TRADITIONAL BRITISH BITTER

These classic British ales have the perfect balance between bitter hops and sweet malts and come in varying strengths.

MUG   PINT

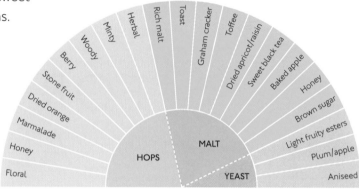

FLAVOR WHEEL

FLAVOR, PROCESS, & STORY

While this style is called Bitter, the overall drinking experience is more of a balance between malts and hops. These beers share an underlying malt flavor, either toasty pale malts or with more toffee and dried fruit flavors. English hops give herbal, woody, spicy, and fruity aromas. Yeast is often an expressive part of the flavor, giving its own fruitiness.

Typically brewed using just British ingredients, the mash is designed to create plenty of malt flavor. Pale ale malts and character malts make up the base, with crystal malts adding a caramelized and sometimes dried fruit quality. English hops give their distinct bitterness and aroma, and these beers usually have a light dry hop. Primary fermentation is usually done with a brewery's house yeast, giving a distinct house aroma and fruity ester flavor profile.

Secondary conditioning produces an elegant and gentle carbonation.

Emerging from an era of vat-aged Porters, new kinds of British ales were served fresh and unaged, giving a more bitter and brighter drinking experience. They came to be known as Bitters, Milds, and Pale Ales and became the everyday British beer, with flavor preferences and regional variety across different counties.

BEER STATS				
Color	Clarity	Ferment	ABV	Bitterness
Gold to brown	Bright	Light fruity	3.5%–5.5%	25–40 IBU (medium)

HARVEY'S BREWERY SUSSEX BEST

4% ABV	BREWED: LEWES, ENGLAND

This ruby-colored Bitter is an orchestral balance of its ingredients: the yeast is expressive, giving baked apple, spice, and vanilla; the malt is molasses, toffee, malt loaf, toast, and tea; English hops are warming and spicy with an herbal, grassy, and faint dried citrus note; the water gives a mineral finish. Every time you drink this, you'll likely notice something different about it, and that's one of the joys of a Bitter: it's familiar yet always interesting.

TIMOTHY TAYLOR'S LANDLORD

4.3% ABV	BREWED: KEIGHLEY, ENGLAND

Landlord, which the brewery call a Pale Ale, is a sweeter and fuller-bodied beer than Harvey's, with malt flavors of bread, caramel, and fudge, all from Golden Promise. The Golding and Fuggle hops give warming honey and dried orange, plus more herbal and fresh minty notes. It's designed to be served with a sparkler (nozzle with holes), which gives it more body and enhances the creamy fudginess of the mouthfeel.

CONISTON BREWING BLUEBIRD BITTER

3.6%/4.2% ABV	BREWED: CONISTON, ENGLAND

A deep golden beer, it has distinct flavors of the richly malty Maris Otter with toast, fudge, and graham cracker depth, and that combines with the snappy lemon pith, orange peel, honey, and floral flavors of Challenger hops. The cask version is lower ABV than in bottle. They have similar drinking qualities, though the cask version enjoys a cleaner and almost creamy and soft mouthfeel. The bitterness really grips at the end and hangs around.

FULLER'S ESB

5.9% ABV	BREWED: LONDON, ENGLAND

Extra Special Bitter (ESB) is a common style in the US but rarer in the UK. Fuller's ESB is seen as the progenitor of the ESB, inspiring all others. Dark amber-ruby, Fuller's distinctive yeast comes first with marmalade and spice. The malts are rich and smooth, with dried fruits, dark toast, caramel, and toffee apple. Golding and Challenger hops are peppery with marmalade, dried citrus, a hop-sack aroma, and a gentle bitterness.

OTHER EXAMPLES TO TRY

THE FIVE POINTS BEST: toasted malts, graham cracker, fresh herbal hops.

BATHAMS BEST BITTER: caramel, bread and butter, dried orange.

DRIFTWOOD NAUGHTY HILDEGARD: piney hops, rich caramel malts, bitter.

BRITISH-STYLE MILD & OLD ALE

These traditional styles of ale have a rich body and flavor of malts, with a low hop bitterness.

MUG   PINT

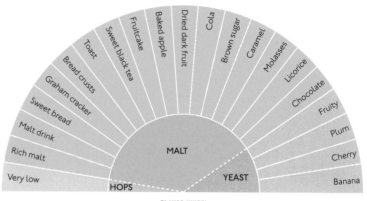

FLAVOR WHEEL

FLAVOR, PROCESS, & STORY

Mild and Old Ales share a rich flavor of malt, from bready pale malts to caramel, fudge, and fruitcake from crystal malts, and lighter roasted cocoa flavors from dark malts. They typically have residual sweetness, giving a rounded mouthfeel. Light and fruity yeast esters are often noticeable. Hops are light. Milds can vary in color and strength, but most common are Dark Milds at 3.5% or 6% ABV. Old Ales are usually brown, with more of a dried fruit than chocolate flavor compared to Milds.

Pale malts are layered on top with crystal malts, dark crystal, brown malt, and maybe some chocolate malt and sugar. Low carbonation is common for these styles, giving a richer impression of the malt flavor. Old Ale has two identities: the British style is low alcohol, richly malty, raisiny, and slightly sweet; an Americanized version is strong and aged, often in wood, making it literally an "old" ale—these are similar to Barley Wines in flavor.

Low-alcohol Dark Milds emerged in the 1900s. Old Ales were once the opposite of Mild, matured to develop a rich aged flavor. Most British Old Ales now just evoke that flavor in low-alcohol beers. Mild enjoyed a renaissance in the early 2020s.

BEER STATS				
Color	Clarity	Ferment	ABV	Bitterness
Red-brown to dark brown	Bright to light haze	Fruity	3%–6%	10–30 IBU (low)

BOXCAR DARK MILD

| 3.6% ABV | BREWED: LONDON, ENGLAND |

Very dark brown in color, this is a perfect example of a modern Dark Mild. It's got lots of lovely smooth malt, which is almost nourishing in its appeal, with chocolate cookies, caramel, licorice, and molasses. It's low in carbonation and high in moreish easy-drinking qualities that define the style. It's a wonderfully simple beer and a joy to drink. Boxcar's Double Dark Mild is a great example of a stronger, more vinous Mild.

THEAKSTON OLD PECULIER

| 5.6% ABV | BREWED: MASHAM, ENGLAND |

Flavor-wise, Old Peculier overlaps Old Ale and stronger Dark Mild styles, though it isn't labeled as either. The aroma leads with fruity esters like banana and black cherry, with some dark cacao malts behind it. The beer is full-bodied and unctuous, with rich malt, graham cracker, dried cherries and raisins, vanilla, dark chocolate, malt loaf, and sweet black malty tea. It's the texture and the depth of malt flavor that makes this so good.

HARVEY'S BREWERY OLD ALE

| 4.3% ABV | BREWED: LEWES, SUSSEX |

Harvey's brew a Dark Mild and Old Ale, and comparing the two reveals the differences. Dark Mild is more cocoa-like, with a light body and dry finish, while the Old Ale, which pours almost black, is richer in malts, with caramel, raisin, date, and molasses with a hint of roastiness. The brewery's distinctive yeast gives its own fruity and spicy aromas to both beers. There's wonderful depth and satisfying moreishness to these great beers.

RHINEGEIST BREWERY UNCLE

| 4.2% ABV | BREWED: CINCINNATI, OH, USA |

Uncle is an antidote to the heavy hoppiness of American beer, and a great example of a British Dark Mild. There's some very British-tasting malty flavors of toast, tea, caramel, and graham cracker, plus some toasted nuts, molasses, and tobacco, with a lightish body and higher carbonation setting it apart from British versions. The bitterness cuts through with a little herbal spice. It has a refreshing restraint and textbook depth of maltiness.

OTHER EXAMPLES TO TRY

ADNAMS OLD ALE: caramel, malt loaf, sweet berries.

SARAH HUGHES DARK RUBY MILD: sweet cherry, cocoa, rich malt.

YARDS BRAWLER: tea, graham cracker, toast.

BROWN ALE

Whether malty British style or hoppy American style, Brown Ales give us a depth of toasted, nutty, and rich malt.

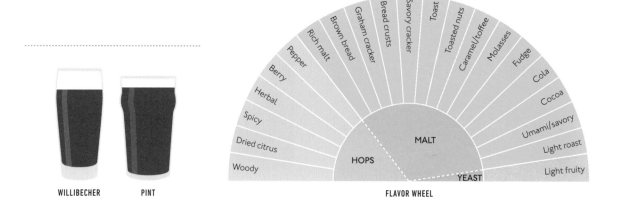

WILLIBECHER   PINT

FLAVOR WHEEL

FLAVOR, PROCESS, & STORY

British-style Brown Ale is dominated by malt flavor, with rich malted barley notes, toasted nuts, dark toast, and light caramel leading toward a light roastiness. American style has all those flavors, often amplified and stronger, plus more bitterness and usually with aromatic dry hops. Overall, they have moderate alcohol and balanced drinking

qualities. On a flavor spectrum, Best Bitters lead to Brown Ales then into Porters, getting more roasted as they go.

Pale malts are joined by caramalts, crystal malts, brown, and chocolate malts. Brewers tend to go either malt led in flavor but with a dry finish, or richly malty with residual sweetness. Bitterness can vary, but they don't tend to be strongly bitter, letting malt be the main flavor. Peppery, herbal, spicy, citrus, and resinous hops are most

common. Most British Browns are not hop aromatic, but many American versions are late hopped and dry hopped, and these tend to have a dried or roasted citrus aroma.

British Brown Ales emerged from the early 20th century as a new bottled style somewhere between Porter, Mild, and Amber. They lost popularity from the 1970s, but a small resurgence in interest came as early American brewers resurrected the style in a new way.

BEER STATS				
Color	Clarity	Ferment	ABV	Bitterness
Brown	Bright to light haze	Light fruity	4%–6.5%	20–40 IBU (medium)

NEWCASTLE BROWN ALE

4.7% ABV	BREWED: TADCASTER, ENGLAND

Newcastle Brown Ale is arguably the most famous Brown Ale. It was conceived in the 1920s to be a lighter-tasting brown beer. It's a light-bodied beer, dry and crisp, with flavors of black tea, caramel malt, brown sugar, banana, dried fruit, and tobacco. It has a cult following, but it's also a singular type of Brown Ale and almost no others are as light as this. "Nut Brown Ale" might be used to describe this kind of Brown.

AVERY BREWING ELLIE'S BROWN ALE

5.5% ABV	BREWED: BOULDER, CO, USA

Stronger than British versions, it has a fuller body and flavor of malts, giving dark toast, cacao, brown sugar, and toasted nuts. The hops are more for flavor than aroma, adding woody, tobacco, light herbal notes, and a lasting bitterness, lifted by the carbonation. It's a beer to drink for complexity of malt without the roastiness of a Stout, and it's a great example of the Americanization of the British Brown.

BIG SKY BREWING MOOSE DROOL

5% ABV	BREWED: MISSOULA, MT, USA

Moose Drool is a deep red-brown beer and it's up front with malt flavors: toasted and nutty, cocoa powder, pretzels, raisin cookie, and light coffee. The malt has some sweetness to it but it has a lightness, and it's kept light by the carbonation and the hoppiness, which is floral, honeyed, peppery, and spicy, leading to a lasting dry finish. In the Newcastle style but with an American accent, it almost drinks like a crisp brown lager.

CIGAR CITY BREWING MADURO BROWN ALE

5.5% ABV	BREWED: TAMPA, FL, USA

Maduro brings more depth of malt than other examples of the style, an American fullness of the palate, and a rounder, deeper flavor overall. There's caramel, cocoa, cacao, brown sugar, toasted bagels, and nut butter, and a coffee-like finish, all with a whiff of sweet cigar-box woodiness. The hoppiness is moderate, with some woody and floral notes, and lasting bitterness that overlaps with the bitterness of the malt.

OTHER EXAMPLES TO TRY

THE FIVE POINTS BRICK FIELD BROWN: toasted nuts, dried citrus hop, toasty.

ALESMITH NUT BROWN ALE: chocolate cookie, toast, light hops.

ANCHOR BREKLE'S BROWN: roast citrus hops, caramel, dark toast.

STRONG ALE & SCOTTISH ALE

These ales all have a full flavor from malts, with each style having its own distinguishing features and qualities.

PINT　　　SNIFTER

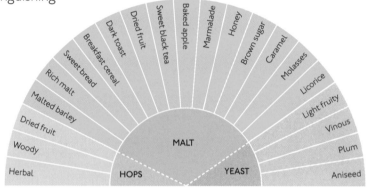

FLAVOR WHEEL

FLAVOR, PROCESS, & STORY

A general category of strong beer rather than a specific style, these are typically deep amber to dark brown, have a lot of malt flavor, and a lasting hop flavor or bitterness, often with British hops but they could be heavily American hopped. They sit between strong Bitters, Old Ales, IPAs, and Barley Wines in flavor.

Many are drunk fresh as strong Bitters, but they are often suitable to be aged. Because of their strength, they will usually have a noticeable ester profile.

Scottish Ales are similar to British Bitters and can range in strength from 3% to 6+% ABV. Typically amber to brown in color, they have a prominent flavor and aroma of malts. While they are malt forward and have some residual sweetness, they are

balanced with dryness at the end and a light bitterness.

Wee Heavy is a stronger category of Scottish-style ales that overlaps with Strong Ale and heads toward Barley Wine, but with a sweeter and more malty flavor profile. Hops are usually light in aroma. The name refers to a "Heavy" (strong) beer, served in a "wee" (small) volume. The name has been appropriated by US brewers for a strong and richly malty beer.

BEER STATS				
Color	Clarity	Ferment	ABV	Bitterness
Dark amber to dark brown	Bright to light haze	Light fruity	4%–10%	20–60 IBU (low–medium)

FULLER'S VINTAGE ALE

8.5% ABV	BREWED: LONDON, ENGLAND

One of the world's finest beers for aging, it can continue to improve for 20 years or more. It pours a bright deep amber to red with a tan foam. When fresh, you get hops and yeast in the aroma, a mix of dried citrus, berry, and spice, sometimes with a hoppy Barley Wine quality. When aged, you get more honey, caramel, vanilla, sherry, and dried fruit aromas. A firm bitterness mellows over time. It's wonderfully complex.

TRAQUAIR HOUSE ALE

7.2% ABV	BREWED: INNERLEITHEN, SCOTLAND

This is a quintessential Scottish strong ale. It's dark ruby colored, there's a lot of sweet and juicy malt flavors with raisin, sherry, a toasted nuttiness, marmalade, vanilla, and an oak quality (it's fermented in wooden vats). There's not much hop flavor, but the yeast adds its own fruitiness with plum and berry notes. Brewed in Scotland's oldest inhabited house, it feels like a hearty, warming beer from a different era.

ORKNEY BREWERY DARK ISLAND

4.6% ABV	BREWED: ORKNEY, SCOTLAND

Pale ale malt and chocolate malt combine here to give a beer with a rich malt depth, with sweet bread, toast, chocolate, dried fruit, roasted nuts, nut brittle, and light coffee, with a noticeable depth of English hops giving it a warming and spicy finish. It's got a wonderful balance between the malt and hops, and it sits somewhere between a stronger Mild and a sweeter Porter, which is the quintessential Scottish Ale flavor profile.

OSKAR BLUES OLD CHUB

8% ABV	BREWED: LONGMONT, CO, USA

This has become an American reference point for strong Scottish-inspired ales. Dark amber-brown, it's a glassful of smooth-bodied malts, with caramel, vanilla, molasses, roasted almonds, dark fruits, and a little savory smokiness. Fermentation adds some yeast fruitiness, but there's not much hoppiness apart from a spicy snap of bitterness at the end. The malt and a low carbonation gives this a comforting richness.

OTHER EXAMPLES TO TRY

ODELL 90 SHILLING: toasted malts, graham cracker, crisp bitterness.

MCEWAN'S CHAMPION: dried fruits, dark cherry, toast.

ORKNEY DARK ISLAND RESERVE: dark chocolate, oak, whiskey.

BARLEY WINE

These wine-strong beers are typically either American style and highly hopped or British style and richer with malt flavor.

SNIFTER   STEMMED

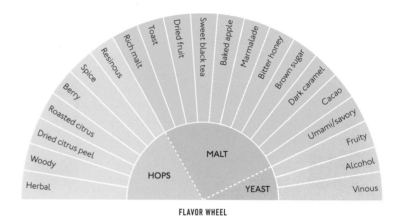

FLAVOR WHEEL

FLAVOR, PROCESS, & STORY

These are strong beers with high malt content, high alcohol, and sometimes a high hop flavor and bitterness. British-style Barley Wine is more malt forward, with dried fruits, caramel, fruitcake, a sherried nuttiness, and a firm bitterness. American versions are typically stronger and have more bitterness and a strong aroma of citrus and resinous hops. Fruity

esters are common. Many can age well for a year or more.

The use of crystal, caramel, and kilned malts alongside pale base malt gives these beers their deep color and distinctive caramel, fruitcake, vinous, and dried fruit flavors. The malts leave behind some residual sweetness. British-style versions use lots of British hops for bitterness; American style have a heavier hop addition and a high bitterness, while large dry hopping gives intense cooked

citrus and resinous aromas. They are often aged in ex-whiskey or bourbon barrels.

The name "Barley Wine" was used from the late 1800s. Over time, it became a rare occasional brew, often a winter special, and at strengths from 7% to 9% ABV. As American craft brewing accelerated, this was one of the first styles to be adopted and then Americanized, adding lots of late hops and dry hops.

BEER STATS				
Color	Clarity	Ferment	ABV	Bitterness
Amber to dark brown	Bright	Fruity esters	8.5%–13+%	40–100 IBU (medium–very high)

ST. MARS OF THE DESERT OUR FINEST REGARDS

9% ABV	BREWED: SHEFFIELD, ENGLAND

A very dark brown beer, there's some fruity yeast and warming alcohol in the aroma, with some vanilla, brown bread toast, and light roast. It drinks rich and hearty, like having malt loaf with a black coffee (with a splash of brandy) on the side, as this has more roasted depth than others. The bitterness is strong and almost minty and fresh. Our Finest Regards is a fascinating roasty-vinous British Barley Wine.

CONISTON BREWING NO.9 BARLEY WINE

8.5% ABV	BREWED: CONISTON, ENGLAND

This is a paler Barley Wine than most, pouring deep gold to amber. It's complex with aromas of marzipan, toasted almonds, vanilla, nutty sherry, caramel, honey, and sweet malts, which all carry through into the flavor. The body is rich and smooth with the malts, with bitter and floral honey, sweet bread dough, orange liqueur, and orange peel, and a clean bitterness. It's arguably best within one or two years of bottling.

SIERRA NEVADA BIGFOOT

9.6% ABV	BREWED: CHICO, CA, USA

First brewed in 1983, this deep red classic American Barley Wine is released annually. It's fresh and intense with grapefruity hops, grilled pineapple, hard herbs, and Campari, with a strong bitterness and grain giving caramel and light dried fruit. When aged, those hops integrate into the malts, giving dried citrus peel and herbal liqueur, plus there's more caramel, nut brittle, raisins, and a long-lasting bitterness.

REVOLUTION BREWING STRAIGHT JACKET

15% ABV	BREWED: CHICAGO, IL, USA

This is a monster of a Barley Wine. A lip-sticking 15% ABV, the base brew is decadent with dark caramel, brown sugar, molasses, and fruitcake. That's all intensified by aging in bourbon barrels for a year, where it picks up vanilla, bourbon, oak, coconut, fig, date, and a sweeter fruity top note like stone fruits. It's a powerful beer with unctuous richness in the mouthfeel and a lasting intensity that makes it one to sip, perhaps with some chocolate.

OTHER EXAMPLES TO TRY

ANCHOR OLD FOGHORN: dried fruit, dried citrus, vinous.

J. W. LEES HARVEST ALE: sweet dried fruit, sherry, bitter honey.

MARBLE BEERS BARLEY WINE: bitter marmalade, rich hop, raisin.

PORTER

Originating in London in the 18th century, Porter has become a popular dark beer style that typically has less roasted barley flavor than a Stout.

PINT   WILLIBECHER

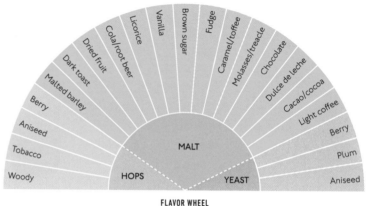

FLAVOR WHEEL

FLAVOR, PROCESS, & STORY

The flavors of Porters and Stouts overlap, but in general, expect more roasted, burned, and almost astringent malt bitterness in Stout. Porter is a little sweeter with more dark fruit and dried fruit qualities and has a higher alcohol content. Porters also have toasty, bready, nutty, chocolaty, caramel, cocoa, brown sugar, and vanilla qualities, with low hop character. American-style Porter is higher in alcohol with more malt and hop flavor.

Brown malt is traditional in Porters. Other common grains are pale ale, crystal, and chocolate, giving the toasty, fruity, and chocolate flavors alongside some residual sweetness. Hops vary from mild to spicy to fruity, with a lasting bitterness, and are often English. An English ale yeast might produce noticeable fruity esters, most often like dark fruits. Porters are sometimes brewed with coffee or other ingredients, and some Porters are Imperial strength.

The name is said to derive from the porters who carried goods around London, stopping for pints of ale on the way. New malting technology and industrialized scale helped formalize Porter as distinct from the sweeter dark brown beers that came before it. Porters had lost popularity by the early 1900s. Like many old styles, craft brewing reintroduced it.

BEER STATS				
Color	Clarity	Ferment	ABV	Bitterness
Brown	Bright to light haze	Light fruity	4.5%–6%	20–40 IBU (medium)

FULLER'S LONDON PORTER

5.4% ABV	BREWED: LONDON, ENGLAND

Considered the archetypal contemporary English or London Porter, and a template for brewing textbooks, it no longer has the old vat-aged qualities and is lower in alcohol than historic versions. A deep brown with tan foam, it has the aroma of dark malts. The body has an almost creamy texture, with caramel, toast, dark fruits, chocolate cereal, and some smooth chocolate notes, with Fuggle hops adding a light herbal bitterness.

ANSPACH & HOBDAY THE PORTER

6.7% ABV	BREWED: LONDON, ENGLAND

If Fuller's is seen as the modern London Porter, this one recalls something older, albeit not long matured. It's a stronger beer in keeping with original Porters, having a full body and a deeply layered malt flavor with cacao, dark chocolate truffles, lighter roasted notes, some smoke and tobacco, and umami savory notes. Dried fruits evoke an old vat-aged quality. There's a mineral dryness and strong, lasting herbal bitterness.

GREAT LAKES EDMUND FITZGERALD PORTER

6% ABV	BREWED: CLEVELAND, OH, USA

Porter was popular with many original American craft brewers, and their brews were stronger and had more malt depth, American hops, and a higher bitterness than English Porter. Edmund Fitzgerald is a great example: smooth-textured, dark cocoa, bittersweet malts, molasses, dark toast, vanilla, and cola notes, with the flavors condensed and full. The herbal, berry, and botanic bitterness is from Northern Brewer, Willamette, and Cascade hops.

MODUS OPERANDI SILENT KNIGHT

5.6% ABV	BREWED: SYDNEY, AUSTRALIA

A dark brown color with some red at the edges, this is a powerful Porter. It's rich with dark malt flavor and depth, and there's a complexity but also a clarity of flavor here, with a smooth body and crisp, dry finish. You get cacao, cocoa, licorice, the flavor of freshly crushed dark malt, and some pastry and a sweet creaminess (think dark chocolate profiteroles), finishing with the lasting flavors of dark malt.

OTHER EXAMPLES TO TRY

FIVE POINTS RAILWAY PORTER: roasted malts, bitter hops, cacao.

DESCHUTES BLACK BUTTE PORTER: cocoa, sweet dark fruit, light roast.

RENAISSANCE ELEMENTAL PORTER: dark chocolate, toasted malt, herbal hops.

BALTIC PORTER

These strong Porters are typically brewed with a lager yeast and are so named because of their popularity in countries around the Baltic Sea, in particular, Poland.

SNIFTER STEMMED

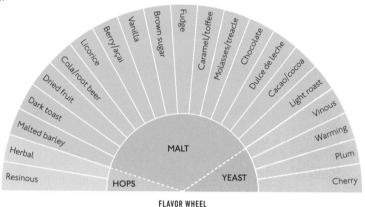

Licorice
Berry/açai
Vanilla
Brown sugar
Fudge
Caramel/toffee
Molasses/treacle
Chocolate
Dulce de leche
Cacao/cocoa
Light roast
Cola/root beer
Dried fruit
Dark toast
Malted barley
Herbal
Resinous
Vinous
Warming
Plum
Cherry

MALT

HOPS   YEAST

FLAVOR WHEEL

FLAVOR, PROCESS, & STORY

Baltic Porters differ from strong and Imperial Stouts by having a less roasted and astringent flavor. They are usually fermented with lager yeast. Most use pale lager malts built up with caramalt, Munich, biscuit, brown, and chocolate plus de-bittered/dehusked darker malts for color and flavor but not roastiness. A longer lagering time lets the flavors mellow and mature, even developing slight aged vinous or sherried flavors, with a lightness in the finish despite the beer's higher alcohol content.

We expect dark fruit, berry, vinous port-like flavors or nutty sherry qualities, molasses, licorice, dark fruity chocolate, and aniseed flavors, perhaps with some fruity yeast esters and higher alcohols in stronger versions. Some can be noticeably hop bitter, but most are rich glasses of dark, smooth malt.

Strong British Porters and Stouts were commonly exported in the 19th century. Many arrived at Baltic ports, having matured new, more vinous characteristics during the journey, and domestic breweries made their own versions of the beer. Later, as most moved to lager production, the strong dark ales became strong dark lagers, and they remained an important local style. Until recently, they were little known outside the region, but their popularity is spreading.

		BEER STATS		
Color	Clarity	Ferment	ABV	Bitterness
Dark brown to black	Bright to opaque	Light fruity	6.5%–11%	25–50 IBU (medium)

BROWAR FORTUNA KOMES PORTER BAŁTYCKI

9% ABV	BREWED: MIŁOSLAW, POLAND

A cold and slow fermentation in open-topped fermenters, and then at least three months maturing in the lagering tank, create the distinct smooth and balanced flavor in this strong Polish Baltic Porter. Black with a rich tan foam, there's cacao and dark chocolate, and it's vinous with some cherry, licorice, prunes, and berries, plus some fruity esters. The body is full but light to drink for its strength.

LOST AND GROUNDED RUNNING WITH SPECTRES

6.8% ABV	BREWED: BRISTOL, ENGLAND

Not to be confused with the brewery's Running with Sceptres, this is a wonderful Baltic Porter. There's dark chocolate, the fruity fermented aromas of cacao nibs, licorice, black currant, and berries. The malts are smooth and rich but there's no roastiness, and a crisp fermentation. It has a higher hop aroma, flavor, and bitterness than others, giving an herbal and aniseed quality that complements the malt and adds complexity.

LES TROIS MOUSQUETAIRES PORTER BALTIQUE

10% ABV	BREWED: BROSSARD, CANADA

This strong Baltic Porter is almost black, and it's a big beer with big flavors, giving something new on each sip while retaining the characteristic balance of a lager fermentation and maturation. There's sweetness first, like molasses and dark maple syrup, and then comes cacao, vanilla, warming sweet alcohol, dark dried cherries, cherry brandy, rye, coffee, and licorice, with subtle smoke weaving all the way through.

PÕHJALA ÖÖ IMPERIAL BALTIC PORTER

10.5% ABV	BREWED: TALLINN, ESTONIA

One of the best-known Baltic Porters, this is Imperial-strength at 10.5% ABV and inky black. When fresh, you get dark malt, very dark chocolate, molasses, warming alcohol, berries, and a firm bitterness. As it ages, there are more dark dried fruits like prune, raisin, and cherry with some port-like flavors, and it develops a new complexity. It's a hearty beer and enjoyable for its complex range of malt and matured flavors.

OTHER EXAMPLES TO TRY

PODGÓRZ 652 M N.P.M.: smooth dark malts, dark fruits, caramel.

BROWAR KORMORAN IMPERIUM PRUNUM: smoke, dried plums, dark chocolate.

JACK'S ABBY FRAMINGHAMMER: chocolate, molasses, oatmeal raisin cookie.

DRY STOUT

These Stouts include Irish Stouts, American Stouts, and Export Stouts, and they share the coffee and dark chocolate flavors of roasted barley.

PINT   WILLIBECHER

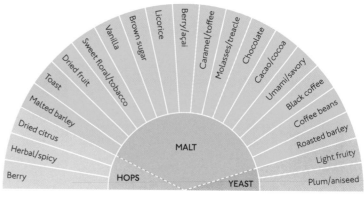

FLAVOR WHEEL

FLAVOR, PROCESS, & STORY

Dark and roasted malts give the main flavors and might make up 10 to 25 percent of the grain bill. Some might include black malt, dehusked malt, chocolate, and crystal malts. We expect flavors of roasted barley, coffee, dark chocolate, cacao, licorice, dark dried fruit, and more. English hops are common in most Stouts and give berry and herbal qualities.

American hops are used in American Stout and might be high in bitterness and aroma. Most should finish dry, not sweet. Some might have notable ester fruitiness from the fermentation. Nitrogen is often added to create a smooth texture and creamy foam.

Irish Stouts are like the classic Guinness. American Stouts are stronger, have more dark malt, hop bitterness, and hop aroma. Export Stouts are like stronger Irish Stouts, with more hop bitterness.

"Stout" originally described a stronger version of a beer, but over time it developed into its own distinct style and sub-styles. Guinness is the archetypal Irish Stout, and the recipe developed in the mid-1900s. Export Stouts were commonly exported to West Africa and the Caribbean and are still popular in those regions. All these Stouts have more roasted bitterness and a drier finish than Porters or Sweet Stouts.

BEER STATS				
Color	Clarity	Ferment	ABV	Bitterness
Dark brown to black	Bright to opaque	Light fruity	4%–6.5%	25–55 IBU (medium)

GUINNESS DRAUGHT

4.2% ABV	BREWED: DUBLIN, IRELAND

Very few beers are as distinctive and famous as Guinness Draught. It's deep ruby-black with a thick white foam, and by drinking through the foam, you feel a velvety texture, while the foam also holds aromas of cacao, roasted barley, and dark berries. Sniff closely and you might notice there's strawberry and candy-like esters. It's lighter bodied than we expect, with some dark roast and a light coffee-like acidity, before a dry, clean finish.

O'HARA'S BREWERY IRISH STOUT NITRO

4.3% ABV	BREWED: CARLOW, IRELAND

Look for this classic Irish Stout on tap or find the nitro cans for the best drinking experience, where you get the creamy foam that's so distinctive of this style. There's roasted barley, coffee, licorice, and very dark cocoa in the aroma. The silky texture has a fullness like a flat white, and there's smooth roast, plenty of dark malt flavor but no harsh roastiness, with Fuggle hops giving it an herbal and almost menthol freshness with the dryness.

DESCHUTES BREWERY OBSIDIAN STOUT

6.4% ABV	BREWED: BEND, OR, USA

More attention-grabbing than the easy-going Irish brews, American Stout is more robust with malt and hop flavor (perhaps as the Irish drink pint after pint, whereas American drinkers often prefer intensity of flavor). Aromas are of roasted barley, cacao, miso, and some berries or cherries, moving to flavors of espresso, cacao nibs, pure roasted barley, fruity vanilla, and dried fruits, with a firm and lasting bitterness from both malt and hop.

THE KERNEL EXPORT STOUT 1890

7.5% ABV	BREWED: LONDON, ENGLAND

Based on a recipe from 1890, this beer has an impactful depth of brown malt, which was classically used for London dark beers (newer versions introduced roasted barley). There's dark chocolate, dark berries, dried fruits, and molasses, plus tobacco, smoke, and old leather, evoking hints of Victorian London. The beer has layers of complexity, a long-lasting bitter finish from hops, and the distinctive dark toast flavor of brown malt.

OTHER EXAMPLES TO TRY

4 PINES STOUT: rich dark chocolate, light espresso, berry.

PELICAN TSUNAMI EXPORT STOUT: cappuccino, dark chocolate, robust.

GUINNESS FOREIGN EXTRA: creamy dark chocolate, berry, smooth.

SWEET STOUTS

Oatmeal Stout and Milk Stout are
the main styles here, and compared
to Dry Stouts, they have sweeter rather
than roasted-bitter flavor profiles.

PINT   WILLIBECHER

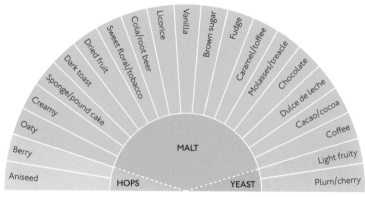

FLAVOR WHEEL

FLAVOR, PROCESS, & STORY

Overall, these tend to be sweeter
and less roasted compared to Dry
Stouts, though they should be
in good balance and not overly
sweet. The sweeter qualities come
from using fewer roasted malts and
adding oats and/or lactose (milk
sugar). They have a full and smooth
texture, with low carbonation, and
some might be infused with nitrogen
(nitro) to make them extra creamy.

In an Oatmeal Stout, 10–20
percent of the recipe is oats, with
darker malts on top to create the
chocolaty flavors. Milk Stouts also
often use oats, as well as lactose,
which might comprise 5–10
percent of the grain bill. Both
have some residual sweetness.
Hops are more for bitterness than
aroma. Additional ingredients like
chocolate, coffee, vanilla, and nuts
are often added.

Oatmeal has been used in
British beers for centuries, but

the Oatmeal Stout didn't arrive
until the late 1800s. It was brewed
and marketed as a nourishing drink
for convalescents and invalids.
Milk Stout was first brewed in
the early 1900s and marketed to
nursing mothers. By the mid-20th
century, these Stouts were
uncommon. Craft beer re-created
them as more flavorful Stouts,
and their popularity lies in their
smooth texture and sweeter
flavor additions.

BEER STATS				
Color	Clarity	Ferment	ABV	Bitterness
Dark brown to black	Bright to opaque	Light fruity	4%–6%	20–40 IBU (low–medium)

LEFT HAND BREWING MILK STOUT NITRO

6% ABV	BREWED: LONGMONT, CO, USA

This has become the textbook-defining example of a Milk Stout. Brewed with lactose, some oats, and a mix of other malts, it's very dark brown with a thick white foam. It's texturally luscious and lovely to drink, with a creamy smooth mouthfeel in the nitro version. There's milk chocolate sweetness, chocolate oatmeal, coffee candy, vanilla, and fudge, finishing with a dusty cocoa and coffee bitterness and a nice dryness.

LOCH LOMOND BREWERY SILKIE STOUT

5% ABV	BREWED: DUMBARTON, SCOTLAND

Silkie Stout is on the roastier side of the style compared to others. Brewed with lots of oats and dark malt, this very dark brown beer with a creamy tan foam has a big flavor of coffee, coffee beans, roasted barley, and dark chocolate oatmeal cookies. It has a robust body, which is both roasted and creamy, with a great complexity of malt depth running through it. High roast works very well with the smoother oats here.

ST-AMBROISE OATMEAL STOUT

5% ABV	BREWED: MONTREAL, CANADA

This beautiful dark beer is regarded as a classic Oatmeal Stout. Aromas are of dark chocolate, cocoa-dusted truffles, sweet coffee, creamy oats, floral vanilla, and molasses. It's got a luxurious chocolate milkshake texture that's silky and smooth but not particularly sweet, and it leaves a lingering dark chocolate and roasted flavor, with some creamy fudge, the distinct flavor of oats, and a dark licorice and berry-like hop depth.

GARAGE PROJECT CEREAL MILK STOUT

4.7% ABV	BREWED: WELLINGTON, NEW ZEALAND

Brewed to evoke the flavors of cereal milk in a Stout, this beer is made with oats, chocolate wheat, lactose, and cornflakes. The aroma is more chocolate cereal than cornflakes, with chocolate, a little sweet roastiness, and some vanilla. While you might not pick out cereal milk if you blind-tasted it, you get a creamy-smooth Stout with background caramel and chocolate notes and an easy-drinking balance for its low ABV.

OTHER EXAMPLES TO TRY

SAMUEL SMITH OATMEAL STOUT: creamy chocolate porridge, light roast.

BRISTOL BEER FACTORY MILK STOUT: milk chocolate, light coffee, creamy.

YOUNG'S DOUBLE CHOCOLATE STOUT: chocolate fudge, vanilla, chocolate syrup.

IMPERIAL STOUT

With an intoxicating mix of rich dark malts and high alcohol, Imperial Stouts are among the best-loved beer styles for those seeking big flavor experiences.

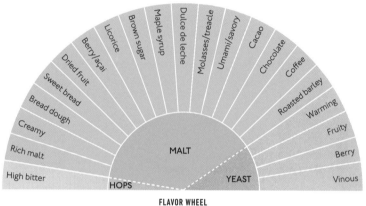

Licorice
Berry/acai
Dried fruit
Sweet bread
Bread dough
Creamy
Rich malt
High bitter
Brown sugar
Maple syrup
Dulce de leche
Molasses/treacle
Umami/savory
Cacao
Chocolate
Coffee
Roasted barley
Warming
Fruity
Berry
Vinous

MALT
HOPS
YEAST

FLAVOR WHEEL

SNIFTER　　**STEMLESS**

FLAVOR, PROCESS, & STORY

Often the strongest and most prestigious beers of a brewery, full-bodied Imperial Stouts give a wide range of dark malt flavors: rich chocolate, cacao, coffee, roasted barley, umami/miso, dark fruits, licorice, aniseed, and sweetness like molasses. Bitterness is often high, though in balance against the higher residual sweetness. They commonly add oats and other ingredients that complement the dark malts, like coffee, vanilla, and chocolate, and are often barrel aged.

Brewers use lots of pale malts, which give the base sweetness. Kilned malts like dark crystal add fruity complexity, then brown, chocolate, and black malt and roasted barley give the dark colors and the roasted flavors. Oats are often used to give a smooth texture, and sugar might be added for flavor and fermentable sweetness. Hops are typically just added for bitterness.

These beers trace their heritage to strong British Porters, or Stout Porters. Brewed for export in the late 1700s, they traveled around the world and were particularly popular in Baltic ports. As tastes changed, Imperial Stout became a rarity by the early 1900s. It was curious and creative craft brewers who brought it back, where it's become a showcase beer style pushing the extremes of brewing.

BEER STATS				
Color	Clarity	Ferment	ABV	Bitterness
Dark brown to black	Bright to light haze	Fruity/warming	8%–15%	30–100 IBU (medium–high)

OSKAR BLUES TEN FIDY

10.5% ABV	BREWED: LONGMONT, CO, USA

A classic American Imperial Stout, it pours a thick black with a dark mocha foam. There's dark chocolate, dark caramel, cacao, espresso, roasted malt, licorice, prunes, some strong hop aromas, and dark fruits, plus spicy vinous alcohol aromas. It's a powerful beer, dark and strong, creamy from some added oats. A high hop bitterness adds some of its own intensity at the end, creating a defining American quality.

FREMONT BREWING DARK STAR

8% ABV	BREWED: SEATTLE, WA, USA

This Imperial Oatmeal Stout is at the lower end of strength for the style, where you get big flavor without the high alcohol. It's a nice contrast to some of the hyper-strong 14+% ABV Stouts. It pours very dark brown with a thick tan foam. There's cacao, vanilla, chocolate-covered raisins, dark chocolate, fermented coffee beans, some miso richness, and an oatmeal texture, plus some floral yeast notes, with the roastiness lasting all the way to the end.

DIEU DU CIEL! PÉCHÉ MORTEL

9.5% ABV	BREWED: MONTREAL, CANADA

This coffee Imperial Stout is great for its depth of flavor, a density of malt richness without it overpowering. It's almost black with a thick dark brown foam. Coffee aroma comes first, with roastiness, mocha, dark chocolate, and some fruity vanilla. The texture has some creamy sweetness that tempers a lot of the dark chocolate, coffee, dark molasses, and the roastiness, which lasts throughout, leading to a strong hop bitterness at the end.

PERENNIAL ARTISAN ALES ABRAXAS

11.5% ABV	BREWED: ST. LOUIS, MO, USA

Imperial Stout allows brewers to be creative with flavor, and Abraxas is inspired by Mexican hot chocolate. It's conditioned on ancho chile, cinnamon, vanilla beans, and cacao nibs. Those ingredients infuse into a beer brewed with lots of dark malts, and it's boiled for a long time to condense those flavors into a richer concentration. The beer has a rich texture and a clever balance of sweet vanilla and chocolate, spice, roast, and warming alcohol.

OTHER EXAMPLES TO TRY

DE STRUISE BLACK ALBERT: dark chocolate, brandy, molasses.

THE KERNEL IMPERIAL BROWN STOUT: cacao, berry, roasted bitterness.

ALESMITH SPEEDWAY STOUT: coffee, fruity cacao, roasted malt.

BARREL-AGED BEER

Barrel aging infuses new characteristics into beers, giving flavors like wood, vanilla, spice, and qualities from the alcohol previously stored in the barrel.

SNIFTER STEMLESS

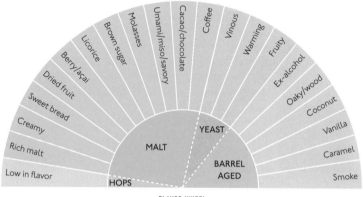

FLAVOR WHEEL

FLAVOR, PROCESS, & STORY

Any beer style can be barrel aged, but it's often Imperial Stouts, Barley Wine, and strong Belgian ales. They are designed to be impactful drinking experiences, combining rich beers with new flavors drawn from the wood (usually oak) and its maturation. Vanillin in oak gives vanilla, and lactones give a creamy nuttiness like toasted coconut and almond.

There's a general fruitiness, some tannin or dryness, dried fruit, caramel, and more alcohol flavor. The alcohol that was previously in the barrel adds its own character, typically bourbon, Scotch whisky, rum, wine, and sherry.

Ingredients depend on the base beer style. After primary fermentation in tank, the beer is transferred into barrels, where it ages for 3 to 12 months or more. As the barrel warms over time, it expands, drawing beer into the wood. As it cools, it squeezes the beer out, which takes the wood flavor with it.

In 1992, Goose Island's Bourbon County Stout was the first beer to be aged in bourbon barrels to take on new flavor, and it created the barrel-aged beer category. Barrels have since become common in breweries. Barrel-aged beers are often made and sold in small volumes, with rareness and a big flavor increasing how highly these beers are rated.

BEER STATS				
Color	Clarity	Ferment	ABV	Bitterness
Deep gold to black	Bright to light haze	Fruity/warming	8%–15%	30–100 IBU (medium–high)

GOOSE ISLAND BOURBON COUNTY STOUT

14.4% ABV	BREWED: CHICAGO, IL, USA

This is decadent, thick black beer, with base flavors of dark fruity cacao, fudge, dark caramel, sweet coffee, and blackberry wine. A mix of ex-bourbon barrels is used to age beer for 8 to 14 months. It absorbs a wide range of new flavors like vanilla (fresh pods and vanilla cake), lots of woody oak, bourbon, aged umami, and sherried nuttiness, cherry, almond, licorice, molasses, and much more. It's an intense, bold, boozy flavor experience.

NEW HOLLAND DRAGON'S MILK

11% ABV	BREWED: HOLLAND, MI, USA

One of the few year-round barrel-aged Imperial Stouts, Dragon's Milk is aged in bourbon barrels for three months, where it picks up the characteristic vanilla, oak, and coconut notes, plus some cola, caramel, chocolate truffle, and roasted barley. It's smooth in texture, but not oversweet, and finishes dry. It's on the restrained side of barrel aging: balanced, nuanced, and more accessible than many others, which can be potent.

HARVIESTOUN BREWERY OLA DUBH 12

8% ABV	BREWED: ALVA, SCOTLAND

Ola Dubh is aged in ex-Highland Park distillery single-malt barrels, and it has an elegance compared to many other Imperial Stouts. The range includes Ola Dubh 12, 14, 16, 18, and 21 (occasionally 30 and 40), with the number denoting the age of the whisky barrels. Each age gives different characteristics to the beer. The 12 is most common, and it's got fruity coffee, vanilla, licorice, and a smokiness that lasts until the end.

LA TRAPPE OAK AGED

11% ABV	BREWED: BERKEL-ENSCHOT, NETHERLANDS

This Trappist Quadrupel is aged for varying amounts of time in different barrels, including virgin oak, toasted oak, whiskey, rum, wine, and port barrels, acacia or cherry wood, and more. Different barrels are blended for each batch, with the brewery's website giving specifics of each blend. Expect dried fruits, berries, spice, vanilla, caramel, and specifics to that blend. They're always interesting, especially if you compare several batches.

OTHER EXAMPLES TO TRY

FIRESTONE WALKER PARABOLA: dark cherry chocolate, rich bourbon.

DE STRUISE CUVÉE DELPHINE: chocolate truffle, berry, vanilla.

ALLAGASH CURIEUX: baked stone fruit, bourbon, vanilla.

SOUR BEERS & FRUIT BEERS

HERE WE'RE CELEBRATING THE great diversity of beer and how it can be both wonderfully traditional and wildly experimental. In this group are some of the world's most traditional and idiosyncratic beer styles, such as Belgian Gueuze and Red-Brown Ales, which are left for years to mature in wooden barrels and develop wonderfully complex flavors. Alongside those are some of the most modern, creative, and fun beers in the world, including refreshingly tart beers that are infused with fresh fruit, and beers using ingredients like chocolate, pumpkin, spices, and so much more.

LAMBIC: A BRUSSELS BEER TRADITION

Lambic and spontaneously fermented beer are a unique expression of a place, taking their character from the brewery's location. Naturally inoculated with wild yeast and bacteria, they're aged and turned sour in wooden barrels until the brewer decides they're ready, then blended to the brewery's desired flavor profile.

BREWING LAMBIC

The fundamentals of brewing a Lambic are the same as for regular ales, but the specifics of each stage are very different. The recipe is 30 to 40 percent unmalted wheat, and classic recipes use a complex turbid mash system, which involves different vessels and temperature steps and breaks down the wheat to leave a milky-looking wort. The wort is high in dextrin sugars that typical ale yeast won't ferment but that wild yeast and bacteria can ferment. The sugars help ensure the beer can age for a long time without spoiling, enabling it to fully attenuate and become very dry.

BREWERS & BLENDERS

In the region around Brussels, where the production of Lambic has been preserved and is now celebrated, there are both brewers and blenders. Brewers make and ferment the wort themselves; blenders buy the wort from different brewers and mature then blend it themselves to sell under their own name.

HOW LAMBIC IS MADE

The Lambic brewing process is unique for letting the wort become inoculated with wild airborne yeast and bacteria.

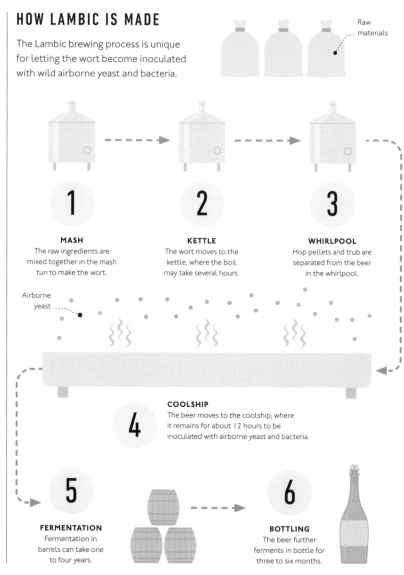

Raw materials

1

MASH
The raw ingredients are mixed together in the mash tun to make the wort.

2

KETTLE
The wort moves to the kettle, where the boil may take several hours.

3

WHIRLPOOL
Hop pellets and trub are separated from the beer in the whirlpool.

Airborne yeast

4

COOLSHIP
The beer moves to the coolship, where it remains for about 12 hours to be inoculated with airborne yeast and bacteria.

5

FERMENTATION
Fermentation in barrels can take one to four years.

6

BOTTLING
The beer further ferments in bottle for three to six months.

The wort moves to the kettle, where the boil may take up to three hours. It uses hops that have been aged for two to three years. The hops have antibacterial qualities—they let good bacteria through but block potentially bad ones—but don't contribute much flavor and bitterness.

The hopped wort travels to the coolship, an open pan often high up in the brewery. It's left there overnight to cool and to allow yeast and bacteria native to the brewery to inoculate and start the fermentation spontaneously. In the morning, the Lambic is poured into barrels where fermentation continues.

Ale yeast is most active at the beginning of fermentation, creating the alcohol over the first two weeks before it runs out of malt sugars. Then the *Brettanomyces* and bacteria take over, slowly converting the remaining sugars and gradually increasing the esters, aromas, lactic acid, and acidity.

The flavor changes throughout, and each individual barrel matures differently thanks to the resident microorganisms in the wood. The beer stays in the barrels until the brewer decides it's ready, which could be up to four years.

BLENDING & BOTTLING

Most Lambic isn't drunk as Lambic: it's blended into Gueuze or a fruited beer. Lambic brewers will taste many different barrels and decide on how to combine them to achieve the correct flavor profile. Most Gueuze is a mix of one-, two-, and three-year-old Lambic, but some older barrels might be used. The beer is blended in a steel tank and put into cork-topped bottles with a priming sugar, where the beer will ferment further for three to six months, when it develops a high carbonation similar to Champagne.

INTERNATIONAL SPONTANEOUSLY FERMENTED BEER

Inspired by the Belgian tradition, brewers around the world have installed, or repurposed, coolships to produce spontaneously fermented beer. They use the same processes as the Brussels brewers and produce new expressions and variations on these much-admired beers.

LAMBIC

Lambic can be drunk young (about a year) or old (more than a year). It's uncarbonated and usually a draft-only product, sometimes decanted into jugs and then into the glass. It's often only found in bars close to Lambic producers.

GUEUZE

Gueuze (also spelled Geuze) usually has a mix of young and old Lambic to create a balanced flavor profile determined by the brewery's own preference. When served, the beer is often opened and laid down in a Lambic basket so that the yeast sediment in the bottom of the bottle isn't disturbed.

KRIEK & FRAMBOISE

Cherries (Kriek) and raspberries (Framboise) can be added to young Lambic, giving more fermentable sugars and imbuing the beer with a bright red or pink color. Other fruits such as different berries, grapes, or apricots can also be added. The Lambic can sit on the fruit for 4 to 12 months.

SPONTANEOUSLY FERMENTED BEERS

These traditional sour Belgian and Belgian-inspired beers are among the most complex and revered beers in the world.

BELGIAN TUMBLER   STEMMED

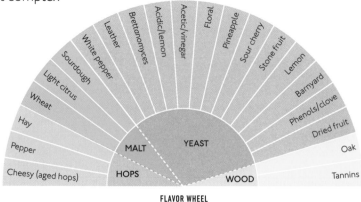

Leather
White pepper
Sourdough
Light citrus
Wheat
Hay
Pepper
Cheesy (aged hops)
Brettanomyces
Acidic/lemon
Acetic/vinegar
Floral
Pineapple
Sour cherry
Stone fruit
Lemon
Barnyard
Phenols/clove
Dried fruit
Oak
Tannins

MALT
YEAST
HOPS
WOOD

FLAVOR WHEEL

FLAVOR, PROCESS, & STORY

These beers undergo a long maturation, when flavors from wild yeast, bacteria, and the aging process produce a wide range of characteristics, from fruity lemon and tropical fruits to funky farm-like aromas and phenolic clove. Each beer shows a unique quality from the microflora that ferments it. Acidity could be tart or puckering, but the best are balanced. They are dry and typically highly carbonated, with tannins from the wood aging rather than hop bitterness.

The base beer in traditional Belgian versions is Lambic (see pp.182–183). It's brewed with pale malt and 30–40 percent wheat and unmalted wheat, plus aged hops. It naturally becomes inoculated with yeast and bacteria, starting a spontaneous fermentation. It might mature in wooden barrels for years, before being blended and bottled, where it carbonates in the bottle. The blended beer is known as Gueuze.

Belgium has a long history of brewing beers with a tart quality. This style almost disappeared in the 20th century thanks to the growing popularity of clean (not sour) dry ales and lagers. A small group of brewers preserved the processes, and in recent years, brewers around the world have been replicating those traditional Belgian methods.

BEER STATS				
Color	Clarity	Ferment	ABV	Bitterness
Straw to deep amber	Light haze	Tart/sour with *Brett*	4%–8%	5–15 IBU (low)

CANTILLON GUEUZE

5.5% ABV	BREWED: BRUSSELS, BELGIUM

Light amber in color, there's funky and preserved lemon, something like earthy ripe cheese (think brie), hay, farmyard, general tart fruits, and some phenolic complexity—it's a beer that is layered with flavor. It's immediately tart with an upfront intensity that mellows as you drink, with some sweeter grain flavors working with fruitier notes to temper the acid. It has a woody and tannic bitterness. The carbonation is bright and refreshing.

OUDE GEUZE BOON

7% ABV	BREWED: LEMBEEK, BELGIUM

Golden amber with lasting foam and lots of bubbles, Boon's Oude Geuze has fresh lemon, fragrant floral citrus notes, berries and stone fruit, and a vibrant tart fruit freshness with a grapefruit complexity that also evokes the dryness and bitterness of grapefruit pith. It's drying at the end, with wood and tannins, an herbal and woody bitterness, with pepper and lemon peel. It's wonderfully elegant, with less farmyard and phenols compared to Cantillon.

BURNING SKY COOLSHIP

6.5% ABV	BREWED: FIRLE, ENGLAND

Classically brewed like a Belgian Gueuze, this beer is a deep amber color, with a freshness and a hint of farminess, flowers and barns, dried lemons, old wood, and leather. It's elegant and balanced, the tartness mellowed by a little sweetness, a woody bitterness softened by a creamy quality on the palate. It's got the kind of complexity that reveals something new with each sip and feels fresher and more vibrant than others.

ALLAGASH COOLSHIP RESURGAM

6.3% ABV	BREWED: PORTLAND, ME, USA

A Gueuze-style beer made with a blend of one-, two-, and three-year-old beer, it has a bright mix of tart apricots, tangy peach skin, dried pineapple, and tepache, with the tropical notes from the local microflora making it stand out from Belgian brews. There's some lemon curd, lemon pith, white wine, floral esters, something a little creamy like lemon yogurt, and an underlying mix of phenols, wood tannins, and oak and a drying crisp finish.

OTHER EXAMPLES TO TRY

3 FONTEINEN OUDE GEUZE: lemon, tart apple, more fruit than funk.

OUD BEERSEL OUDE GEUZE VIEILLE: grape, tart tropical, peach, wood.

RUSSIAN RIVER SONAMBIC: tart lemon, white wine, oak tannin.

FLEMISH-STYLE RED-BROWN ALES

These beers have an acetic and vinous quality from yeast, bacteria, and a long maturation, giving some the nickname the "Burgundy of Beer."

BELGIAN TUMBLER **STEMMED**

FLAVOR WHEEL

Flavor wheel labels: Cola, Dried fruit, Berries, Brettanomyces, Vinous, Plum, Banana, Acetic vinegar, Sour cherry, Phenols/clove, Dried fruit, Vanilla, Oaky, Tannins, Ex-alcohol, Caramel, Sourdough, Wheat, Peppery, Hay, Floral, MALT, YEAST, HOPS, WOOD

FLAVOR, PROCESS, & STORY

These soured and aged red to brown beers have a flavor mix of sweeter malt, fruity fermentation, acetic tartness, and the character of maturation. They should be in sweet-sour balance overall, where a residual sweetness gives flavors of berry, apple, cherry, cola, caramel, and chocolate. Aged in steel tanks or ex-wine or bourbon barrels, they show a balsamic vinegar, vinous, and sherry-like flavor. They could have different fruits added. Compared to Lambic, they have more malt flavor, more berry fruits, and a different acidity.

Color comes from pale and colored malts together. Hops are for light bitterness but not aromatic impact, and aged hops might be used. Most of these beers have a primary fermentation with ale yeast in steel tanks, before moving into another vessel. There they mix with wild yeast and bacteria during their maturation. Brewers might add fruit, often berries or cherries. Young and old beers are blended together to create the intended balance.

These beers emerged as a way of storing and maturing beer, with vinous notes developing over time. It was a well-regarded Flemish style until the mid-20th century, and a few dedicated brewers have maintained it, with craft beer creating a renewed interest.

BEER STATS				
Color	Clarity	Ferment	ABV	Bitterness
Amber red to brown	Light haze	Tart/sour with *Brett*	4%–9%	5–15 IBU (low)

RODENBACH GRAND CRU

6% ABV | BREWED: ROESELARE, BELGIUM

The classic Flemish Red-Brown, *Grand Cru* blends two-thirds *foudre*-matured beer (aged up to two years) with one-third fresh beer. It's layered with fruitiness, then sweetness, then tartness, and given character through the aged flavor. It has an expansive palate of cherries, berries, vanilla, cola, apple and pear, strawberry candy, cherry brandy, sherry, sweet balsamic, vinous dark chocolate, a wine-like fruitiness, and a lasting dry finish.

VERHAEGHE DUCHESSE DE BOURGOGNE

6.2% ABV | BREWED: VICHTE, BELGIUM

Fermented in tanks, then matured in oak, Duchesse de Bourgogne is another classic Red-Brown beer. A blend of young and *foudre*-aged beer, it has a palate of red fruits, cherries, and berries, giving sweetness and tartness at the same time. There's some light spice and tangy Bramley apples, it's vinous with sherry and oak, caramel and balsamic, and wood tannin, with underlying malt flavor keeping it in sour-sweet balance.

NEW BELGIUM LA FOLIE

7% ABV | BREWED: FORT COLLINS, CO, USA

A classic American interpretation, La Folie is matured in large oak *foudres* and has its own particular *terroir* (accent), having been produced for many years. It's got a fruity sweetness and sourness, like cherry, plum, apple, and cranberry. The body has a fullness and richness, carrying some toast, caramel, and raisin, before it all dries out to a quenching tartness at the end, which might make you pucker on the first sip, but mellows as you drink.

DE DOLLE BROUWERS OERBIER

9% ABV | BREWED: ESEN, BELGIUM

Oerbier is different. It's a deep red-brown color, and it develops a tartness as it ages in bottle with its house culture of bacteria. It's not intensely soured and nor is it wood matured. It undergoes a long boil, creating a caramelized depth in the beer, alongside dark cherry, plum, cola turned tart, vanilla, toast, and dried fruit, all cut through and lifted by a hint of almost creamy acidity. Golding hops give a spicy and notable bitterness.

OTHER EXAMPLES TO TRY

LIEFMANS GOUDENBAND: dried fruit, cherry, apple, vinous, sherry.

RUSSIAN RIVER SUPPLICATION: cherry lemonade, vanilla, wood tannin.

WICKED WEED OBLIVION: rich fruit, berry jam, balsamic, oak.

TRADITIONAL FRUIT SOURS

These are traditionally brewed Belgian-style soured beers, Lambic or Red-Brown, aged with fruits, giving a fresh fruitiness above a tart base.

BELGIAN TUMBLER   STEMMED

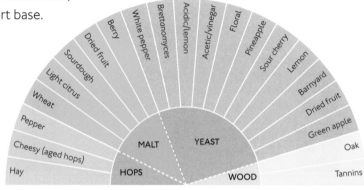

FLAVOR WHEEL

FLAVOR, PROCESS, & STORY

Alongside the funky, tart, and naturally fruity flavors of the base beer, the addition of fresh fruit contributes new flavors and changes the color. The best balance fruitiness with tartness and are not oversweet. The fruits present with secondary qualities like fruit pips and stones. Cherries (Kriek) and raspberries (Framboise) are most common, but you'll also find berries, peaches, apricots, grapes, and plums. They finish dry, crisp, and refreshingly tart.

The base beer is a regular Lambic or Red-Brown, matured for several months up to a couple of years. Fruit is added into the maturing vessel, wood or steel, then the beer is further aged for a few months up to a year. The addition of fruit continues the fermentation as the yeast consumes the fruit sugars. The beer is usually blended with unfruited base beer before bottling.

Kriek (cherry Lambic) has been brewed around Brussels since the early 19th century. Whole stone-in fruit is the typical method, though some larger brewers might use fruit juice, puree, or even flavorings. Most traditional fruited sour beers should be drunk soon after they're put on sale by the brewery, especially those made with stone fruit, to get the best expression of the fruit.

BEER STATS				
Color	Clarity	Ferment	ABV	Bitterness
Yellow to red/purple	Light haze	Tart/sour with *Brett*	4%–8%	5–15 IBU (low)

BOON KRIEK MARIAGE PARFAIT

8% ABV	BREWED: LEMBEEK, BELGIUM

Kriek Mariage Parfait is a strong aged Lambic with 14 oz (400 g) per liter of cherry added. It's deep red and abundant with cherries in the aroma: tart cherry, cherry jam, and cherry Bakewell tart, which leads to almond and vanilla notes. The tartness is subtle, like a sour cherry, while the natural fruit sweetness gives body and depth. The carbonation is like a rosé Champagne, with underlying oak complexity.

CANTILLON FOU'FOUNE

6% ABV	BREWED: BRUSSELS, BELGIUM

Brewed with Bergeron apricots, the fruit is macerated with aged Lambic in steel tanks for a few months, then blended with more Lambic when it's bottled. It's a hazy apricot-colored beer with a wide spectrum of apricots in the aroma: fresh, fleshy, dried apricot and apricot and lemon marmalade. It's tart but balanced by the fruitiness. There's oak, apricot skin, and wood tannins, plus some underlying wheat cracker malt.

OUDE QUETSCHE TILQUIN À L'ANCIENNE

6.4% ABV	BREWED: BIERGHES, BELGIUM

Oak-aged Lambic of one to two years old has fresh purple plums (which are closely related to the damson) added and is further aged in steel for four months. It's got a floral and fresh aroma of biting into a ripe plum. There's some tartness, sweetness like a tangy prune, and some tannin from the plum skin and oak aging, with some vinous, tartly fruity, tangy apple and aged cheese complexity beneath it all.

NEW GLARUS RASPBERRY TART

4% ABV	BREWED: NEW GLARUS, WI, USA

Where some soured and aged beers can be challenging, Raspberry Tart is a glass of pure, fresh raspberries. It's a deep red beer, brewed in the Red-Brown style, and aged in wood, giving some oak, vanilla, and lemony funk. The beer is more sweet than sour, in a natural fruit-sweet way, and smells like raspberry jam. The tartness is light like a zingy raspberry candy, while the texture is both refreshing and also quite full and smooth.

OTHER EXAMPLES TO TRY

3 FONTEINEN SCHAARBEEKSE KRIEK: bright sweet cherry, almond, lemon.

CANTILLON SAINT LAMVINUS: red grapes, vanilla oak, berry, tart.

ALLAGASH COOLSHIP RED: raspberry lemonade, vanilla, oak, berry tartness.

MIXED FERMENTATION & WILD ALES

Brewed using a mix of yeast and bacteria and matured in wooden barrels, these are craft beer's evolution of traditional Belgian sour beers.

STEMLESS   STEMMED

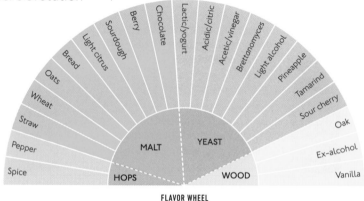

FLAVOR WHEEL

FLAVOR, PROCESS, & STORY

There's no single way to describe these beers. They are usually fermented with more than a typical beer yeast and are matured to develop aged character plus wild yeast's aromas and bacteria's acidity. The base beer determines underlying flavor. Yeast and bacteria give fruity or funky esters and sometimes spicy phenols. The beers could be lightly tart to mouth-puckering. Carbonation is often quite high. They might use fruits. Wood, if used, can be part of the flavor profile.

Recipes vary depending on the base beer. Hops are usually very low. Many beers undergo a primary fermentation using a regular yeast. Then they are matured, becoming inoculated with different yeasts and bacteria. They are often aged in ex-wine or whiskey barrels, though some are also made in stainless steel tanks. Adding fruit is common. Blending is an important part of getting the right flavor profile.

These beers could be called Mixed Fermentation, Wild Ale, American Wild/Sour, or Brett Ale (made with just *Brettanomyces* and no bacteria). They're often inspired by the flavor profile of Lambic but could also be like a soured Stout. The best achieve a wonderful balance of flavor, depth, and complexity without any single part of the process overpowering.

BEER STATS				
Color	Clarity	Ferment	ABV	Bitterness
Straw to dark brown	Bright to light haze	Tart/sour with *Brett*	4%–8%	5–15 IBU (low)

RUSSIAN RIVER TEMPTATION

7.5% ABV	BREWED: WINDSOR, CA, USA

Made in barrels that previously held Sonoma County Chardonnay, the wine and a grape quality are evident alongside fresh lemon and dried lemon. There's floral vanilla, a rich palate of light tart fruits, and a little tangy orange. The acidity spikes early, then it eases back and gives a freshness to the underlying fruity flavors, with some alcohol and sweetness in the back. Some wood tannins and a hint of peppery spice give a nice cut to the finish.

CASCADE BREWING APRICOT

7%–8% ABV	BREWED: PORTLAND, OR, USA

Apricot is a blend of Blonde Ales soured in old wine barrels with fresh local apricots. It's got a vibrant apricot aroma—tart fresh fruit, sweet dried apricots, a creamy quality, apricot jam, and the floral and tannins of apricot skin. Around that there's some lemon yogurt-like acidity, fermented pineapple, and light woody spice. The finish is like biting into an underripe apricot, with tannins, tartness, and fruit and some lactic acidity.

LOVERBEER BEERBERA

8% ABV	BREWED: MARENTINO, ITALY

This "Italian Grape Ale" is a reddish base brew with Barbera grape juice and skin added into wooden barrels, and microflora on the grapes spontaneously starting the fermentation. It has a vibrant red fruit nose of cranberry, cherry, and red grape, but around that is the wild yeast and aged character, giving tart lemon, balsamic vinegar, vinous dried fruit, and some wild yeast funkiness like old leather or hay. Tannins keep it dry at the end.

THE KERNEL BIÈRE DE SAISON

4.4%–6% ABV	BREWED: LONDON, ENGLAND

Brewed with the Kernel's house mixed-culture yeast, it gets tart and dry in tank before being aged in different wooden vessels. It usually contains additional fruit (often apricot, damson plum, apple, or cherry) or might be dry hopped (check the details on the label). The beer is always tart and dry, there's underlying wood, black pepper, and some curry spice, with the added fruit or hops giving their extra flavors.

OTHER EXAMPLES TO TRY

CROOKED STAVE PETITE SOUR RASPBERRY: fresh berry, refreshingly tart.

SIDE PROJECT FUZZY: juicy peach, lemon zest, tropical, oak.

THE BRUERY TART OF DARKNESS: tart espresso, berry, oak, vanilla.

BERLINER WEISSE & GOSE

The "fast sours" are light German-style wheat beers with a refreshing acidity, often brewed with added fruits or dry hops.

BELGIAN TUMBLER   STEMMED

FLAVOR WHEEL

Flavor wheel segments: Straw, Bread, Light citrus, Lemon, Lactic/yogurt, Acidic/citrus, Fruity esters, Stone fruit, Plum, Banana, Berry, Pineapple, Coriander (Gose), Salt (Gose), Added fruits, Oats, Wheat, Citrus, Tropical, Floral, Low to no bitter. MALT, YEAST, HOPS, OTHER.

FLAVOR, PROCESS, & STORY

These low-alcohol, light, dry, and refreshingly tart beers have become a favorite with many brewers. Berliner Weisse could be brewed with *Brettanomyces* but is rarely aged so is more fruity than funky. *Brett* or not, it has a crisp, lemony finish. A classic Gose is similar at its base and contains added coriander and salt, giving a floral and fruity aroma and a light salinity against a lactic acid tartness. Additional ingredients can become a major part of the flavor profiles.

This style is brewed with around half and half Pilsner malt and wheat. Hops are very light in bitterness but might be used aromatically as a dry hop. Acidity can come from the kettle sour method (see p.65), adding *Lactobacillus* (or a mixed fermentation with *Brettanomyces* in a Berliner Weisse), or from simply adding lactic acid. As "fast sours," they are brewed within a few weeks.

North Germany has a long history of brewing light, tart wheat ales. Berliner Weisse used to contain *Brettanomyces*, but as a taste for cleaner beers spread, it became like a tart Pilsner. Now Berliner brewers are bringing back the old-style Weisse, while craft brewers add fruit. Gose is known as a beer from Leipzig but has history in Goslar before it.

BEER STATS				
Color	Clarity	Ferment	ABV	Bitterness
Straw to yellow	Light haze to cloudy	Fruity/tart sometimes *Brett*	3%–5+%	5–15 IBU (low)

BRAUEREI LEMKE BUDIKE WEISSE

3.5% ABV	BREWED: BERLIN, GERMANY

An old-style Berliner Weisse brewed with *Brettanomyces* and *Lactobacillus*, it's very pale yellow with a light spritz of bubbles. The aroma is fresh with green apples, tart raspberry lemonade, light lemon, lemon zest, and a floral note, and as the *Brett* is young, it gives only a hint of farmhouse funkiness with some tart and tangy apples. It's light and refreshing, with a little zing of lemon candy at the end.

DIEU DU CIEL SOLSTICE D'ÉTÉ FRAMBOISE

5.9% ABV	BREWED: MONTREAL, CANADA

This raspberry-infused Berliner Weisse is a kettle sour, with a restrained lactic yogurt-like acidity and a dry, crisp, and refreshing finish. The addition of fresh raspberries turns the beer bright pink and gives a lovely mix of raspberry flavor—fruit, pips, jam, and sorbet. It's fresh but not sweet. There's some light wheat character, a creaminess to the texture, some fruit sweetness, and it's all in a wonderful balance of fruity and tart.

DÖLLNITZER RITTERGUTS GOSE

4.2% ABV	BREWED: LEIPZIG, GERMANY

In this classic Gose, the toasted coriander is floral and spicy with orange peel and dried lemon aromas, while an underlying wheat dough sweetness enhances that orange note. The saltiness is quite prominent—it's not salty, but you know there's salt in there. It adds a savory background that seems to mellow the acidity while also suggesting a richer mouthfeel. It's refreshing with a lasting spicy finish and a quench of lactic acid.

WESTBROOK BREWING GOSE

4% ABV	BREWED: MOUNT PLEASANT, SC, USA

Westbrook brews a rare example of a straight-up Gose. It has a rich fullness to the texture, more so than Goslar-brewed versions, aided by the salt in the beer, which gives a greater depth—in the same way salt enhances food flavor. The coriander is distinctively of toasted seeds, plus some dried orange and floral notes. There's a lemony freshness and tartness, and something reminiscent of salted yogurt drink. It's very moreish.

OTHER EXAMPLES TO TRY

SCHNEEEULE MARLENE: lemon tart, stone fruit, light fruity *Brett*.

SIREN CALYPSO: tropical hops, light lemon, zingy fresh.

CREATURE COMFORTS TRITONIA: cucumber, lime, light lemon tart.

MODERN FRUIT & ADJUNCT SOURS

Inspired by desserts and dominated by the flavor of fruits and other ingredients, these beers are often more sweet than sour.

STEMLESS   STEMMED

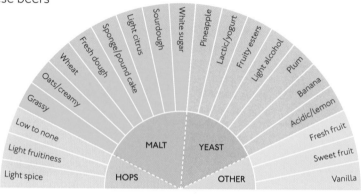

FLAVOR WHEEL

FLAVOR, PROCESS, & STORY

Fruit or other adjuncts give the main aromas and flavors. They can range from lightly tart, dry, and refreshing all the way to beers reminiscent of a boozy fruit smoothie. They are typically designed more for their fruity flavors rather than for depth and complexity, and the best versions tend to be those with the highest volume of fruit.

Base beers are usually approximations of the Berliner Weisse or Gose style with color coming from the fruit. Wheat and oats add more texture. The additional ingredients might be fresh, frozen, puree, extract, or essence; the fruitiest versions use puree. Acidity is low in many, with most tending toward a sweeter flavor profile, though some have a more subtle fruit addition. Some might be hopped for aroma.

As brewers seek more impactful flavored beers, they often add large amounts of flavorful ingredients. Adding fruits and spices to beer has a long history. A shift occurred in the late 2010s, however, and now these beers are intensely fruity rather than subtly flavored. They are more likely to take inspiration from candy, cereals, and tropical smoothies than from historical brewing. Brewers are constantly innovating with the flavors they put into their beer.

BEER STATS				
Color	Clarity	Ferment	ABV	Bitterness
Depending on style/fruit	Light haze to opaque	Fruity to tart	3%–8+%	5–15 IBU (low)

OMNIPOLLO BIANCA MANGO LASSI GOSE

6% ABV	BREWED: SUNDBYBERG, SWEDEN

Omnipollo helped create the genre of intensely flavored, adjunct-packed, dessert-inspired beers. Bianca is a Mango Lassi Gose brewed with mango, lactose, and salt. It's a thick beer that looks and has the texture of mango juice. It's got a creamy mango nose, like mango ice cream, and it's a sweet fruit beer with the salt adding just a little richness, before an acidity reminiscent of green mango and a squeeze of lemon.

MORTALIS BREWING CO. MEDUSA

5% ABV	BREWED: AVON, NY, USA

This opaque red sour ale is brewed with passion fruit and dragon fruit. It's a sweetly tropical aroma, mostly of passion fruit, but also some general fruitiness like pineapple and overripe mango and the sweetly floral and melon-like aroma of dragon fruit. It's got a characteristic juice-like texture, rich with fruit sweetness, but it's not too heavy and has a background acidity that cuts through as a sharp contrast to the sweetness.

VAULT CITY STRAWBERRY SKIES

8.5% ABV	BREWED: EDINBURGH, SCOTLAND

Think strawberries and cream—fresh Scottish strawberries are pureed and mixed into a sweet, strong base beer along with hibiscus and vanilla. The sweet beer enhances the fruitiness, and you get a strawberry candy kind of flavor, thick strawberry smoothie mouthfeel, lots of lovely creamy vanilla, which also makes it seem more dessert-like, a creamy oat richness, and just a little bit of acidity to cut it at the end.

SIERRA NEVADA WILD LITTLE THING

5.5% ABV	BREWED: CHICO, CA, USA

At the crisper and lighter end of the style's spectrum, this is brewed with guava, hibiscus, and strawberry. In many ways, it drinks like a glass of fresh, low-alcohol rosé wine. It's a light blush pink, the aroma is nostalgic of children's sodas or ice pops, with the guava and strawberry coming through clearly. It's got the sweetness and tartness of a just-ripe strawberry. The base malt is crisp, leading to a dry finish with some lasting fruit flavors.

OTHER EXAMPLES TO TRY

J. WAKEFIELD BREWING DFPF: dragon fruit, passion fruit, tropical tartness.

THE VEIL NEVER SERIES: thick fruit smoothie, juicy and tart.

CERVEJARIA DOGMA SOURMIND SERIES: sweet and sour, creamy tropical fruit.

FLAVORED BEERS

A long list of ingredients can be added to beer, transforming the base style with new flavors that range from light and refreshing to the beer equivalent of dessert.

STEMLESS   STEMMED

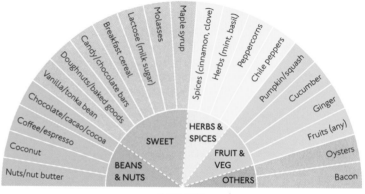

FLAVOR WHEEL

FLAVOR, PROCESS, & STORY

Any beer style can have other ingredients added to it. The underlying beer style should be evident, but typically the primary flavors are from the additional ingredients. Classic examples use, for example, coffee and spice to enhance other qualities in the beer, while the most highly flavored beers now veer into a new, very sweet category known as Pastry (usually Pastry Stout).

The most common ingredients include coffee, chocolate, coconut, vanilla, maple syrup, lactose, nuts and peanut butter, vegetables, fruits, spices, and much more. Sometimes the pure ingredient is added and infused—like shots of espresso, whole coffee beans, or roasted pumpkin. Other times, it's an extracted flavoring for maximum impact.

The style comes from craft beer's never-ending search for beers with ever-more flavor. In the past, the flavors were subtle

additions, and many examples still exist like this. Alongside them are many beers that have gotten sweeter, richer, and stronger. The ones listed opposite are a mix of common types of flavor additions. Along with Modern Fruit Sours, Flavored Beers have become among the highest-rated beers in the world, often esteemed by newer drinkers, though lovers of traditional styles tend to dislike these beers.

		BEER STATS		
Color	Clarity	Ferment	ABV	Bitterness
According to base style	According to base style	According to base style	0.5%–12+%	0–100 IBU (none–very high)

SIREN BROKEN DREAM

6.5% ABV	BREWED: FINCHAMPSTEAD, ENGLAND

This "Breakfast Stout" is brewed with oats, milk sugar, and espresso. The aroma is like walking into a coffee shop, with espresso and freshly ground beans, a hint of old coffee grounds, and some toasting bread. The coffee flavor runs through it but it's nicely balanced and weaves in and out of the dark malt flavor, which gives some chocolate, toast, chocolate oatmeal, and roasted and light smoked notes. Residual sweetness gives some extra body.

MAUI BREWING COCONUT HIWA PORTER

6% ABV	BREWED: MAUI, HI, USA

One of the original beers to use toasted coconut, it's still one of the best examples of how well coconut works in a beer. Toasting it gives a nuttiness alongside the coconut flavor, which also brings a hint of creaminess. It's perfect in a chocolaty porter, which has notes of fudge, mocha, and cocoa and is low in roast and bitterness. Some residual sweetness pushes forward the coconut flavor. It has a light, dry finish for a mid-strength dark beer.

ELYSIAN BREWING NIGHT OWL

6.7% ABV	BREWED: SEATTLE, WA, USA

Pumpkin Beer is one of North America's main seasonals, arriving in early fall and running until Thanksgiving. Elysian has become a pumpkin specialist. A deep orange color, Night Owl is made with lots of pumpkin puree, pumpkin seeds, ginger, cinnamon, nutmeg, cloves, and allspice. The spices dominate the aroma with a hearty and warming scent, and the pumpkin adds sweetness, texture, and earthiness to the base brew.

OMNIPOLLO NOA PECAN MUD CAKE STOUT

11% ABV	BREWED: SUNDBYBERG, SWEDEN

A thick black pour, this is liquid chocolate pudding and a heady smell of nostalgia. The beer is decadently rich and sweet, thick in texture, oily, with flavors of chocolate, molasses, brown sugar, pecan pie, some darker fruits, and a boozy chocolate finish. Most of those flavors seem like they're from flavorings, and not exactly natural, but that's what this beer is trying to evoke: the flavor of childhood chocolate bars.

OTHER EXAMPLES TO TRY

SALTAIRE TRIPLE CHOC: cocoa, milk chocolate, light roast.

TREE HOUSE BREWING IMPERMANENCE: creamy milk chocolate, maple syrup.

SAINT ARNOLD BREWING PUMPKINATOR: intense pumpkin, pumpkin spice, molasses.

LOW- & NO-ALCOHOL BEERS

Low- and no-alcohol brews are growing in variety and quality, becoming an exciting new category of beer.

INGREDIENTS & PROCESS

Beer with 0.0%–0.5% ABV or less is classed as being alcohol free in most countries. Many nonalcoholic beers have a trace amount of alcohol in them, mostly for flavor. Low-alcohol beer is typically anything under 2% ABV, but there's not often a legal guideline. Any beer style can be made low alcohol or alcohol free.

Brewers typically use the standard ingredients. They sometimes add lactose to give more body, while higher protein grains like wheat might also be used to help with the beer's body. Sometimes brewers add hop oils to create the hop aroma.

Four different methods are used to brew low- or nonalcoholic beer. In **dealcoholization**, a regular beer is brewed to about 5% ABV and allowed to ferment and mature as usual, then the alcohol is removed. One process is reverse osmosis, which essentially separates water and alcohol from the beer, leaving a kind of beer concentrate. The alcohol is stripped away and the water is blended back to the concentrate. The other technique involves boiling the alcohol out. Alcohol has a lower boiling point than water (172°F/78°C), so heating beer can "boil" or vaporize the alcohol, but heating to such a high temperature can also cook and change the beer flavors.

A better process for keeping flavor is vacuum distillation, which holds the beer at a lower pressure, and that lowers the alcohol boiling point closer to 104°F (40°C).

Limited fermentation is a method that limits the fermentable sugars in beer and controls fermentation to a low percentage. It's done by a combination of using grains with fewer fermentable starches (like certain malts, rice, and corn), using mash techniques that produce fewer sugars, using special yeasts that don't ferment maltose, and by stopping the fermentation by lowering the temperature.

Dilution and **fermentation free** are less common methods that tend to produce inferior beer. Dilution blends water into an alcoholic beer to get it to 0.5% ABV. Fermentation free are essentially beer-flavored sodas, using extract ingredients to mimic beer.

GUINNESS DRAUGHT 0.0

0.0% ABV	BREWED: DUBLIN, IRELAND

This is an impressive brew that captures the aroma, flavor, and drinking qualities of Guinness without the alcohol (it's removed by reverse osmosis). Pouring ruby black with bubbles cascading up to a white foam, it has Guinness's lightly fruity aroma mixing with some dusty cocoa notes. It has the smoothness initially, though a little lighter in texture overall, with a hint of coffee or berrylike tartness and a woody, peppery dryness at the end.

LUCKY SAINT

0.5% ABV	BREWED: GERMANY

Brewed in Germany and sold in Britain, this is reminiscent of great Bavarian lagers minus the alcohol. A hazy golden color with a lasting foam, it's brewed using vacuum distillation, which allows it to maintain a malty flavor, while modern German hops give a light fruity and dried lemon quality that combines with lemony fruitiness in the beer's finish. The carbonation and texture are exactly what you want from a lager.

ERDINGER ALKOHOLFREI

0.5% ABV	BREWED: ERDING, GERMANY

Alcohol-free Hefeweizen is very popular, and it works well as a nonalcoholic style because of its fuller texture and natural perceived sweetness. This pours a hazy orange-gold color with lots of foam. It has aromas of orange and lemon, almost like orange sponge cake. The fullish body has a light wort-like sweetness, a hint of citrus acidity, and then some fruitiness at the end. It's refreshing, thirst-quenching, and satisfying.

ATHLETIC BREWING CO. RUN WILD

0.5% ABV	BREWED: STRATFORD, CT, & SAN DIEGO, CA, USA

This hazy, deep gold American IPA leads with citrus peel, pine, grapefruit, and floral honey aromas. Those are above a body that has a satisfying and smooth texture plus a refreshing carbonation, leaving behind tangy citrus, black tea, and some resinous, peppery pine. There's a touch of sweetness in this but it's balanced with a lasting hop bitterness. Athletic also brews many other great alcohol-free beers.

OTHER EXAMPLES TO TRY

BROOKLYN SPECIAL EFFECTS: sweet citrus, honey, sweet tea.

BREWDOG HAZY AF: juicy tropical fruits, wheat, crisp.

LOWTIDE BREWING WEST COAST HOP LOCK: orange, peach, dry bitterness.

WHEAT BEERS & BELGIAN ALES

THE DEFINING CHARACTERISTICS OF these beers are those of yeast and fermentation, giving distinctive fruity and spicy aromas. In this group are many classic beer styles that come from old European brewing traditions, including German Hefeweizen, Dunkelweizen, and stronger Weizenbocks, plus the wonderful and wide range of Belgian-style ales, from zesty Witbiers and refreshing Blondes to spicy Saisons, raisiny Dubbels, bitter and fruity Tripels, and strong, rich Quadrupels.

HEFEWEIZEN

Especially popular in Bavaria, these German-style wheat beers are known for their distinct banana-like yeast aroma, high carbonation, smooth mouthfeel, and refreshing finish.

WEIZEN

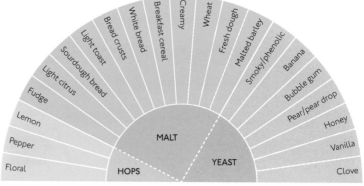

FLAVOR WHEEL

FLAVOR, PROCESS, & STORY

Bananas! That's often the first impression of a Weissbier (or Weizen, Hefeweizen), thanks to a yeast that produces isoamyl acetate, an ester that is a flavor compound in bananas. The yeast makes other esters such as pear, rose, honey, and vanilla, plus varying amounts of spicy, clove-like phenols. The wheat imparts a smooth, sometimes creamy texture and a hint of fruity tartness. Hefeweizen might initially seem sweet, but they finish dry and refreshing with a high carbonation.

Wheat is typically 50–60 percent of the grain bill, with pale/colored malts making up the rest. Classic German brews might use a decoction mash to enhance mouthfeel and dryness. Traditionally, shallow, open fermenters are used for Weissbier in Germany, and fermentation temperature is warmer than a regular ale. Tank geometry and temperature produce the great range of fruit esters and phenolic spice aromas.

Wheat was a common grain in European brewing nations. The exception was Bavaria, where, from 1516, wheat was banned from breweries apart from those owned by the royal family, who exclusively brewed Weissbier for centuries, until they decided to give up their sole brewing rights (the beer was waning in popularity) in the late 1800s. A few dedicated Bavarian brewers rejuvenated the style, and today it's one of the most common beers in Germany.

BEER STATS				
Color	Clarity	Ferment	ABV	Bitterness
Pale yellow to amber	Hazy to cloudy	Fruity/spicy	4.5%–6%	10–20 IBU (low)

SCHNEIDER WEISSE ORIGINAL WEISSBIER

5.4% ABV	BREWED: KELHEIM, GERMANY

In the 1870s, Schneider was one of the original brewers to get civilian rights to brewing with wheat, and its Original evokes old late 19th-century brews. It's a rich amber color, and the grain gives toffee and toast, some sweetness initially, even a heartiness, which also sweetens the banana aroma, and some stone fruitiness from the yeast. The spiciness is elegant. Few other brewers make a Weissbier like this.

WEIHENSTEPHANER HEFEWEISSBIER

5.4% ABV	BREWED: FREISING, GERMANY

Pour this next to Schneider Original and the difference is striking. Weihenstephaner is cloudy yellow with a bright white foam. There's creamy banana and banana candy, vanilla, citrus, a little cracker and cracked pepper, and just a pinch of smoky clove. A fleeting fudge-like sweetness dries to leave a light and refreshing beer—a real feature of this style is its round body at first, ending crisply with a snap of dryness and carbonation.

AYINGER BRÄUWEISSE

5.1% ABV	BREWED: AYING, GERMANY

Ayinger is lighter overall than Schneider and Weihenstephaner, again showing the style's nuance and range. The fruitiness is more like a subtle banana bread. There's some creamy spice, such as vanilla and cardamom; some sweeter tropical fruits; and a spritz of lemon. The wheat is like fresh bread. The body is crisper and leaner than others, with the wheat and high carbonation combining to suggest a little tartness, which is refreshing.

COEDO SHIRO

5.5% ABV	BREWED: SAITAMA, JAPAN

This Japanese brew is on the creamy-smooth side of the style. It has an appealing fruitiness with candy banana, stone fruits, and a touch of crème caramel, and is light on the clove. Like a German brew, it starts out with a smooth fullness, which gives bready malts, dough, graham cracker, and brioche toast. Then the carbonation cuts in, lifts it all, mixes in more fruitiness, and dries out and ends with a gentle finish and a hint of citrus.

OTHER EXAMPLES TO TRY

ERDINGER WEISSBIER: light fruitiness, crisp refreshment, low spice.

LIVE OAK HEFEWEIZEN: banana pudding, toast, light spice.

TOIT BREWPUB WEISS: sweet wheat, banana candy, anise.

DUNKELWEIZEN & WEIZENBOCK

This extended family of German-style wheat beers is darker, stronger, or hoppier than regular wheat beers.

WEIZEN   SNIFTER

FLAVOR WHEEL

FLAVOR, PROCESS, & STORY

Dunkelweizen are dark wheat beers brewed in the same way as a Hefeweizen with a large percentage of wheat, but with added dark and specialty malts like Munich and Vienna. They add toasty, roasty, nutty, and cocoa flavors alongside the yeast fruitiness and spice.

Weizenbock and Weizendoppelbock are stronger wheat beers, which can range in color from pale yellow to dark brown. Imagine a regular Weissbier or Dunkelweizen, only a few percent stronger, giving more alcohol flavor, body, and richness, and generally amplifying the flavors. The extra alcohol strength tends to put more stress on the yeast during fermentation, which in turn pushes forward more esters and phenols and a broader range of aromas. First brewed in 1907, Schneider Weisse's Aventinus is said to be the originator of this style.

A Hopfenweisse has the flavors of a Weizenbock or Weizendoppelbock but with loads of aromatic hops. It was a style created by Schneider Weisse in 2008 in collaboration with Brooklyn Brewery. The sweeter base flavors, extra fruity yeast aromas, plus a stronger phenolic element work with the citrusy hops to give aromas that are unique to a Hopfenweisse. This is a complex and fascinating beer style, marrying old German traditions with a modern American hop influence.

		BEER STATS		
Color	Clarity	Ferment	ABV	Bitterness
Gold to dark ruby brown	Hazy to cloudy	Fruity/spicy	5%–8+%	10–40 IBU (low–medium)

ANDECHSER WEISSBIER DUNKEL

5% ABV	BREWED: ANDECHS, GERMANY

Ruby-amber in color, the dark malt addition is light, but it adds a tasty, toasty depth of cocoa powder, some roasted nuts, bread crusts, and pretzels. Along with the banana esters—like banana milkshake—there's some dried fruit, woody spice, and ripe tropical fruit, which is part of this beer's unique yeast character. The finish brings a combination of slight yeast spiciness, peppery German hop bitterness, and crisp dryness.

BIRRIFICIO ITALIANO VÙDÙ

6% ABV	BREWED: LIMIDO COMASCO, ITALY

This Dunkelweizen is brewed with a heritage Italian wheat. There are the classic banana and clove aromas, plus sweeter stone fruits, then the dark malts transform the aroma and make it more caramelized, more chocolaty, like toast rather than bread, with a hint of chocolate panettone. The richness up front is full-bodied, giving some cocoa and toffee, followed by a firmer, more herbal, floral bitterness than most versions of the style have.

SCHNEIDER WEISSE AVENTINUS

8.2% ABV	BREWED: KELHEIM, GERMANY

The original Weizendoppelbock, and still the textbook example, it pours a color unlike any other in the world of beer—a rich ruby-orange with a thick, creamy foam. Along with roasted banana, banana custard, or chocolate-coated banana, there's a hint of cola, caramelized bread pudding, figs, raisin pastries, some dried citrus peel, and medicinal clove. It leaves you with sticky lips from residual sweetness.

SCHNEIDER WEISSE HOPFENWEISSE

8.2% ABV	BREWED: KELHEIM, GERMANY

Schneider invented the astonishing Hopfenweisse, essentially a heavily hopped Weizenbock. It's hazy amber with lots of foam. The aroma is intense: floral-like fresh hops, pithy citrus, clove-studded oranges, roasted banana, fermented pineapple, a hint of phenolic smokiness. The body is boozy, oily with all those hops (Hallertau Saphir), and rich with the yeast. The bitterness (40 IBU) is sharp at the end, powerful but restrained.

OTHER EXAMPLES TO TRY

ERDINGER WEISSBIER DUNKEL: subtle, cocoa, dried fruit, pepper.

LIVE OAK PRIMUS: chocolate banana, vanilla, spiced banana bread.

BRAUEREI MICHAEL PLANK HELLER WEIZENBOCK: creamy banana, rich spices, sweet bread, orange peel.

WITBIER

These refreshing and light Belgian-style wheat beers are often brewed with orange peel and coriander for a fruity, floral flavor and a spicy, dry finish.

TUMBLER   STEMMED

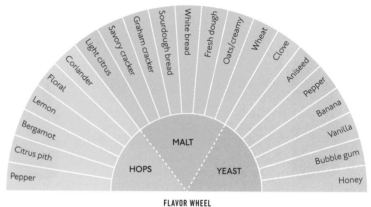

FLAVOR WHEEL

FLAVOR, PROCESS, & STORY

Unfiltered, light, highly carbonated, and easy drinking, these beers are designed for refreshment rather than complexity. A prominent yeast aroma and flavor are joined by the addition of spices, typically dried orange peel and coriander, giving a citrus, floral, and spicy depth that complements (or is complemented by) the yeast.

Other fruits and spices are also seen but are kept subtle and are not the dominant flavor.

Wheat is usually 30–60 percent of the recipe, with a mix of pale malts and oats comprising the rest, giving a full, smooth texture. Sweetness can be low to medium, and bitterness is usually very low, allowing more of the yeast and spices to come through. The expressive yeast can range from fruity to spicy. Hops are very light.

Wheat beers (Wit, Witbier, Witte, Bière Blanche, White Ales) have a long history in Belgium. Mostly low alcohol and tart, they disappeared as cleaner ales and lagers became popular. There isn't a straight line between the old wheats and modern Wits, but we can date the contemporary era to Hoegaarden in the 1960s. It created what has become a global favorite and was one of the first craft beer styles to gain prominence in North America.

BEER STATS				
Color	Clarity	Ferment	ABV	Bitterness
Yellow	Hazy	Fruity/spicy	4%–5.5%	10–20 IBU (low)

HOEGAARDEN WIT

4.9% ABV | BREWED: HOEGAARDEN, BELGIUM

The phenolic breadth to this beer runs deep—you can smell it at arm's length and taste it long after swallowing. Peppery clove (almost like a deli counter or bathroom cleaner) gives intensity to the floral coriander and makes the orange peel taste perfumy, like sticky candied peel. It may sound unappetizing, but countless drinkers love it. It's the original modern Witbier and one of the most important beers ever brewed.

BRASSERIE LEFEBVRE BLANCHE DE BRUXELLES

4.5% ABV | BREWED: QUENAST, BELGIUM

A lovely light, uncomplicated Witbier, this is on the fresher side of the style, with more fruity aromas than others, including bubble gum, strawberry, vanilla, candied apricot, and sweet tropical fruits. The coriander is more toasty than floral, and the dried orange is a background depth and a lasting flavor at the end. The texture has a creamy wheat smoothness to it, carrying a bit of floral honey. The carbonation adds to the pleasing refreshment.

ALLAGASH WHITE

5.2% ABV | BREWED: PORTLAND, ME, USA

Allagash White is a perfect expression of the Belgian Wit with a hint of an American accent. It's a hazy pale yellow with a distinctive white foam. Coriander and dried orange are immediate, along with dried lemon, cardamom, lemon cake, bitter lemon, vanilla, and light clove. The texture is luscious, creamy smooth, and silky. A firm bitterness and peppery hop quality at the end mark it apart from many Belgian examples.

LOST AND GROUNDED HOP-HAND FALLACY

4.4% ABV | BREWED: BRISTOL, ENGLAND

Hop-Hand Fallacy is a classically styled Witbier, perfectly balanced between the light yeast esters, peppery spiciness from the yeast and hops, fragrant toasted spiciness and floral aroma of ground coriander, and the fruitiness of dried orange peel. The body is pale yellow and lightly hazy, with a soft creaminess to the texture and a tingling kind of fizz that bounces across the palate. At the lower range of alcohol, it's refreshing with a dry, spicy finish.

OTHER EXAMPLES TO TRY

BLUE MOON: lemon, vanilla, cracker, seltzer-like, orange soda.

UNIBROUE BLANCHE DE CHAMBLY: floral coriander, honey, wheat, clove.

HITACHINO NEST WHITE ALE: nutmeg, sweet orange, wheat, refreshing.

SAISON

This range of well-attenuated, yeast-forward
beers is brewed in—or inspired by—an
old Belgian farmhouse tradition.

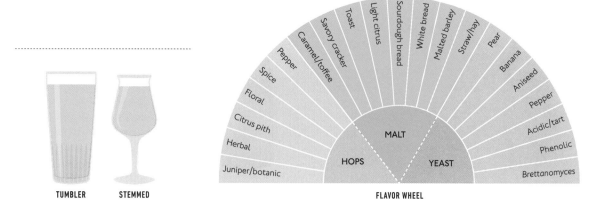

TUMBLER STEMMED

FLAVOR WHEEL

FLAVOR, PROCESS, & STORY

The more you drink Saisons, the
less you understand them, but the
more you love their complexities.
They vary broadly in character,
from under 4% ABV to more
than 9% ABV, bitter or tart, with
different levels of sweetness and
hoppiness. What connects them
is a very dry finish and a complexity
of yeast flavor and aroma.

Yeast—and sometimes
bacteria—tends to define these
beers. They have a full spectrum
of fruity ester aromas and usually
an underlying phenolic, peppery,
or clove-like depth. High attenuation
leaves a dry finish, and carbonation
is high. *Brettanomyces* yeast and
bacteria are used in some. Barley
is sometimes joined with other
grains such as wheat, oats, and
spelt. Hops are a background depth
in most, adding extra peppery or
pithy flavor. A hard-water profile
leaves a crisp, dry character.

Saisons ostensibly come from a
preindustrial domestic farmhouse
tradition. Those beers were
made using local ingredients and
passed-down processes, and
probably didn't taste very good.
As large-scale brewing developed
and beers became more tasty and
consistent, the farmhouse
traditions were abandoned. What
we now consider Saisons date from
the mid-20th century, and took
until the turn of the 21st to grow
in popularity and be developed by
craft breweries.

BEER STATS				
Color	Clarity	Ferment	ABV	Bitterness
Straw to deep gold	Bright to light haze	Fruity/spicy, sometimes acidic	4%–9.5%	20–50 IBU (medium)

BRASSERIE DUPONT SAISON DUPONT

6.5% ABV	BREWED: TOURPES, BELGIUM

An archetypal Saison, it's hazy gold, expressive, and expansive. Fruity banana esters come first with some peppery spice behind. The first taste is like caramelized grain, but it dries out, almost mineral-like, almost savory, diving into herbal and citrus pith hops, which really grip and last. It's elusive to describe but uniquely recognizable once you've come to love it. Try also Dupont's Moinette Blonde and Avec Les Bons Voeux.

BRASSERIE FANTÔME SAISON

8% ABV	BREWED: SOY, BELGIUM

This displays a wildness of character compared to Dupont's rustic charm, driven by the enigmatic and idiosyncratic yeast, giving lemon, pineapple, sour mango, peaches, tangy fruit candy, tart apple, and more. Honeyed malt gives some sweetness and richness, which plumps up the fruitiness, then it gets really dry as the yeast comes back with a fruity zinginess. Its complexity is somewhat baffling and that's the joy of a beer like this.

BURNING SKY SAISON PROVISION

6.7% ABV	BREWED: FIRLE, ENGLAND

Magically complex, this is a beer defined by its place and process. First fermented with a Saison yeast, then aged in large wooden *foudres* for several months with a house culture of yeast and bacteria, it matures to a refined tartness and complexity that feels supremely integrated. Always interesting, there's sometimes lemon, hay, gooseberry, creamy underripe apricot, Bramley apple, dried citrus peel, and a peppery bitterness.

BOULEVARD BREWING CO. TANK 7

8.5% ABV	BREWED: KANSAS CITY, MO, USA

This is heavily hopped like an IPA, making it a great example of an American Saison. Golden in color, the base beer has a fullness to begin that dries out to a lasting bitterness, with some clove, pepper, and playful fruitiness, like sweet banana plus alcohol. The hops are strong, combining a Belgian brew with the American love of hops. Hoppiness plus yeast give funky fermented pineapple, dried orange peel, pithy grapefruit, and fizzy lemon candy.

OTHER EXAMPLES TO TRY

BRASSERIE DE BLAUGIES LA MONEUSE: toffee, peppery spice, very dry.

HILL FARMSTEAD ARTHUR: Champagne, tart tropical fruit, mouthwatering.

LA SIRÈNE SAISON: tart, lemon, complex.

FARMHOUSE & RUSTIC ALES

These varied Belgian- and French-style ales defy easy categorization and come from a romanticized farmhouse tradition.

TUMBLER   STEMMED

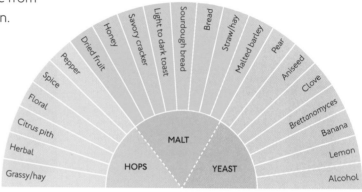

FLAVOR WHEEL

FLAVOR, PROCESS, & STORY

These beers vary greatly in flavor profile, from low alcohol and quenching to malty and strong, and from pale gold to dark brown. Some are bitter; others, tart and wild. The main character that connects them all is a dry finish, often with a "rustic" fermentation profile (the opposite of the clean or neutral fermentation profile of a pale lager or ale), either fruity, phenolic, or wild and funky with

Brettanomyces yeast. They should have complexity and depth.

Barley is often joined by wheat, oats, spelt, or rye, giving a greater depth of malt character. Few of these beers are aromatically hoppy, but many have a firm bitterness, often from German hops with a spicy, peppery finish. Some brewers may mature these beers in wooden barrels for extra depth or acidity.

Historically, Bière de Garde, France's famous beer style, was stored in barrels, where it turned

vinous and tart. Now it's more like a lagered strong ale, robust with malt and alcohol, low in esters, and with a drying finish instead of bitterness or tartness. Table Beer, or Grisette, is also a common style. It's low alcohol, very dry, and usually either tart or bitter. These styles are gaining new interest from drinkers who like the farmhouse and Saison style.

BEER STATS

Color	Clarity	Ferment	ABV	Bitterness
Straw to brown	Bright to light haze	Fruity/spicy	3.5%–8.5%	15–45 IBU (low–medium)

BRASSERIE 3 MONTS BIÈRE DE FLANDRE

8.5% ABV | BREWED: ST-SYLVESTRE-CAPPEL, FRANCE

A classic French Bière de Garde, it is robust with deep malt flavor, a bit like chewing on a handful of malted barley. There's some fruity yeast character and a little phenolic clove and black pepper, plus an underlying light tropical aroma, all enhanced by a richness of alcohol. The finish is warming and drying but low in bitterness. Compare with Dupont Moinette to taste the stylistic difference from a Saison.

BRASSERIE THIRIEZ LA BLONDE D'ESQUELBECQ

6.5% ABV | BREWED: ESQUELBECQ, FRANCE

A lighter French farmhouse ale, hazy yellow with a brief crown of foam, it has an intriguing low-level mix of fruitiness, with hints of banana, vanilla, pear, dried citrus peel, cooked stone fruit, plus white pepper, clove, and something floral—it seems like a lot of the flavor is hop-derived, but there's yeast in there adding extra depth. The malt is up front and has a soft richness to it, while the carbonation is brisk and light.

JOLLY PUMPKIN BAM BIÈRE

4.5% ABV | BREWED: DEXTER, MI, USA

In a wonderful way, this Michigan-brewed beer is as anachronistic as something brewed deep in the Belgian countryside. It takes some flavor inspiration from old farmhouse ales (aged, tart, dry) and does something new by dry hopping it. It's crisply refreshing with its mix of dryness, lemon, and pineapple yeast character, some fermenting stone fruits, tart green apple flavor, and Prosecco-like zing at the end.

JESTER KING LE PETIT PRINCE

2.9% ABV | BREWED: AUSTIN, TX, USA

This is a Belgian-inspired Table Beer, a low ABV, dry, highly carbonated and bitter ale designed to be the daily drink on a farm table. Jester King's version remains true to an old rusticity, with its house yeast adding wild notes, peppery spice, lemon peel, and pear, with hay-like and floral hops. The carbonation is briskly refreshing, which is emphasized by a light tartness, high attenuation, and an absence of any sweetness.

OTHER EXAMPLES TO TRY

CUVÉE DES JONQUILLES: floral, fragrant, refreshing.

BRASSERIE THEILLIER LA BAVAISIENNE: toasted, fruity alcohol, dry.

LA GOUDALE: honey, floral, light spice, toasty malt.

BELGIAN BLONDE & PALE ALE

These Belgian-style ales are moderately strong and have a refreshing, easy-drinking quality, accented by hop or yeast.

TUMBLER   STEMMED

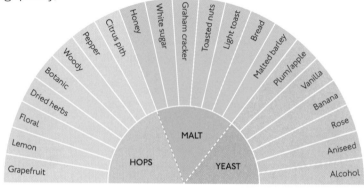

FLAVOR WHEEL

FLAVOR, PROCESS, & STORY

Everyday drinking beers, Blondes are sweeter than Pales, stronger, and have a more prominent fruity yeast aroma and flavor, while Pales have more hop flavor and aroma, with less malt. These are brilliant golden beers with a crown of white foam. Refreshing, they maintain interest with complex yeast and/or hops. Hop character tends toward spicy, peppery bitterness, but some highly hopped examples express citrus and floral qualities. Alcohol can vary a lot, as can sweetness.

They use base recipes of pale malts, typically Pilsner, sometimes with colored malts or wheat, and sometimes pale candi sugar to add dryness. Hops are typically German, Belgian, or British, and bitterness varies by brand: Pale Ales are drier and more bitter. Some Blonde beers include spices like coriander. Many will be bottle conditioned, which adds to their depth of flavor.

Blondes and Pales represent the shift in Belgium from a country of localized and idiosyncratic beer types, often tart and using lots of wheat, toward cleaner, more bitter beers that spread in popularity. They are a group of easy-drinking, moderately strong beers with more character than a typical Pilsner or Pale Ale. The Belgian Pale has become an important beer style for those who love hop flavor and bitterness.

BEER STATS				
Color	Clarity	Ferment	ABV	Bitterness
Straw to gold	Bright to light haze	Fruity/spicy	5%–7.5%	20–45 IBU (low–medium–high)

ST. FEUILLIEN BLONDE

| 7.5% ABV | BREWED: LE ROEULX, BELGIUM |

This lightly hazy golden-amber beer is perfumed with yeast and spices, giving aromas of coriander, honeysuckle, lemon, apples, pears, and marmalade. The fizz is lively and bright, bursting on the tongue, and beneath that there's a creamy quality to the malt, like unsweet fudge and toasty malts. Yeast flavors layer through the beer, with hops adding a light fruitiness and peppery note. The finish grips with hoppiness.

LEFFE BLONDE

| 6.6% ABV | BREWED: LEUVEN, BELGIUM |

There can be few drinkers who haven't seen or heard of Leffe Blonde. It's a sweet, honey-like beer. The spice is pronounced, with clove, pepper, and a phenolic honey quality—sometimes even a baked ham note, which some drinkers might find unpleasant. It's not bottle-refermented and, overall, it lacks the depth and character of most Belgian Blondes, but it is worthy of consideration, and comparison, for its ubiquity.

THE LOST ABBEY DEVOTION

| 6% ABV | BREWED: SAN MARCOS, CA, USA |

Somewhere between a Belgian Blonde and Pale, Devotion harmonizes grassy, floral, hay, citrus peel, and fresh herb aromas of European hops with underlying yeast pepper and fruitiness. The texture has a distinctly American fullness of malt, cut with carbonation, and in the middle are citrus and melon notes, white bread, plus more of those grassy hops. The finish suggests it's going bitter, but there is spice instead.

BRASSERIE DE LA SENNE ZINNEBIR

| 5.8% ABV | BREWED: BRUSSELS, BELGIUM |

Hops and yeast playfully combine in this orange-gold Belgian Pale Ale. It's not always clear which ingredient is providing the dried orange, stone fruit, pear, or peppery aroma, although a soft clove note is a signature of the brewery's yeast. In the flavor, the hops are more direct, being grassy, perfumed, citrus pithy, and bitter. The malt gives structure without demanding attention, and the bitterness is lasting and strong.

OTHER EXAMPLES TO TRY

WESTVLETEREN BLONDE: orange peel, pepper, vanilla, toast.

AFFLIGEM BLONDE: sweet bread, banana, zesty.

DE HALVE MAAN BRUGSE ZOT: honey, pepper, light fruity esters.

BELGIAN STRONG BLONDE & TRIPEL

These strong pale Belgian ales have high carbonation, a very dry finish, and powerful aromas from the yeast.

SNIFTER   **GOBLET**

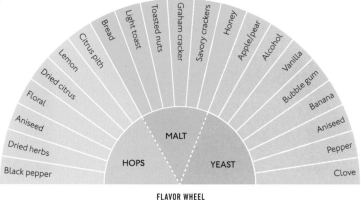

FLAVOR WHEEL

FLAVOR, PROCESS, & STORY

The yeast gives the personality to these styles, and esters and phenols define the uniqueness of each beer. The prominent yeast aroma can be fruity, spicy/phenolic, or both. The use of sugar helps create a very dry and "digestible" beer, often with medium bitterness and fruity, floral, spicy hop flavors. They are high in carbonation. Perceived sweetness ranges from low to moderate, and alcohol flavor is usually evident. These are among the driest finishers, and Strong Blonde/Golden tend to be drier than Tripels. Tripels tend to be sweeter and richer overall, with more phenolic yeast character.

Classic recipes use Pilsner malt, candi sugar, Belgian, German, or English hops, an expressive yeast, and sometimes added spices like coriander. Sugar increases alcohol while keeping the body light and leaves the dryness. They are typically bottle conditioned.

Beer style guides try to distinguish between Strong Blonde, Strong Golden, and Tripels, but they're more of a continuous spectrum of flavor. Tripels date from the 1930s (Westmalle Tripel) and were strong, pale beers that combined old dark ale traditions with the ever-growing taste for lighter-looking beers. Strong Blonde or Golden Ales are usually dated from the 1970s. They are among the most popular in Belgium.

BEER STATS				
Color	Clarity	Ferment	ABV	Bitterness
Gold to amber	Bright to light haze	Fruity, fruity/spicy	7.5%–9.5%	20–50 IBU (medium)

TRIPEL KARMELIET

8.4% ABV	BREWED: BUGGENHOUT, BELGIUM

Brewed with barley, oat, and wheat, plus undisclosed spices, this is a floral, fruity, spicy, and phenol-driven beer—think dried lemon and clove. There's floral and citrusy coriander-like spice alongside the phenols, with a creamy banana ester adding suggestions of sweetness. The carbonation is Champagne-like, giving a lightness above the rich depth. The clove can be challenging for some drinkers.

WESTMALLE TRIPEL TRAPPIST ALE

9.5% ABV	BREWED: WESTMALLE, BELGIUM

This and Tripel Karmeliet are classic examples of the style yet are strikingly different. Westmalle hits with alcohol first, a warming, spicy aroma, with an expansive yeast-derived aroma of dried banana, creamy vanilla, almond essence, and pear drops without the phenolic clove. Carbonation is moderate, the body is lean, with alcohol adding a richness and a mouthwatering quality, before it ends with a very dry finish.

RUSSIAN RIVER DAMNATION

7.5% ABV	BREWED: WINDSOR, CA, USA

This Strong Golden Ale is at the weaker end of the alcohol range. Banana esters and a flourish of fruitiness (light tropical stone fruit, vanilla) come first. The texture is smooth and almost creamy, with the banana esters teasing that creaminess further with a slight pale malt sweetness. It's noticeably American compared to Belgian versions, where the malt profile has a richer quality, and the bitterness is more forceful.

DUVEL MOORTGAT

8.5% ABV	BREWED: PUURS, BELGIUM

The world's finest Strong Blonde Ale, it is brilliant gold and paler than most others in its category. Lasting white foam holds on to aromas of pear, apple, floral hops, and some alcohol. The carbonation is brisk and lively, and it bounces along the tongue, popping with stone fruit and an oily citrus quality from the hops. It's very lean in body, some alcohol supports the background malt flavor, and it's very dry at the end.

OTHER EXAMPLES TO TRY

ST. BERNARDUS TRIPEL: more fruity, orange, honey.

LA CHOUFFE BLONDE: floral, honey, herbal, clove.

ALLAGASH TRIPEL: bitter, peppery spice.

BELGIAN BRUNE & DUBBEL

These moderate to strong dark Belgian ales have a wonderful range of flavors, with a refreshing carbonation and expressive yeast character.

SNIFTER

GOBLET

Woody/herbal
Floral
Spice
Pepper
Sweet black tea
Berry/baked fruit
Licorice
Dried fruit
Tea cake
Toasted nuts
Cocoa
Dark chocolate
Caramel
Dark toast
Bread
Vinous
Dried fruit
Plum
Aniseed
Vanilla
Pepper/clove

MALT

HOPS

YEAST

FLAVOR WHEEL

FLAVOR, PROCESS, & STORY

Brune is usually sweeter and lower in alcohol than a Dubbel. They share similar flavor profiles, mostly focused on the interplay of malt and aromatic yeast. While they sound sweet with dried fruits, chocolate, and festive spices, these beers tend toward a dry finish with a peppery hop character. Alcohol is moderate to high, but should never be overly noticeable.High carbonation adds a briskness to the texture and lightness to the drinking experience.

Traditionally, a dark candi sugar produces the darker colors, though darker malts are also used for color and flavor. The sugar creates caramelized and dried fruit flavors and helps the dry finish. The brewery's yeast and brew processes create the unique aroma and flavor profiles. They are typically bottle conditioned.

These dark ales can be traced back to early brewing in the Middle Ages. Their modern relevance dates from the reopening of the Belgian monasteries in the mid-19th century. They were modernized in the early 20th century and have since developed the flavor profiles we expect. "Dubbel" refers to "double-strength" beers, used when it was common to have a weaker and a stronger beer. Tripel and Quadrupel followed in the 1930s and 1990s respectively, representing a modern shift in brewing and drinking.

		BEER STATS		
Color	Clarity	Ferment	ABV	Bitterness
Dark red to dark brown	Bright to light haze	Fruity/estery	6%–8%	15–30 IBU (low–medium)

WESTMALLE DUBBEL TRAPPIST ALE

| 7% ABV | BREWED: WESTMALLE, BELGIUM |

Westmalle's Dubbel doesn't fit the description of a classic Dubbel—dried fruits, festive spice, toffee, vanilla—with the expected sweetness or richness. Instead, there's a crispness to this lean and restrained beer. All the expected flavors are there, but they are compacted tightly in. High carbonation keeps the rounded fruity flavors balanced, and then you're left with an almost seltzer-like dryness at the end.

CHIMAY RED

| 7% ABV | BREWED: CHIMAY, BELGIUM |

There's a subtlety to the Chimay beers (which may be a compliment or a suggestion that other Dubbels are more complex and interesting). Red-brown in color, there is some dried fruit, fruit esters, floral vanilla and clove, ripe stone fruits, caramel, and banana candy. The body is surprisingly light, with some honey sweetness and a light bitterness, though sometimes with an umami or iron-like character. Easy going, but not the most interesting.

TYNT MEADOW ENGLISH TRAPPIST ALE

| 7.4% ABV | BREWED: COALVILLE, ENGLAND |

Although it's made with all British ingredients, including a British ale yeast, it's a very Belgian-tasting ale. Yeast leads aromatically with dried fruit, freshly fermenting dough, fermenting apples, and a floral ester. The full body has hints of toffee apple, fruity dark chocolate, dried figs, sweet black tea, licorice, and a roasted flavor. Every bottle has a slightly different quality to it, which makes it an engaging beer if you drink it regularly.

OMMEGANG ABBEY ALE

| 8.2% ABV | BREWED: COOPERSTOWN, NY, USA |

Brewed with sweet orange peel, coriander and cumin, star anise, and licorice root, this is a Dubbel-style beer that leads with spice instead of yeast. Spices are warming, wrapped in honey and toasted sweetness, which leads to a dryness at the end. Overall, it is drier and spicier than Belgian versions, with a clarity of flavor that's less complex than other Dubbels, but it is a great example of how styles travel.

OTHER EXAMPLES TO TRY

WESTVLETEREN 8: fresh sweet bread, dates, brown sugar.

TRAPPISTES ROCHEFORT 8: molasses, baked figs, vinous.

UNIBROUE MAUDITE: caramel, stewed stone fruit, orange, clove.

BELGIAN STRONG DARK ALE & QUADRUPEL

Among the world's best-loved styles, these beers are associated with monastic and abbey brewing, and have a thrilling depth and complexity.

SNIFTER

GOBLET

Tea cake
Brown sugar
Caramel/toffee
Dark toast
Bread
Dried fruit
Licorice
Dried fruit
Plum/apple
Umami/miso
Aniseed
Cocoa
Vanilla
Chocolate
Pepper/clove
Pepper
Sherry/port
Spice
Vinous
Woody
Alcohol

MALT

YEAST

HOPS

FLAVOR WHEEL

FLAVOR, PROCESS, & STORY

Among the most wonderfully complex beers, these dark, strong ales tend to have prominent yeast character, giving a broad range of esters and occasionally some phenols. The yeast interweaves majestically with a rich depth of malt, which gives dried fruit, cocoa, and baked goods, while caramelized sugar adds flavors like rum raisin and molasses and a lightness to the body. Alcohol is often noticeable, and carbonation is usually high.

For such complex beers, they tend to have simple recipes; character comes from process and yeast. They use mostly Pilsner malt plus a small addition of wheat, dark or caramel malt, and various sugars depending on the brewery. Dark sugar gives color, flavors (caramel and dried fruit), and extra alcohol, which creates a drier beer. Each beer's yeast is distinctive and an integral flavor in the beer. They are most often bottled, and bottle conditioned and matured before sale. They can age handsomely, and after a couple of years, they tend to taste sweeter and vinous with more dried fruit.

Usually associated with monastic beer, Quadrupel is the strongest of a brewery's lineup. Strong, dark Belgian ales have long existed, but it wasn't until 1991 that the term "Quadrupel" was first used, credited to La Trappe monastery.

BEER STATS				
Color	Clarity	Ferment	ABV	Bitterness
Dark red to dark brown	Bright to light haze	Fruity/estery	8%–12%	25–50 IBU (low–medium)

TRAPPISTES ROCHEFORT 10

| 11.3% ABV | BREWED: ROCHEFORT, BELGIUM |

There's a volume and depth of flavor that makes Rochefort 10 stand above others in its class. It's layered with flavor, with raisin, prune, fig, vanilla, crème caramel, port wine and nutty sherry, and fruit and nut chocolate. The carbonation majestically mixes all those flavors and lifts them off the palate, leaving a beer that satisfies without ever sitting heavy. It's endlessly interesting to drink.

ST. BERNARDUS ABT 12

| 10% ABV | BREWED: WATOU, BELGIUM |

Quadrupel lovers could argue for hours over their favorite, fighting between Westvleteren, Rochefort, and St. Bernardus. St. Bernardus Abt 12 is boozy baked figs and strawberry candy, with a strong rose or violet floral character, vanilla, raisin, malty black tea, and a pinch of clove at the end. It's strong on the palate to begin but disappears quickly, leaving a feeling that it's lighter than the 10% on the label.

DE HALVE MAAN STRAFFE HENDRIK QUADRUPEL

| 11% ABV | BREWED: BRUGES, BELGIUM |

The hoppiness is striking in this Quad, reminiscent of Black IPA or American Barley Wine. It's like herbal liqueur, minty, peppery, richly spicy, intense. The malt has more richness and intensity to balance those hops, giving a full body, with a ranging palate of flavors of licorice, aniseed, booze-soaked berries, sloe gin, fermented dark fruits, woody herbs, and hop cones. It has evolved the Quad style in a new hop-forward way.

UNIBROUE TROIS PISTOLES

| 9% ABV | BREWED: CHAMBLY, CANADA |

Deep red and lightly hazy, there's dried cherry, rum raisin, baked figs, caramelized plums, plus a spiciness throughout with nutmeg, pepper, anise, and allspice notes. It has a rounder, fuller texture than Belgian brews, with caramel and chocolate sweetness and a slickness to the body, which is enhanced by a lower carbonation than other examples. Overall, though, it finishes with a nice dryness and herbal, spicy bitterness.

OTHER EXAMPLES TO TRY

WESTVLETEREN 12: tea cake, fig, cherry, sweet bread dough.

HET ANKER GOUDEN CAROLUS: banana, high sweetness, alcohol, spice.

LA TRAPPE QUADRUPEL: fig, pepper, sweet malt, less complex.

INDEX

ABOUT THE AUTHOR

Mark Dredge is an award-winning beer writer and TV host. He has won numerous awards from the British Guild of Beer Writers and the American Guild of Beer Writers. Mark was shortlisted for the André Simon Drink Award in 2020. His published works include *A Brief History of Lager*, *Beer and Food*, *Cooking with Beer*, *The Best Beer in the World*, *The New Craft Beer World*, *The Beer Bucket List*, and *Beer and Veg*. Mark appears on the TV program *Sunday Brunch* as Channel 4's beer expert and is an international beer judge, attending top competitions such as the World Beer Cup and the Great American Beer Festival. Mark is a certified cicerone and runs beer education classes and regular online tasting events. He also runs the website BeerDredge, where he continues to share knowledge on all things beer.
www.beerdredge.com

AUTHOR'S ACKNOWLEDGMENTS

Thanks to Marta Bescos and Charlotte Beauchamp for contacting breweries and collecting all the images. Thanks to Vanessa Hamilton's brilliant work on the design of this book, and especially being able to interpret my doodles and scribbles and turn them into excellent visual diagrams. To Dawn Titmus for all the work in editing and pulling this book together—thanks for your smart and thoughtful edits. Thanks to Steph Milner for commissioning the book and allowing me to write all about the wonderful flavors of beer. Thanks to the brewers who took the time to look over or comment on illustrations or text that I'd put together. And thanks to Emma for always asking to try the beers I'm drinking and always being curious about how they taste the way they do. This book is for anyone who's ever picked up a beer and wondered why it tastes the way that it does.

PUBLISHER'S ACKNOWLEDGMENTS

DK would like to thank the beer companies for their kind permission to reproduce images of their products, Marta Bescos and Charlotte Beauchamp for picture research, Niyran Gill for the cover illustration, John Friend for proofreading, and Vanessa Bird for the index.

p.36 Composition of Beer: © 2021 Anheuser-Busch InBev all rights reserved twitter.com/abinbev/status/588008852882194432
p.37 Historic Levels of Minerals in Brewing Water: howtobrew.com/book/section-3/understanding-the-mash-ph/balancing-the-malts-and-minerals
The Practical Brewer, p10
Wahl-Henius, *American Handy Book*, 2:790, 1902
Westermann and Huige, *Fermentation Technology*, p.13
p.42 Enzyme Targets: byo.com/article/the-science-of-step-mashing
p.43 Decoction Mash: brulosophy.com/2016/12/08/in-defense-of-decoction-a-german-purists-perspective-on-an-age-old-brewing-method
p.56 Dry Hopping Hazy IPA: Utopian Brewing www.utopianbrewing.com

PICTURE CREDITS

DK LONDON
Senior Designer Glenda Fisher
Jacket Designer Eloise Grohs
Jacket Coordinator Jasmin Lennie
Production Editor David Almond
Production Controller Luca Bazzoli
Senior Acquisitions Editor Stephanie Milner
Editorial Manager Ruth O'Rourke
Design Manager Marianne Markham
Art Director Maxine Pedliham
Publishing Director Katie Cowan

Senior Project Editor Dawn Titmus
Senior Project Designer and Illustrator Vanessa Hamilton
Senior US Editor Megan Douglass

First American Edition, 2022
Published in the United States by DK Publishing
1745 Broadway, 20th Floor, New York, NY 10019

A catalog record for this book
is available from the Library of Congress.
ISBN: 978-0-7440-6128-4

Printed and bound in Slovakia

For the curious
www.dk.com